ArtScroll Series

Rabbi Nosson Scherman / Rabbi Meir Zlotowitz
General Editors

*The enduring lessons
of the legendary
Rosh Yeshivah,
Rabbi Mendel Kaplan*

Published by
Mesorah Publications, ltd

MENDEL
and his wisdom

by

Yisroel Greenwald

FIRST EDITION
First Impression ... November 1994
Second Impression ... October 1995
Third Impression ... July 1999
Fourth Impression ... September 2007
Fifth Impression ... June 2012
Sixth Impression ... May 2019

Published and Distributed by
MESORAH PUBLICATIONS, Ltd.
4401 Second Avenue
Brooklyn, New York 11232

Distributed in Europe by
LEHMANNS
Unit E, Viking Business Park
Rolling Mill Road
Jarrow, Tyne & Wear NE32 3DP
England

Distributed in Australia & New Zealand by
GOLDS WORLD OF JUDAICA
3-13 William Street
Balaclava, Melbourne 3183
Victoria Australia

Distributed in Israel by
SIFRIATI / A. GITLER — BOOKS
POB 2351
Bnei Brak 51122

Distributed in South Africa by
KOLLEL BOOKSHOP
Northfield centre, 17 Northfield Avenue
Glenhazel 2192, Johannesburg, South Africa

Typography by Compuscribe at ArtScroll Studios, Ltd.

Printed in the United States of America
Bound by Sefercraft, Quality Bookbinders, Ltd. Brooklyn, N.Y.

◄§ Introduction

בס"ד
כסלו תשנ"ה

ותהי אסתר נשאת חן בעיני כל ראיה (אסתר ב:טו)
And Esther would captivate all who saw her
(Esther 2:15)

Chazal (*Megillah* 7b) explain this to mean that she found favor in the eyes of people of every nationality. Each nation's people believed she was one of them. Reb Mendel would explain that each nation has its specific quality and character, and Esther possessed the positive qualities of all the nations, so each saw in her their particular uniqueness. So it was with Reb Mendel. Everyone had *his* Reb Mendel. To a *chacham*, he was **the** *chacham*; to a *lamdan*, **the** *lamdan*; to an *iluy*, **the** *iluy*; to a *mentsch*, **the** *mentsch*; to an *anav*, **the** *anav*. Whatever quality one had in himself, it was that quality that he saw in Reb Mendel.

Every *talmid* and friend felt he was *my* Reb Mendel. He could reach up to the greatest and bow to the simplest. He was whatever the situation or the person warranted or needed. Reb Mendel always shunned the limelight; it is very doubtful he would ever have agreed to have anything written about himself. However, for another's good or satisfaction he would go against his own wishes or difficulties. We hope these recollections of Reb Mendel will bring about good, by leading us to emulate his traits and actions, by bringing satisfaction to *talmidim,* friends and family, and by having a remembrance of a Rebbe, friend and father like our Reb Mendel.

יהא זכרו ברוך
הכ"מ
משפחתו

◀§ Table of Contents

❦ **Author's Introduction**

A renowned *rosh yeshivah* once commented on Reb Mendel Kaplan's unique success with his students: "I make *talmidim*. Reb Mendel makes *mentschen*."

A recent *baal teshuvah* once came to study at a large yeshivah of several hundred students. Since he did not know anyone when he arrived, he was left to fend for himself. Fortunately, a number of *bachurim* independently took an interest in the newcomer and assisted him in various ways. It later emerged that the one thing his benefactors had in common was that they had all been close *talmidim* of Reb Mendel Kaplan.

Every morning, fifteen minutes before *Shacharis*, Reb Mendel taught the Alter of Kelm's *Chachmah U'Mussar* to a select few students. One snowy winter morning he walked in and said to the group, "Today we're going to learn a different form of *mussar* — shoveling snow." He directed each *bachur* to a shovel and sent the group outside to clear a path in the snow for the other boys who would soon be on their way to *Shacharis*.

Noticing that one boy was growing tired, Reb Mendel went to relieve him. "Here, let me have your shovel," he insisted. The boy hesitated for a moment, but Rebbe assured him, "Don't worry, the doctor says I need the exercise."

Rabbi Mendel Kaplan, *zt"l*, was one of the most gifted *roshei yeshivah* and Torah educators of his time, as well as an outstanding *mussar* personality, yet little is known about him in the broader Jewish community. He served two generations of American yeshivah students as a bridge between the "old" world of the Lithuanian yeshivos and the "new" world of post-war

American yeshivos, and was renowned throughout the yeshivah world as a master teacher and a living example of Torah ethics.

In the heyday of the renowned Baranovich Yeshivah, he was one of its finest students. When Rabbi Elchonon Wasserman, *zt"l*, was abroad for half a year collecting funds he chose Reb Mendel to deliver the highest *Gemara shiur*. At that time, Reb Mendel was only in his mid-twenties. Rabbi Yeruchem Levovitz, the famed *mashgiach* of the Mirrer Yeshivah in Poland, called Reb Mendel a true *shomei'a* (someone skilled in the art of listening and comprehension), an exemplar of Torah and *mussar* in their purest form. Despite being a thorough product of the European Torah world, Reb Mendel developed a panoply of inventive — and sometimes unorthodox — methods to inculcate Torah values in American yeshivah *bachurim*.

Reb Mendel adhered scrupulously to the traditions he had received from his distinguished teachers, and he had a gift for expressing complicated concepts in seemingly simple terms. With a casual remark or sharp witticism he could convey deep messages based on the teachings of his mentors, Reb Elchonon, Rabbi Shimon Shkop, the Brisker Rav, and Reb Yeruchem Levovitz. He once told his class at the Talmudical Academy of Philadelphia: "I am your Rebbe, and I was a *talmid* of Reb Elchonon. Reb Elchonon was a *talmid* of the Chofetz Chaim, and the Chofetz Chaim was a *talmid* of Reb Nochum of Horodna, and Reb Nochum was a *talmid* of Reb Lazer Yitzchok Frid, a grandson and *talmid* of Reb Chaim Volozhiner, and Reb Chaim Volozhiner was a *talmid* of the Vilna Gaon. So you now have a direct *mesorah* that stretches back to the Vilna Gaon!"

He was a man of untold resiliency, fierce determination, incisiveness, and tremendous "heart." At the Philadelphia Yeshivah, where he taught for close to twenty years, Reb Mendel moved simply and inconspicuously. He never allowed anyone to hold a door open for him. He wore a blue frock instead of the customary rabbinical black, and he personally drove and repaired his own car. Yet the more he fled from honor, the more his students adored him.

He possessed a rare ability to make others feel good about themselves. That ability, combined with his warm and colorful personality, deeply affected the lives of his students. A recent visitor to Chicago, where Reb Mendel once taught post high-school students, found that the mere mention of his name evoked tears in the eyes of those who had not seen him for forty years. Hundreds of students in yeshivos across the country still trade *vertlach* of Reb Mendel and reminisce about the old days. He could be a *lamdan,* counselor, father, mother or mechanic, depending on the needs of the student. To Reb Mendel there was no such thing as great or small when it came to humanity; he honored everyone with respect and love.

> An obese gentile woman of advancing years lived on Reb Mendel's block. Each morning she would walk slowly to a restaurant several blocks away for breakfast. One wintry Sunday morning, as this woman was plodding through the deep snow to the restaurant, Reb Mendel drove by. From the other side of the avenue, he rolled down his window and called to her, "Mary, wait! I'll take you!" With some difficulty, he turned his car around in the snow and gave her a ride to the restaurant. After she finished eating, she was shocked to see the rabbi's car still at the curb in front of the restaurant. He had waited the whole time to take her back home. She later met Reb Mendel's wife and recounted the entire episode. "Your husband is not a person," she concluded, "he's an angel."

Sometimes when Reb Mendel returned to the Philadelphia Yeshivah from visits to New York, the *bachurim* would see him accompanied by shabby vagabonds he had picked up on the road and given a meal and a place to stay. Once, for instance, on his way back to Philadelphia, he noticed a young man lying on the street freezing in the cold. Reb Mendel took him into his car, gave him a warm drink, and brought him to the yeshivah. There, he gave him food and a place to sleep in his own room. After learning that the boy was Jewish and the member of a cult, he made him promise to leave the cult and return home. Reb Mendel arranged a ride home for the young man, and kept in contact with him to see how he was doing.

Despite the severe hardships and suffering he endured in his life, Reb Mendel possessed an incredible joy in life. His thoughts transcended this world, but at the same time he felt very much a part of it and took a heartfelt interest in the people and events around him. He delighted in unraveling the secrets of a mechanical device or in striking up a conversation with his seat mate on a train ride. He felt both the joy and sorrow of others as if they were his own. When Reb Mendel smiled as he picked up a little child, it was impossible to tell whether the child was his or someone else's.

His body moved swiftly and naturally, as if to a silent rhythm which only he could hear, yet always seemed calm and composed. The slight smile fixed at the edge of his lips expressed an inner tranquility — a tranquility experienced by anyone who encountered him. As one former student recalls, "When you walked into a room where Reb Mendel was, you immediately felt relaxed. When you came to him with a problem, your problem started to melt away as soon as you saw him."

He often said in the name of Reb Yeruchem Levovitz: "When you look at different people, you see different qualities. This one

Reb Mendel holding a talmid's child

is a *masmid*, that one a *tzaddik*, a *baal chesed* and so forth. But someone who is well rounded in all areas is a *mentsch*." Reb Mendel was such a *mentsch*. And of all the titles that could be applied to him, I believe that is the one by which he would wish to be remembered.

᠙᠙᠙

This work is only a profile of Reb Mendel's life and a sample of his *mussar* teachings. While much has of necessity been omitted, I have tried to capture the music that was Reb Mendel's. From the time I first entered his *shiur* until the time of his passing, I cherished my relationship with him. I seized every opportunity I could to speak with him, to learn from him, or simply to be with him. Until this day, those moments stand out as the most precious of my life. His words were priceless to me, and I always made an effort to write them down as soon as I could, for fear that I would later forget them. After his passing, I eagerly sought any story about him or anything he had said, not with the intention of publishing them, but to help me internalize his wisdom.

The plan to write this book developed over the course of time, as many people asked me for copies of my notes, and several *roshei yeshivah* encouraged me to share what I knew of his way of life and teachings with the general public. This book is a compilation of personal notes and memories, and interviews with former students, friends and members of his family. I have also drawn upon notes of a number of former students, to whom I am deeply indebted for sharing them with me.

I would like to particularly thank my dear friend Yossi Kirsch for sharing with me his extensive and meticulously recorded personal notes from which I have drawn extensively. I would like to also thank Rabbis Aharon Sonnenshein, Dovid Klugman, Avrohom Dov Owsianka, Yossi Jacobs, Chaim Mittleman and everyone else who provided me with stories and information for inclusion in the book.

The close relationship I shared with Reb Mendel is greatly due to my parents who through their example instilled in me an appreciation and love for Torah scholars. May Hashem bless them with many years of health and *nachas* from all their children and grandchildren. I am also indebted to the Rebbeim of Mesivta Toras Emes Kamenitz and particularly Rabbi Naftali H. Basch who originally introduced me to Reb Mendel through encouraging me to study at the renowned Philadelphia Yeshivah upon graduating high school.

In the production of the book I would like to thank Mrs. Chanie Simins and Michoel Lesher for editing the early drafts of the book and Pinchos Rohr and Yonason Rosenblum for their editorship of the final drafts. I would also like to thank Dov Kahan for reviewing the book and offering his enlightening insights.

We appreciate the assistance of Rabbi Yecheskel Leitner who graciously allowed us to use photographs from his book, "Operation Torah Rescue."

I express my heartfelt thanks to Rabbi Nachman Wolfson who took the cover photo and whose photos grace many pages of this book.

This book presented me with the privilege to meet the special people who work at ArtScroll, notably Steve Blitz, Rabbi Moshe Lieber, Avrohom Biderman and most of all Rabbis Nosson Scherman and Meir Zlotowitz. May Hashem bless them all with strength to continue with their great and holy work.

Lastly, I would like to thank a great friend who carefully reviewed the manuscript numerous times and in his humility wishes to remain anonymous.

Yisroel Greenwald

◄§ Preface

by Rabbi Berel Wein

[R]eb Mendel was a unique and unforgettable individual. Whatever little my classmates and I have become we owe in large part to him. He knew how to build a person; I have never seen his equal in that respect.

Writing about Reb Mendel is nearly impossible: he was such a complex person, and he appeared so different to so many different people. Reb Mendel was hard to get a handle on. When he first began teaching a *shiur* in Chicago in 1946, I was thirteen or fourteen. He told me not to go to a certain co-ed camp, and yet he did not prevent other boys in the *shiur* from going. He once told a certain boy never to bring a newspaper into *shiur*, but he would read a newspaper in the class together with the boys.

There was one boy in *shiur* who was a great basketball player, and he used to come into the *shiur* room dribbling a basketball. For a long time, Reb Mendel watched him without ever saying a word. Then one Sunday morning, he told him not to bring the ball into *shiur* again. It was totally out of the blue — why he told him then and not at a time when he was dribbling

Reb Mendel Kaplan, zt"l

the ball I don't know. But the boy accepted it. Today he is a *rosh yeshivah*.

Reb Mendel was an incredibly astute person — a master psychologist — and he had remarkable power over people. Eventually we stopped trying to figure him out.

S *S* *S*

He was completely unpretentious and natural. I remember when he first learned to drive a car. No other *rosh yeshivah* drove or even thought of driving, and certainly none of them would have considered asking a student to teach him. But Reb Mendel did not fear that he was lowering himself in his students' eyes.

He was the only *rosh yeshivah* we ever saw with his jacket off on hot summer days. He was a master in *shtik,* but it wasn't part of him — it was just a tool he used. He had no hang-ups. When we visited him at home, he acted like a perfectly normal person and talked to us while at the same time feeding a baby or washing a dish or replacing a light bulb.

S *S* *S*

Whatever you asked him, his answer always threw you off. He knew how to show just what he wanted of himself, and keep what he wanted hidden. That was his genius.

If you asked him a question in talmudic learning, he often told

Reb Hertzl Kaplan

you to ask his brother Reb Hertzl (who also taught a class at the yeshivah), and when you asked Reb Hertzl, he would tell you to go back to Reb Mendel. That was part of the game — he would pretend that the question was too deep for him. Someone in *shiur* once asked a question, and Reb Mendel said, "Go ask Reb Hertzl." Later, he was walking with me somewhere and said, "You know why I told him to go ask Reb Hertzl? Because I didn't have an answer to his question. Now that I've had time to think, the answer is probably like this . . ." Whether that was the truth, I don't know. By the time I left his *shiur*, the only thing of which I was sure was that I could never take anything he said *only* on face value — never!

ᔨ ᔨ ᔨ

Sometimes Reb Mendel seemed to take two or three different approaches to the same issue. In our time, there was a very strong *Shomer HaDati* Bnei Akiva in Chicago and many of the best *bachurim* of our yeshivah were leaders in it. Someone once complained to Reb Mendel about this organization and he answered, "It's better than standing on Roosevelt Road watching television." (In those days television was a big novelty and *frum* Jews used to stand around on Shabbos afternoon watching it in the window of an appliance store on Roosevelt Road.)

In *shiur*, he once commented about the same organization, "They'll outgrow it." He didn't say there was anything wrong, just, *"Men vert elter* — We get older." And that's what happened. By the time they were seventeen or eighteen, ninety percent of them outgrew it.

I don't remember him ever saying anything negative about any Jew. He used to say, "You can't truly estimate what a Jew is; no matter what kind of Jew."

He once said during *shiur*, "The _____ (a certain religious anti-Zionist group) is one hundred percent right. It's just that its adherents are missing a capful of love for their fellow Jews. But if that's missing, then it doesn't help to be one hundred percent right."

All his students, therefore, make very poor haters. It was very hard to be a hater if you were around him for any period of time. His ironic demeanor had no venom in it. Once a great but controversial *talmid chacham* came to Chicago, and there was a great deal of controversy concerning him. Reb Mendel said, "Even his *lashon hara* has *geshmak*!" While criticizing this person for his loose tongue, he still built him up by saying that everything about him was *geshmak*.

Reb Mendel had a very sharp way of expressing himself and a keen sense of humor from which no one escaped completely unscathed. When I had moved up to the higher division of the yeshivah, I once asked him about something he had told me a few years earlier. He told me to forget everything he told me when I was fifteen because much of it was just for the shock value.

Once we had a discussion in class about Thanksgiving. When I was growing up, Thanksgiving was a "Jewish" holiday as well and even important European-born rabbis in Chicago had a Thanksgiving dinner. (The attitude among Jews was different then. People were so grateful to America for having taken them in. Today you don't see this any more; it's all taken for granted.)

Reb Mendel made a joke about eating turkey on Thanksgiving, and one very serious boy asked, "Do you mean we shouldn't have a Thanksgiving dinner?" Reb Mendel replied, "If you go home and tell that to your mother, I'll slap you." At the time, we were left confused. In retrospect I see that he wanted to temper our enthusiasm about Thanksgiving, but, at the same time, he didn't want to cause fights at home. He wanted to make us think about things we wouldn't normally think about. He was the true iconoclast.

S➤ S➤ S➤

Reb Mendel always had a different perspective on things than others did. When Israel's first Prime Minister came to Chicago on a fund-raising trip, Reb Mendel went to the banquet at the Palmer House. He stood in the back and watched as Jews lined up to give money for Israeli Bonds. "That's the Jewish people," he later said to the class. "That's the children of Avraham — they have such a love for doing kindness that they'll stand in line to give away their money."

When the State of Israel was proclaimed, he spoke to us about what *Eretz Yisrael* meant and what a historical moment it was. He used to read to us articles about the battles being fought and say, "The little helpless Jews are going to beat the Arabs, they're going to beat the whole world — that's the strength of the Jews." In later years he once said, "The hatred between the Arabs and Israel is really a hatred between Eisav and Yaakov, and the war they're fighting against the Jews is really a war against Hashem."

When Reb Mendel first came to Chicago, our *shiur* taught him to read English and he even took an interest in our high school studies. Yet once during class he saw a secular book that argued that *Yeshayahu* was written by two different prophets. He took the book and tossed it directly into the wastepaper basket on the other side of the room — a fifty-foot shot without even hitting the backboard! No one could ever even imagine the existence of "two" Yeshayahus again.

҉ ҉ ҉

Reb Mendel wanted us to learn things from life around us. When Chief Rabbi Isaac HaLevi Herzog came to Chicago, Reb Mendel went to greet him together with the other *rabbanim*. A week later, the Ponevezher Rav came and spoke. Rebbe told the *shiur*, "You've had a chance to see two great Jews. They both have *atzilus* (the quality of nobility)." The following week, he reviewed for us the lessons we should have learned from seeing these two great men.

One incident illustrates how much emphasis he placed on deriving lessons from experience. Two survivors from Europe got into a dispute and one of them hired me as his lawyer. Before Yom Kippur, I asked Reb Mendel whether I should ask forgiveness from the opposing party, since I was representing his opponent. Reb Mendel recommended that I call the man. I did, and he was not at all friendly. I happened to see Reb Mendel before Succos and he said to me, "You should always remember that it was a great thing you did in calling him, even though it didn't help." Then he added a very strange comment: "The *churban* (destruction in Europe) was wasted on him; he didn't learn any lessons from it."

҉ ҉ ҉

Reb Mendel's exceptional strength was his ability to influence people. He was concerned about what type of *shidduchim* the *bachurim* would make. Even though we were just above bar mitzvah age when we were in his *shiur*, he always told us we should strive to marry the daughter of a *talmid chacham*, and his words had great influence on us.

Once he went to an engagement party for a former student at which the *kallah* wore a beautiful red dress. The next day Reb Mendel called the boy over and told him, "She's a terrific girl and it's a marvelous *shidduch* you've made. Just one thing — you should tell her not to wear red dresses." And the boy accepted it. Reb Mendel was the only one who could have said such a thing without giving offense. And people listened to him.

Reb Mendel was the *Kohen* at the *Pidyon HaBen* of my oldest grandson, and he said to me then, "Berele, do you remember when we first started thirty years ago? I'm sure you never thought we would be here today!" To me that sums up Reb Mendel's whole outlook. Thirty years earlier, I would never have dreamed that he would be at my grandson's *Pidyon HaBen*. But he always saw further than most people.

All of us who were privileged to be his students still hear his words echo in our ears, still see the flash of his blue eyes and the warmth and humor of his smile. Reb Mendel was a unique and unforgettable individual.

REB MENDEL

CHAPTER ONE

A Biographical Sketch

REB YISRAEL MENDEL KAPLAN was born in 1913, in Baranovich, Poland, just prior to the outbreak of World War I.

Baranovich Baranovich was home to 30,000 people, of whom 25,000 were Jewish. The Baranovich Yeshivah, led by Rabbi Elchonon Wasserman, attracted budding young scholars from all over Europe. But Torah study was not limited to the confines of the yeshivah. Many local laymen studied late into the night, and often spent the entire night in the town *beis midrash*, where they would doze on the hard wooden benches.

The greatness of Baranovich's men in Torah scholarship was matched by the *chesed* and piety of its women. One day, when Reb Mendel was a young boy learning in *cheder*, he and his classmates were busy chanting the *Chumash* in unison, when the door unexpectedly swung open. In walked a middle-aged woman, her eyes afire with determination.

"I have a very important announcement to make," she proclaimed in a stern voice. Without waiting for permission from the rebbe to speak, she proceeded: "No one is to play in the restricted areas."

"We all immediately understood where she meant," said Reb Mendel later. "During the war, large areas had been heavily bombed, and there were menacing signs and barbed-wire fences warning people to keep away. The warring armies had left a lot of ammunition behind since they were running through the town quickly. But we children viewed those areas as our own private playgrounds.

"To our astonishment, the woman took a bloody handkerchief out of her purse and unfolded it before our eyes, revealing several small mutilated fingers.

" 'These are the fingers of my son,' she cried out. 'He was playing in the rubble and a bomb accidentally went off in his hands. No one, but no one, should set foot in those places again. This is what happens if you play with ammunition.'

"She left the room and proceeded to the next class, and then to all the other *chadarim* in the city, each time repeating her solemn message." Reb Mendel noted, "Can you imagine how difficult it was for this woman to contain the pain and suffering she felt after her child's horrid injury? But she did it anyway, for the benefit of other children. This was the greatness of a mother in Europe."

It was in this atmosphere of Torah and communal concern that Reb Mendel was born and raised. Jews performed acts of *chesed* not only with their money. Reb Mendel's wife had a great-aunt who could always be seen doing large amounts of laundry. Her niece came to visit her one day and found her standing over several large pots of soaking laundry.

"Who are you doing all this laundry for?" the niece asked.

She just shrugged her shoulders and replied innocently, "You know how laundry is — it collects." Not even her closest relatives realized that she did laundry for the boys in the yeshivah.

Nor was doing *chesed* limited to happy times. When this same woman was struck by overwhelming tragedy — the loss of nine of her children, leaving her with only one surviving child — she refused to withdraw into self-pity. Instead, she appointed herself guardian over a group of orphans who lived next door. She would knit late into the night, completing two pair of socks each day — one for the summer, one for the winter — which she would give to poor yeshivah students.

REB MENDEL'S FATHER, Reb Avraham Kaplan, was an honest and pious man who would *daven* for hours every morning, with a sweet soulful song, before going out to work. He earned his living as an attorney and was accorded great love and respect by Jew and gentile alike. A gentile client once took Reb Avraham to court in his wagon. The wagon had a high step that made it difficult to mount, so the gentile lay down on the ground and motioned for Reb Avraham to climb on his back into the wagon. As a child, Mendel would sometimes accompany his father to court, and there he formed his first impressions of the contrast between the Jewish and the non-Jewish worlds. His father impressed upon him the importance of honesty and integrity, even in situations where those values were trampled upon by others.

Parents

Reb Mendel's mother, Esther, was known in the city as an extremely pious woman. She lived her life by the adage: "I am not

Reb Avraham Kaplan

going to wait for my children to save me from *Gehinnom* — I will take precautions to save myself!" In the early 1900's, relatives in America used to send her fifty dollars a month — a colossal sum of money in those days — and she distributed it all to the poor of Baranovich. Every year she planted and tended a vegetable garden in her backyard, and she would fill up large sacks of potatoes and other vegetables to carry to poor people throughout the city. She was not content with buying hay to feed the animals of the poor; she would first buy samples of each type of hay to test on the animals to find out which they preferred. On Shabbos she did not go to *shul* to pray; instead, she went from house to house (within the local *eiruv*) collecting cooked food for the poor. One household gave a few eggs, another prepared a small package of meat, and so on. Once she finished her "rounds," she delivered all her booty to the homes of the needy.

Esther Kaplan was as brave as she was pious. While raising money for the poor, she was not afraid to enter the estates of the wealthy, undaunted by the large dogs protecting these homes. Once when someone disgraced the rabbi in *shul* she rose from the women's gallery and loudly berated the man for his misconduct.

Reb Mendel's Maternal Grandparents

Reb Mendel always spoke of his mother as a *tzadeikes*. She often said, "Summer vacation is like Elul. You have to grab every minute [to enjoy yourself in order to improve your physical well-being]." It was self-evident to her that in the month of Elul every moment was to be used for work on spiritual improvement.

Esther Kaplan provided the initial impetus to start a yeshivah in Baranovich. One day she met a *sofer* named Reb Chaikel[1] and said to him, "What will be with Baranovich? We need a yeshivah, we need living *sifrei Torah*!"

"You are right," he said. "But who will help me?"

"I will," she answered.

From that time on, Reb Chaikel dedicated himself completely to establishing a yeshivah in Baranovich, going around town to recruit students while Esther Kaplan went through the neighborhood collecting food and provisions for them.

Yeshivah Ohel Torah in Baranovich

During World War I, when famine was widespread, Esther Kaplan once saw Reb Chaikel digging for potatoes in a field. Reb Chaikel had always collected food for the boys in the yeshivah, but now he needed potatoes to save himself and his family from starvation. Esther Kaplan asked him, "If you are looking out for yourself, who will worry about the starving yeshivah boys?"

Reb Chaikel responded sadly, "What should I do? My family is also starving!"

Esther Kaplan replied, "I'll tell you what to do. Go on collecting for the yeshivah, and you can take some of what you get to feed yourself and your family." Reb Chaikel took her advice and

---

1. Reb Chaikel (*Sofer*), although an ordinary layman, was considered one of the great *tzaddikim* of Baranovich. Once the Chofetz Chaim passed through Baranovich by train, and many people went to the train station to catch a glimpse of the holy sage. The Chofetz Chaim was already old and weak and did not have the strength to make a public appearance. He inquired, however, if Reb Chaikel was present. "If Reb Chaikel is here I will appear at the window in his honor," he said.

immediately left the field, and went back to collecting food for the hungry yeshivah students.

Esther Kaplan's greatest desire was that her young Mendel should grow to study Torah. If Mendel did not go to *cheder* for a day, she would fast. When Mendel asked his mother why she was not eating, she told him, "*Oib du lerenst nit, ken ich nit essen* — If you don't learn, I can't eat."

Esther Kaplan went to extreme lengths to ensure that her son studied Torah diligently. Once she refused to give him money to buy a ball, so he collected pieces of rags and made his own home-made ball. When his mother saw him playing with it, she made sure it "disappeared." Mendel took the hint and from that time on never played ball again. Once, in his later years, he remarked, "I don't take any credit for my success with my students. *Es iz altz in zechus fun mein mameh* — It's all in my mother's merit."

Esther also kept a close watch on little Mendel's playmates and was very happy when her son became best friends with the son of the town's *rav*.
Mendel and the boy used to review their studies together and play in each other's homes. Reb Elchonon Wasserman, the *rosh yeshivah* of Baranovich Yeshivah, often visited the *rav's* home to discuss communal matters. Sometimes when the discussion grew intense, Reb Elchonon felt the need for a cigarette, but he was careful to send only the *rav's* son for the errand. Mendel was a *Kohen* and even though he was

Reb Elchonon Wasserman, zt"l

only ten years old at the time, Reb Elchonon would not let a *Kohen* serve him.

SHORTLY AFTER his bar mitzvah, Mendel entered the Baranovich Yeshivah where, despite his tender age, he quickly

The Lion of the Group

won high esteem. Reb Elchonon used to say that Mendel's mind worked like a fine-tuned violin — whatever he said came out beautiful, true and pure.[2] In his humility, Mendel often pretended not to know very much. He would sit quietly while listening to a heated discussion in learning or pretend to be playing with a string under his desk. But despite his efforts at concealment, he was considered by his peers to be "the lion of the group."[3] His fellow students used to relate their *chiddushim* to Mendel for his evaluation. He had the ability to hear meanings in their words that even they were not fully aware of and to ferret out errors that might have crept into their ideas.[4]

Reb Elchonon arranged for his son Naftoli to learn with Mendel as his exclusive study partner. He also chose Reb Mendel to help him prepare for his daily *Gemara shiur*. During the week following Reb Mendel's wedding, Reb Elchonon came to his house. Receiving no reply to his knocking, Reb Elchonon began to bang loudly on the shutters. "Come," he called, "nowhere does the Torah say that a *chasan* is exempt from Torah study."

Reb Elchonon told Reb Mendel's mother that her son would one day be a *maggid shiur* in the yeshivah. Although the outbreak of World War II prevented this dream from being realized, Reb Mendel did give Reb Elchonon's *shiur* when the latter went to America in the late 1930's to raise money for the yeshivah.

In the yeshivah, Reb Mendel distinguished himself by his concern for others as well as by his scholastic achievements. Rabbi Simchah Sheps, *rosh yeshivah* of Yeshivah Torah Vodaath in Brooklyn, recalls from his days as a student in Baranovich: "Whenever a *bachur* in the yeshivah was sick, Reb Mendel was the one who brought food to him. Often this caused him to be late for

---

2. Related by Rabbi Aharon Eisenberg.
3. Related by Rabbi Shmuel Berenbaum, *rosh yeshivah* of the Mirrer Yeshivah in Brooklyn and a former student in Baranovich.
4. Related by Rabbi Aharon Eisenberg.

his study session with Reb Naftoli Wasserman, but in his humility he never disclosed the true reason for his tardiness."

Rabbi Sheps, who shared a room in the yeshivah with Mendel, once returned to his room late at night to find a strange man sleep-

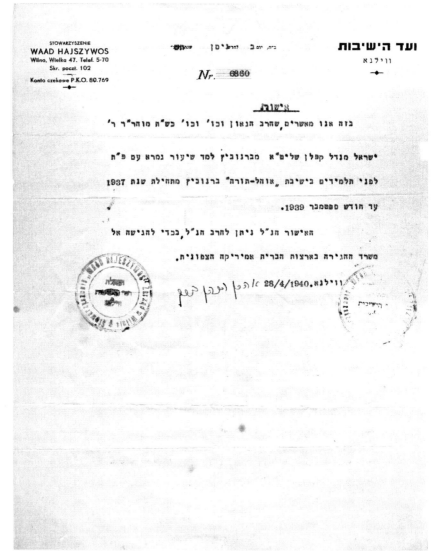

A letter from the Vilna Va'ad HaYeshivos attesting to Reb Mendel's having taught at Baranovich Yeshivah

ing in Mendel's bed. The following morning, Reb Simchah awoke to see the same man still sleeping soundly and undisturbed. He pressed Mendel for an explanation, but to no avail. Only later did he discover that the man had nowhere else to sleep so Mendel, who had just met him, gave him his own bed and spent the whole night awake learning.

ဿ ဿ ဿ

When Reb Mendel's father grew older, he found his law practice too difficult to maintain by himself. His failing eyesight forced him to cut back on his activities and he strongly desired that his son join him in his practice. He arranged for Mendel to take the admission test for law school. Seeing that his father would be greatly grieved if he did not obey his wishes, Mendel dutifully studied for the examination. His mother, however, desired that he continue his full-time Torah studies.

On the day of the test, she brought a large amount of bread to the yeshivah and begged the students to pray that Mendel fail the examination. Although Mendel was very capable and had done all the required studies, his mother's wish was fulfilled: Mendel failed and was able to continue his Torah studies without interruption.

WHEN REB MENDEL was twenty and learning in the Mirrer Yeshivah, Reb Zvi Hirsch Gutman, the *menahel* of the Baranovich

Marriage Yeshivah, began looking for a *shidduch* for his daughter, Sarah Baila. He asked Reb Elchonon Wasserman for his opinion of Reb Mendel, as well as several other eligible young men, including Reb Elchonon's own son, Naftoli. Reb Elchonon chose Reb Mendel. Reb Zvi Hirsch, who was very close to Reb Elchonon, pressed him: "Isn't your son Naftoli a little better?" Reb Elchonon put aside his personal feelings and answered honestly, "*Mine Naftoli iz a gutte bachur, ober tsu Mendele kumt er nit* — My Naftoli is a good boy, but he doesn't come up to Mendel." The match was arranged, and Reb Mendel was soon engaged.

Reb Mendel's father-in-law was an exceptional individual, wise in Torah and saintly in his conduct. He was reputed to know by heart the entire *Shulchan Aruch Orach Chaim* with its major commentators. As *menahel*, he was responsible for managing the financial affairs of the yeshivah and dealing with the physical

| *Reb Hirsch Gutman's father* | *Reb Hirsch Gutman, Reb Mendel's father-in-law* | *Reb Mendel's brother-in-law, Reb Lipa Gutman, Rav of Na-Lubok* |

needs of the students. Until he could arrange proper accommodations for new students, they stayed in his home as guests.[5]

After the engagement, Reb Mendel returned to his studies at the Mirrer Yeshivah. During the year and a half he and Sarah Baila were engaged, Reb Mendel interrupted his learning to visit his *kallah* only once. She had been ill for several days, and then one day there was a knock at the door. Reb Zvi Hirsch opened the door and was surprised to find Reb Mendel standing before him.

"How did you know my daughter is sick?" he asked. (At that time, there was no direct communication between the two cities.)

"I didn't," Reb Mendel answered. "I don't know why I came, but I had a strong feeling that I was needed here. So I came."

After a short time in the Gutman house, Reb Mendel went to visit his parents. Reb Mendel's mother immediately prepared some nourishing food and admonished him to take it back to Sarah Baila, whose illness had robbed her of her appetite. (Sarah

---

5. Rav Gutman's hospitality was known far beyond the boundaries of Baranovich. Whenever a travelling yeshivah student needed a place to stay in Baranovich, which was a junction for a number of railroad lines, he knew to go to the Gutman home. The Gutman children were put to sleep early and once they were safely asleep, their pillows were gently taken away for use by the guests. When there were more guests than beds, as often happened, Reb Hirsch would nimbly take doors off their hinges and rest them on two chairs to serve as makeshift beds.

A *bachur* once came to the Gutman home late at night to ask if he could sleep there. Reb Hirsch apologized, saying that there weren't any more beds in the house. The *bachur* replied, "I meant to ask if you have any *doors* left."

Baila's mother was no longer alive.) Reb Mendel stayed at the Gutmans' home for a number of hours, preparing Sarah Baila's food and tending to her needs. Once she started to feel better, he returned to Mir to resume his studies.

Mendel and Sarah Baila's wedding took place in Baranovich in the home of Rabbi Yisrael Yaakov Lubchansky, in the winter of 1935. The *chupah* was held outdoors in knee-high snow. Reb Elchonon displayed his deep affection for his beloved student by dancing with all his might above the snow. During the wedding feast, Reb Elchonon performed a unique dance of his own. He would dance a short distance with his knees bent and his *kapota* spread across the floor. Then he quickly raised himself to full height, danced for a

Reb Mendel and Sarah Baila as Chasan and Kallah

בעזה״ית

אתכבד להזמין את הו״כ להשתתף בשמחת כלולתי את ב״ג

מרת **שרה בילה גוטמן** תחי׳

בת הר״הג ר׳ **צבי הירש** שליט״א מנהל דהישיבה הק׳ .אוהל תורה׳ בברנוביץ

שתהי׳ ברצות ד׳ ביום ו׳ עש״ק פ׳ תצוה י״ב אדר ראשון תרצ״ה בבית הר״הג
ר׳ ישראל יעקב שליט״א בעיר ברנוביץ רחוב נרוטוביץ 66

בהוקרה רבה

מנדל קפלן

Kapłan Gutman Baranowicze Narutowicza 66 :הכתבת

The wedding invitation - larger than actual size!

bit and then once again lowered himself. This continuous alternation between full height and kneeling was famed as Reb Elchonon's "Torah dance," for on Simchas Torah he danced before the Torah in the very same manner.[6] In later years, Reb Mendel smiled whenever he recalled Reb Elchonon's dancing.

After the wedding, the young couple lived for some time in the same building as Reb Elchonon. Apart from the countless hours they shared in Torah study, Reb Mendel benefited even more from this opportunity to study his

Reb Mendel as a young man

rebbe's behavior in all aspects of life. A door connected their two apartments, and the prized student was welcomed as a member of the Wasserman family. Reb Mendel's rebbetzin often cooked meals for Reb Elchonon when his wife was away, and he would send his son with a message praising her excellent cooking: *"Gay zug far Sarah Baila es is geven zayer gishmak — Go tell Sarah Baila that it was very tasty."* On Shabbos morning, Reb Mendel took his children to Reb Elchonon's home for *kiddush,* where they would climb onto the *rosh yeshivah's* lap. Despite the poverty they endured, their Torah studies sustained them with joy and

---

6. Although Reb Elchonon was known for almost never laughing (see *Nedarim* 50b-51a), Reb Mendel's wedding was a rare exception. Reb Elchonon loved Reb Mendel dearly, and although he always refrained from showing his inner feelings, at this special moment they came to the fore. The catalyst was a comedy skit performed by the *mashgiach* of the yeshivah, Rabbi Yisrael Yaakov Lubchansky, and Rabbi Shmuel Charkover, one of the top students of the Mirrer Yeshivah. The skit portrayed a tailor trying to sell a customer an ill-fitting jacket. The skit was so funny that Reb Elchonon could not restrain his laughter, and motioned pleadingly for them to stop.

tranquility. But that glorious epoch came to an abrupt end with the outbreak of World War II.

GERMANY INVADED POLAND in September of 1939, quickly taking half the country for itself, and leaving the other half for

The War Years Russia under the terms of the Ribbentrop-Molotov Pact. The Bolsheviks were bent on destroying every trace of religion in their half of Poland, and quickly set out to accomplish this goal. The existence of all the yeshivos in the Russian-controlled Poland was threatened, and Reb Elchonon instructed all his students to flee to Vilna, which briefly remained the capital of independent Lithuania, under neither German nor Russian control.

Immediately after Succos 5700 (1939), the mass exodus to Vilna began. Reb Mendel arranged for his wife and three small children to travel on ahead, while he remained behind to transport their possessions. When Rebbetzin Kaplan arrived at the railroad station in Vilna, there were thousands of people milling around without any idea of where to go. Rebbetzin Kaplan hired a horse and buggy to take her family to the home of an acquaintance. Arriving at the small apartment, she found it already occupied by nearly thirty refugees. Since there was barely any room to move, she quickly left. Throughout the Jewish quarter, the same story repeated itself wherever she went. All the houses in the area were packed. Exhausted and lacking anywhere else to go, she returned to the house of her acquaintance and went to sleep in the hallway. The owner, overcome with compassion for the young mother and her children, took them into the already overcrowded apartment.

Reb Mendel and his family in a village near Vilna on their flight from the Nazis

Despite the difficulties faced by the refugees, life for yeshivah students in Vilna soon returned to normal. Rabbi Chaim Ozer Grodzenski, the undisputed leader of world Torah Jewry at that time, was confined to bed by his declining health. Nevertheless, he was able to help the many yeshivos that came under his protective care to re-establish themselves in Vilna. The yeshivos, located in thirty *battei midrash* in and around the city, resumed their regular study schedules and *shiurim*. While in Vilna, Reb Mendel studied under Rabbi Yitzchok Zev Soloveitchik, the famed Brisker Rav.

One day Reb Mendel was chopping wood for their cooking oven when four huge policemen suddenly surrounded him. "Don't you know it's forbidden to chop wood today? Today is our holiday!" the officers barked. Reb Mendel apologized and explained that on Jewish holidays it is permitted to chop wood for cooking purposes. The officers, unimpressed by his talmudic reasoning, took him directly to police headquarters where he was placed under arrest. A judge sentenced him to a term in prison, and only through the swift intervention of Reb Chaim Ozer, together with Reb Elchonon and Reb Yisrael Yaakov Lubchansky, was he released.

Vilna's status as a city of refuge did not last long. In June 1940, the Red Army invaded Lithuania and placed the country under Soviet rule. All yeshivos were abolished and Torah students persecuted. Reb Elchonon moved his yeshivah to a quiet village near Vilna, hoping to escape attention. The Communists, however, extended their edicts to the small villages as well. Reb Mendel once told the story of a Jewish Communist official who came to Reb Elchonon demanding that he close his yeshivah. Reb Elchonon asked him, "How is it possible to be without Torah?"

The Communist answered arrogantly, "Of what use is a yeshivah? There's no Judaism left in Russia anyway."

Reb Elchonon retorted, "You don't know what will happen in another year from now. In another year the situation may change completely."

Reb Mendel commented, "This *Yid*, even though he was a Communist, was a better sort of person and didn't force them to close the yeshivah. Reb Elchonon's warning proved to be entirely justified. We don't know what will happen in another year." The following year Germany declared war on Russia and pushed the Red Army out of Poland and Lithuania.

Yeshivah students were subject to constant harassment and persecution at the hands of the Communists. The yeshivos which had dispersed to the villages had special difficulties. For example, when a student wished to telephone his home, he had to travel by train to Vilna since there were no telephones in the smaller villages. The Communists did not allow yeshivah students on the bus, and the boys were forced either to hire horses and buggies or walk several miles. There were bread lines, but the Communists ordered that no bread be given or sold to yeshivah students. Such was the state of affairs in the "new Communist order."

Through the workings of Divine Providence, however, the Communist persecution resulted in saving the lives of hundreds of Torah scholars, including Reb Mendel and his family. It had become impossible to continue Torah studies under the Russians, and the yeshivos made every effort to escape, thus saving themselves from an incalculably harsher fate at the hands of the Nazi beasts who were soon to overrun Lithuania.

The Kaplans' final destination visa

When the Russians seized control of Lithuania, all foreign consuls moved out, except for that of Japan. The Japanese consul gave many Jews transit visas that allowed them to travel to Japan on their way to an undefined ultimate destination. Those transit visas were valid only if accompanied by visas granting them entry into another country. Reb Mendel obtained such a visa but was never able to secure a Japanese transit visa. Nevertheless, when it came time to leave, he and his family joined the many members of the Mirrer Yeshivah on their trip across Russia. Two weeks later, they reached Vladivostok, a port at the eastern end of Russia, and boarded a boat for Japan.

When the boat docked in Japan, the Japanese checked everyone's documents. Since Reb Mendel could not produce the necessary papers, he and his family were separated to be sent back to Russia and Siberian exile. An officer was appointed to guard

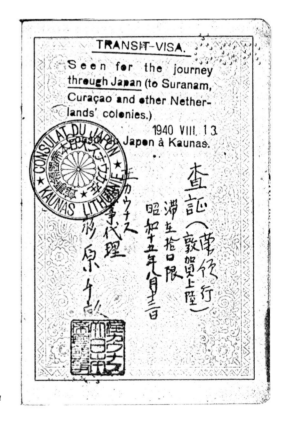

A Japanese transit visa

them constantly. The Rebbetzin, who kept her three small children and a little baby constantly by her side, taunted the officer, "Why are you guarding me? Do you expect me to run off a boat with four children?"

While the other passengers boarded a train for the ongoing journey, the Kaplans, together with others who also lacked proper papers, were forced to remain behind. The boat was ready to take them back to Russia when Rabbi Yisrael Kaplinsky, a colleague of Reb Mendel's, furtively handed him an extra visa which he possessed.

They quickly changed the name on the visa from Kaplinsky to Kaplan, but their efforts at forgery were obvious. Reb Mendel was afraid to present the document. The penalty for possessing forged papers might have resulted in an even worse punishment than Siberian exile.

Reb Mendel and his wife watched their friends slowly leaving the landing area to freedom. With nothing else to do, Reb Mendel quietly walked to a deserted stairway, leaned on the railing, and buried his head in his arms. Sapped of all energy, he stood there at the railing.

In the meantime, the Rebbetzin, ill from the long journey and contemplating their dismal prospects, began to weep bitterly. Her children sensed that something was amiss and quickly joined the chorus. By this time almost all the officers had already departed,

leaving only one commander to oversee operations. The commander strolled towards the Rebbetzin and, seeing her and the children crying, felt compassion for them. Bending down to the young mother he asked softly, "Don't you have some sort of valid paper?"

The Rebbetzin replied with a choking voice, "We had one but it was misplaced with the luggage."

The commander called to Reb Mendel and ordered him to find the papers. Reb Mendel looked through his luggage and, with no choice, "found"

Approaching harbor in Shanghai

the forged visa and begrudgingly handed it to the commander. The commander quickly glanced at the papers, then summoned an officer to his side.

"Go accompany the rabbi to the office of the registrar and get these papers stamped."

The officer was unwilling to comply with the order, explaining that it was already six in the evening and all the clerks were preparing to leave for the day. The commander cut him off, "I don't need any excuses. Go call the office and have them await your arrival."

The officer called the office and then rushed with Reb Mendel to a building near the piers. The clerks were in a hurry to get

The Kaplan children on the boat

home, and did not bother to look at the forms before stamping them and passing Reb Mendel and his family through.

Meanwhile, Rabbi Kaplinsky had detained the train in the hope Reb Mendel and his family would somehow get through. When he suddenly saw them running toward the train, he burst into tears of joy! The Kaplans went with the Mirrer Yeshivah group to Yokohama and Kobe in Japan, and later to Shanghai in China, where they remained for five and a half years.

THE EUROPEAN REFUGEES found it very hard to adjust to the hot and humid climate in Shanghai. The streets were filthy, food **Shanghai** was scarce, and the sight of people falling dead in the streets all too common. At the end of each day, a truck toured the streets with workers who picked up the dead bodies and threw them onto the truck like sacks of garbage.

Reb Mendel's papers in Shanghai

In the Mirrer *beis midrash*, however, the sound of Torah study resounded from early morning till late at night. During the day the students hung towels from their belts to wipe the unceasing perspiration from their bodies, and continued their studies even

A telegram sent to Reb Mendel at Jewcom – the Jewish communal organization in Japan

when they had to lie down, overcome with exhaustion.

In both Kobe and Shanghai, the Kaplan house was open to anyone in need. A student related how Reb Mendel once saved his life. One Shabbos morning in Japan, on the long walk from his lodgings to the yeshivah for *davening*, he was suddenly overcome with a dreadful exhaustion. With his last bit of strength, he dragged himself to the yeshivah, where *davening* was in progress. He felt himself on the brink of collapse from hunger and exhaustion. Reb Mendel appeared at that moment in the hallway. Realizing the state this *bachur* was in, Reb Mendel immediately brought him to his home. There, he placed a pot of rice, which was to have fed the entire Kaplan family that Shabbos morning, in front of the *bachur* and with loving care stood over him urging him to finish it "till the very last kernel." When

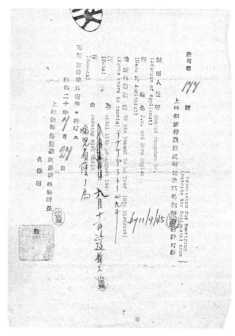

A permit allowing Reb Mendel to stay out of the assigned areas in Shanghai to care for his ailing son

Reb Mendel's son Shimon, born in Shanghai

the *bachur* left Reb Mendel's home, he felt like a new person. Half a century later, he still relates this story with unbridled gratitude.

In Shanghai, Reb Mendel spent many a day caring for his wife and other family members who were often ill with various diseases. Nevertheless, as soon as he came into the *beis midrash*, he was able to resume his learning as if he had been involved in the topic all day. He also gave a *Gemara shiur* for some younger students. Reb Zev Tikotzky, who was a student in his *shiur* at that time, recalls that what impressed him most was Reb Mendel's ability to admit when he did not know

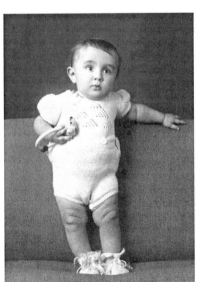

something. "He knew a lot more than his students did, and found it easy to give satisfying answers to our small questions. But still he was big enough to say frequently, 'I don't know.' "

In Shanghai, the younger of Reb Mendel's two sons, two-year-old Chaim Ozer, died. Reb Mendel followed the coffin in complete calm, as if he were returning an object given to him for safekeeping

Reb Mendel's son Chaim Ozer. He was born while his mother was standing between cars on the train leaving Vilna because his parents' compartment was filled with drunken soldiers.

to its owner. On the gravestone he had inscribed only the words, "אוי לנו כי חטאנו" — "Woe to us for we have sinned."

AFTER THE WAR, Reb Mendel and his family emigrated to America and settled in Chicago. Before long the Kaplan family
America had no food in the house. Outwardly, Reb Mendel's demeanor remained unchanged, and no one imagined how desperate their situation actually was. For several months he did not pay the rent. His landlord met him on the steps one day. "Rabbi Kaplan," he intoned, "you know that in America if you don't pay the rent they make you move out!"

Reb Mendel knew the landlord was really a kindhearted man and replied, "If you have a neighbor with little children who doesn't pay his rent, might you think that possibly they don't have anything to eat either?"

The landlord was taken aback and immediately arranged for one of his wealthy children to lend Reb Mendel several hundred dollars, thus saving the family from starvation.

Shortly thereafter, Reb Mendel was asked to give a *shiur* at the local yeshivah high school. The first *shiur* he delivered was a disaster. Aside from the language barrier, the American mentality was completely foreign to him. It was then that his extraordinary ability to adapt himself to new situations saved him.

The next day he came into *shiur* with a *Chicago Tribune* tucked under his arm. "*Kinderlach*," he told the class, "today I will teach you how to read a newspaper," and for the next two hours he held the class spellbound. Although he still could not read English well (the class helped him with that), Reb Mendel gave the class a running commentary on every topic, showing them how to read between the lines and analyze what the events really meant. From then on, the class looked at their rebbe in a new light — here was someone who could not only explain difficult *Gemaras*, but who also understood the world and life itself.

Reb Mendel had a great impact on the lives of his students. One student from that era confesses that he was then in doubt whether to remain religious. Reb Mendel sensed his personal conflict and worked hard to win the boy's confidence. Over the course of time the boy's whole outlook changed, and eventually he became a *rosh yeshivah*.

As a rebbe, Reb Mendel could be stern at times, and other times humorous and lovable. He had received the recipe for this delicate blend from his own teachers. Rabbi Yisrael Yaakov Lubchansky, the Baranovich *mashgiach*, for example, used to give solemn *mussar* discourses throughout the month of Elul. On Simchas Torah, however, he would don a doctor's cap and stethoscope and make all the *talmidim* form a long line in front of him. He would cock his head and, with his stethoscope on each boy's chest in turn, he would listen carefully, in deep concentration. After the "examination," he gave each student a "diagnosis." To one boy he said, "You have to learn an extra twenty minutes of *mussar* every day and come to *Shacharis* on time. Then you'll be okay." Another one was told, "Your problem is that you learn too much *mussar* and you don't eat enough." And so he would continue down the line, prescribing for each boy the "medicine" he needed.

Despite being a newcomer to America, Reb Mendel immediately began to find ways to help those in greater need than himself. Once a group of refugees was due to arrive in Chicago from Europe. As soon as they arrived at their lodgings, Reb Mendel came to greet them, and brought them soft pillows and blankets.

Once, while the Rebbetzin was out of town visiting relatives, a group of *bachurim* who had been in Shanghai passed through Chicago on their way from California to New York. That night, Reb Mendel invited them all to his home. The Rebbetzin returned to the small apartment late at night, and found dozens of sleeping *bachurim*. She was unfazed — if anything, it reminded her of life in Baranovich as a young girl — and she spent the night sleeping on one of the few remaining chairs.

Throughout his life, Reb Mendel was the softest of men. But if ever a situation arose involving the dignity of the Torah, he was equal to it. He considered the Jewish education available in Chicago at the time inadequate to produce Torah-true sons and daughters of the highest caliber. When his daughters were ready to enter high school, he sent them and the Rebbetzin to New York where the girls could attend the Bais Yaakov in Williamsburg. Later the Rebbetzin rented an apartment in Brooklyn to stay with them. Because there were no teaching positions available in New

York, Reb Mendel stayed behind in Chicago, visiting his family only twice a year.

The girls' tuition was more than his teaching salary could cover, so he started a small winery to supplement his income. He hoped to be able to confine most of his business activities to the yeshivah vacations — producing wine in Tishrei and selling it in Nissan.

When Reb Mendel's oldest son was only ten years old, he was sent to learn at Telshe Yeshivah in Cleveland. The *rosh yeshivah*, Rabbi Elya Meir Bloch, *zt"l*, was at first reluctant to accept such a young student, but Reb Mendel and his Rebbetzin were persistent. The Rebbetzin took her son to Cleveland and stayed with him for three weeks. When the time came for her to return home, the boy came to the train station and pleaded to be taken home. He chased after the train as it pulled away and continued running and crying for as long as the Rebbetzin was able to see him from the window.

Reb Mendel and his wife suppressed their sympathy for their son, and many times listened in silence as he cried to them over the telephone and pleaded to be allowed to return home. Reb Mendel promised his son that, in the merit of these hardships, he would someday become a great *talmid chacham*. In later years, when his son was already a *rosh yeshivah*, Reb Mendel explained to him that he had sent him away to show the Jewish community that if they wanted their sons to be successful in learning, they had to send them away. To drive his point home, he had to make a personal sacrifice — an *Akeidas Yitzchak* — even though it was his own precious son. By setting this example, he inspired other parents to send their sons away to yeshivah, and many of these boys grew up to become Jewish leaders and educators.

In those days, every American boy went to college to learn a profession. Reb Mendel, however, inspired a number of students to forgo college. Indeed, many of them went on to study in the famous yeshivos of higher learning in America and abroad.

His "success" in this regard was not greeted with enthusiasm by many parents of students in the Chicago Yeshivah. The mother of one of his students informed him in a scathing letter, "America is not Europe and we don't do these things here." (Reb Mendel saved the letter for its sentimental value.) Reb Mendel's detractors even called a board meeting for the specific purpose of pressuring the yeshivah to fire him for his "un-American" ideas.

On the day of the board meeting, Reb Mendel's two leading opponents met with their supporters to prepare their presentation. They left the house confident of success, and got into the car to drive to the board meeting. As they pulled out of the driveway, the driver inexplicably fell from the car onto the driveway. The driverless car continued, with its passengers, out of the driveway and across a busy street, where it hit a tree and finally came to a halt. Miraculously no one was injured, but everyone was considerably shaken. They recognized Divine intervention and decided to cancel the board meeting and drop the issue entirely. When Reb Mendel heard about the incident, his only reaction was relief that no one had been injured.

Reb Mendel showed no concern for the threat to his livelihood and continued to teach in the only way he felt proper. When the school announced a holiday for the Fourth of July, he insisted that his *shiur* continue on that day as well. Later when they planned for a girls' school to open near the boys' building, he went on strike.

Such actions finally led the school to ask Reb Mendel to deliver his *shiur* just one day a week, although it offered to continue paying his full salary. Reb Mendel refused to accept this offer, since it would prevent him from properly guiding his students. As a result, he was left without his principal means of support.

In his farewell talk to his students, he told them, "Always be one of the pursued, rather than the pursuer." Later in life he said, "Three times in my life was I treated unjustly. But in each case it turned out for my benefit."

Reb Mendel ran a winery which provided a supplement to his income, at best. It did not even cover his children's tuition and other expenses out of town. A

wealthy man in Chicago, however, was impressed with Reb Mendel's intelligence and talent. He considered investing a large sum of money to expand the Kaplan winery, in the hope that it would one day rival Magen David, a major Chicago-based winery. After observing Reb Mendel for a while, however, he had one reservation. He explained to Reb Mendel that for a business to be successful, *"Men darf lieb habben dem daller —* One has to love the dollar." Reb Mendel replied, *"Dos vet ir mir shoin kein mahl nisht ois lernen —* That you will never succeed in teaching me."

The man continued to invest small sums in the winery to help Reb Mendel, but the humble Kaplan winery remained a local endeavor that produced neither wealth nor fame. Reb Mendel's spiritual "wine of Torah" was soon to be enjoyed elsewhere.

SHORTLY AFTERWARDS, Reb Mendel moved to New York to be with his family. He held several temporary teaching positions until
The Yeshivah of Philadelphia 1965, when the Talmudical Academy of Philadelphia invited him to give a *Gemara shiur.* Reb Mendel was fully content teaching the youngest post-high school class and continued to

The building of the Talmudical Academy of Philadelphia where Reb Mendel gave shiur for nearly 20 years

give that *shiur* for the rest of his life. The *rosh yeshivah* of Torah Vodaath, Reb Yaakov Kamenetzky, *zt"l*, marveled at his modesty. "*Ahza kuntz! Ahza kuntz!* — Such a feat! Such a feat!" he once exclaimed to one of Reb Mendel's sons-in-law. "He is greater than famous *roshei yeshivah*, and he can still work quietly under younger men!"

At the Philadelphia Yeshivah, Reb Mendel taught with the same total dedication and self-sacrifice he had shown all his life. He lived in a dorm room in the yeshivah during the week, returning to his home in the Bensonhurst section of Brooklyn for Shabbos only after giving his Friday morning *shiur*. He drove back to Philadelphia early each Sunday morning, despite the strain this schedule placed on him. At times, he would drive to Philadelphia just to give a single *Gemara shiur* and then return home the same day.

Whatever stresses he may have borne in his heart, he always appeared happy and calm to the outside world and was careful to shield even his wife from anything that might upset her. Once he had a kidney stone attack in the middle of the night and bore the extreme pain in silence so as not to worry the family. Another time he made an eight-hour drive to visit a sick relative in Virginia, leaving directly from the yeshivah so that the Rebbetzin would not worry about his undertaking such a difficult trip at his age and in his condition.[7] Several months before he passed away, he was involved in a serious auto accident and was taken to the hospital for observation and testing. Although the incident agitated him greatly, he still returned home with his usual composure. When his wife noted that he was not driving the same old car, he said only, "A car also has to take a rest sometimes."

೬♪ ೬♪ ೬♪

Reb Mendel passed away on 13 Nissan, 5745 (April 4, 1985), just two days before Pesach. Earlier that week, he had finished the

---

7. He made the trip the day before Rosh Hashanah so that he would not have to miss a *shiur* in yeshivah. He returned to his home in Brooklyn only a few hours before Rosh Hashanah, totally drained and exhausted. That night when he prayed in the Mirrer Yeshivah on Ocean Parkway, a student noticed that he looked pitifully tired, and often placed his head on his lectern for a few moments' rest between prayers. At the time, the student thought it odd that he entered the Day of Judgment tired and worn out, unable to pray with his usual energy. But Reb Mendel obviously felt that it was more important to enter the New Year with the merit of that good deed.

winter term in the Philadelphia Yeshivah and returned home to prepare for Pesach. On his first night home, there was a terrible storm raging outside. Though tired and weak from the trip, Reb Mendel took care of a few things at home and prepared to go out. The Rebbetzin asked incredulously, "Where are you going in this weather?! You just came home!" Reb Mendel said he knew of an old *talmid chacham*, a friend from Europe, who was in the hospital, and he wanted to visit him to cheer him up. The Rebbetzin asked him to wait until the morning, but to no avail. He felt his friend's anguish with such vividness that it was unthinkable to push off the visit.

Pesach preparations are hectic for everyone, but for Reb Mendel the burden was tenfold. Aside from helping his immediate and extended family with preparations for Pesach and squeezing in whatever time he could for Torah study, he coordinated an effort to supply *Yom Tov* needs for the poor and needy. The very night he passed away, he went out to personally deliver large food packages to several poor families. The Rebbetzin saw how exhausted her husband was from working the entire day, and tried to stop him. Reb Mendel was undeterred and told her simply, "You don't put off *mitzvos*."

When Reb Mendel returned home later that night, he heard one of his grandsons having difficulty falling asleep. He got two glasses of water, and went into his grandchild's room. Together they made a blessing on the water. After putting his grandson back into bed, he returned to his room and prepared to go sleep himself. During that sleep, Reb Mendel's pure soul was quietly returned to its Creator.

The *levayah* was held at the cargo section of Kennedy Airport just a few hours after his passing to allow burial in *Eretz Yisrael* before Pesach. There was virtually no time to publicize Reb Mendel's passing, and although there was a sizable crowd of *talmidim,* it was nowhere near the outpouring there would have been had there been more time. Rabbi Shmuel Kamenetzky, *rosh yeshivah* of the Philadelphia Yeshivah, told those gathered, "This is the way Reb Mendel would have preferred to leave this world. Just as during his lifetime he fled from all honors and never allowed others to serve him in any way, so too in his passing." Rabbi Shmuel Berenbaum, the Mirrer *rosh yeshivah*, viewing the distraught faces of Reb Mendel's students, commented, "They look like they have just lost their own father."

תנצב"ה

Reb Mendel's grave

*Reb Mendel's lifelong
friend, Reb Simcha
Wasserman, at
Reb Mendel's grave*

CHAPTER TWO

Reb Mendel's Shiur

REB MENDEL viewed his classroom as a Temple in miniature and zealously guarded its sanctity. He did not allow his *shiur*-room to be used for anything other than Torah study; secular subjects had to be taught elsewhere. The seats were arranged in a semicircle around his desk, as prescribed by the *Rambam* (*Hilchos Talmud Torah* 4:2).

He ran his class according to the timeless methods described in *Tanach* and *Gemara*. His reputation as a *gaon*, his mastery of the *Gemara* and his unworldly piety made him among the most popular *roshei yeshivah* of his time. Even students of an age when boys tend to be undisciplined sat quietly, even reverently, in his presence.

Reb Mendel's teaching techniques were derived from the great leaders of the previous generation. When he saw the class was having difficulty comprehending the *Gemara's* intricacies, he would assure us that the subject was indeed one of the most difficult in the entire Talmud. This boosted our spirits enormously. We no longer felt like uncomprehending fools, but that our lack of comprehension was totally appropriate given the depth of the topic. Only years later did we realize that he always used the same introduction, regardless of the true difficulty of the subject. He once confided to a student that he had learned this technique from Reb Elchonon.

When teaching a difficult concept, he could put on a marvelous act of showmanship to save the students' feelings. At first he would feign a look of confusion, and then, with a shake of his head, he would say, "*Noch a mohl!* — Once more," in a tone that implied that he needed to clarify it further for his own benefit. He always acted as though the *Gemara* he was teaching was completely new to him, and he needed our help to understand it.

He once told me how Rabbi Shimon Shkop, under whom he had studied for two years in Grodno, Poland, never looked at the clock to know when to end his *shiur*. Instead he looked at the faces of his students. When he saw that they were tired and distracted, he knew it was time to stop. Reb Mendel did the same.

From the very first day of his *shiur* we had a good feeling about his class, ourselves and learning in general. One year Reb Mendel began his *shiur* in the middle of August. One student was dismayed to have to leave summer camp while it was still in full swing. He did not want to return to yeshivah in the middle of the summer. Perhaps sensing the student's feelings, Reb Mendel opened the *shiur* by quoting the *Mishnah* (*Avos* 3:7): "One who walks on the road reviewing [a Torah lesson] but interrupts his review and exclaims, 'How beautiful is this tree, how beautiful is this plowed field,' Scripture considers it as if he bears guilt for his soul." He continued, "*Chazal* teach us that Hashem's mercy far exceeds His justice (*Yoma* 76a), so you can imagine what a reward one receives if he interrupts the idle pursuits of the summer to come and learn Torah."

Reb Mendel's *shiur* was an adventure, in which the words and ideas of the Sages were constantly alive and vibrant. One day, for instance, he told the class to bring Reb Chaim Brisker's classic work on the *Rambam* to *shiur* the next day. He began the next *shiur* discussing Reb Chaim and how he had strained to get each word and expression exactly right. Then he learned with us Reb Chaim's introduction to give us a feeling for his greatness, and to teach us that the great Torah works were the products of human beings like ourselves. Learning about the authors whose works we

Preparing for Shiur

studied, and the times in which they lived, helped us view their words differently.

"The *Gemara* is not a hook to hang your fancy *p'shatim* on," Reb Mendel would say. Although he never attempted to demonstrate his sharpness of mind and vast knowledge, we sensed his genius in his ability to present complicated concepts in the simplest of terms. His *shiur* could be understood on many levels. Even the weaker students could grasp the main points, while the more advanced students used them as a springboard for further thought and discussion.

Reb Mendel's *shiur* was not a lecture but a structured dialogue. He had a gift for involving even the weakest students. Once he said to a boy whose attention seemed to be wandering, "Are you listening? Why aren't you playing the game? It's like playing ball — I throw something out at the class, you have to throw it back."[1]

Another time, a shy *bachur* who was having problems understanding the topic at hand whispered to the boy next to him. Reb Mendel looked toward him and said, "What are you saying? Speak up, it's time to stand up and be counted! That's how you say it in English, isn't it? *Al tihi anav* — Don't be humble. If you don't understand something, don't keep quiet about it; scream, 'Rebs, I don't understand!' "

---

1. See *Tosafos Sanhedrin* 26a.

Then he mused, "In Chicago that's what they called me: 'Rebs.' Here I don't know what they call me."

§► §► §►

He understood American youth, and appreciated that unorthodox methods might be needed to transmit the tradition to them.

Rebbe once witnessed a snowball fight in the yeshivah yard and observed to one student, half jokingly, half sadly, "In our generation, a *rosh yeshivah* has to smile when he sees *bachurim* having a snowball fight. In the next generation, the *rosh yeshivah* will have to pick up a snowball and join in."

His greatest strength as an educator was the ability to find the right expression for each person. "Just say whatever you think is the right explanation," he would tell us. "You don't have to worry; I never get angry. I'm just a salesman. A salesman has to be very clever; he'll tell his customers any kind of foolishness as long as he makes a sale."

Once Rebbe noticed a boy fooling around in class and exclaimed in exasperation, "What are you doing? Drawing pictures? Look, at least it's better than throwing spitballs. It's all because of your 'school' mentality. I go to one *bachur* and ask him to learn with another *bachur*. And he tells me, 'I can't learn with him because I DON'T LIKE HIM!' I can't believe that *bachurim* tell me these things. It says explicitly in the Torah, 'Do not hate your brother in your heart' (*Vayikra* 19:17). How could you not like someone? Suddenly I realize that I'm still living back in Baranovich two generations ago."

Reb Mendel once said that learning *Chochmah U'Mussar* can make a person five years more mature, and attending his *shiur* did the same. It helped counteract all the foolishness and vanity of American society.

The Art of Teaching

ALTHOUGH EVERY REBBE has the same goal, there are many variations in style. Reb Mendel spoke about two diverging approaches.

"When Reb Aharon Kotler spoke, it was like the Giving of the Torah on Mount Sinai — with fire and thunder. Reb Shimon Shkop, on the other hand, taught Torah in a way the listener could easily absorb. His *shiur* was 'ultrasonic' in that everything sounded so simple and easy that it was hard to see that any new thing was being said."

"I didn't have a rebbe like Reb Aharon (Kotler)," he told us once. "Once when he was visiting Baranovich, he gave us a *shiur*. He was like a lion. We were about seventeen and didn't know what was happening. After the *shiur*, we all felt ashamed because we didn't understand a thing. Then, about the same time — it was around Elul — Rabbi Isser Zalman Meltzer came and also gave a *shiur*. It was nice and soft, and we all followed.

"The same is true in *mussar* as well. Rabbi Naftali Amsterdam, a *talmid* of Reb Yisrael Salanter, used to give *mussar* in Elul with a nice soft melody. On the other hand, the *mashgiach* in Baranovich,

Rabbi Yisrael Yaakov Lubchansky

Reb Yisrael Yaakov, a son-in-law of the Alter of Novardhok, used everything at his disposal to work us up to a fever pitch. Reb Yisrael Salanter had a full arsenal of methods for conveying *mussar*, and each of his students used different combinations of his methods."

Reb Mendel clearly felt that our generation needed the softer, more soothing approach. Once a student told Reb Mendel that the Alter of Slobodka was said to have spoken in a deliberately boring monotone in order to force the students to concentrate on the content of what he was saying. Rebbe said that this was quite possible, but then added, "Today we have to speak to the people like a nice hot shower."

"Look at this *Rashi*," Reb Mendel once exclaimed in class. "He added a whole title and commentary to put in a couple of simple words to prevent us from blundering in the *Gemara*. Sometimes with just one word *Rashi* can encompass a problem and solution that takes *Tosafos* a whole paragraph. *Rashi* was a real live person, not just a commentary, and he wrote what he did to explain the *Gemara* even to the simplest child — unlike *Tosafos* which teach us the *lamdus*. That's why children all learn *Rashi*. He starts off leading us by the hand through the complexities of the *Gemara*, like a father leads his son. He did it just in order to do the Jews a favor.

"I learned from my teachers that you are obligated to help someone who can't learn, and this we see from the way *Rashi* is always there to help with an outstretched hand. *Rashi* is filled with goodness. Reb Elchonon would read *Rashi* along with the *Gemara*; and he would say that in every word of *Rashi* he saw his pure goodness to others."

Reb Mendel taught in a similar fashion, filled with love and goodness.

The Treasured Student

"DO YOU THINK THIS IS A COLLEGE LECTURE?" Rebbe once asked. "Someone asked me, 'Don't you keep attendance?' I told him that I know in advance who's going to come and who isn't. Even before *shiur*, I know already."

The Jewish people are compared to stars, each Jew with his own unique purpose (*Megillah* 16a). Reb Mendel felt strongly that every student was a star with a special role in the class. No one was expendable.

"The whole *shiur* sounds to me like an orchestra. Like a conductor, who immediately knows if someone is off-key, and even more so if he's not there at all, if a student is missing, I feel that the music is just not the same. A *bachur* thinks he can leave the *shiur* as often as he likes, that he's like the background drums and no one will notice if he's not here. Who knows? Maybe he's really a very fine-sounding violin."

℘ ℘ ℘

Reb Mendel literally suffered over students who failed to progress as they should have. Among the few possessions Rebbe left behind were numerous cards, on which were written the names of the many students for whom he had *davened*.

One day during *shiur*, Rebbe spoke to a student who had attended a wedding the night before. "You're not listening to *shiur* — what can I do for you? You think the 'Reb' is like a teacher, and if you're not here I'll just mark you absent. You don't begin to understand what a rebbe in a yeshivah is; you don't understand that a rebbe can feel pain just because you're not here. I say this because I see you are not following, and it hurts me."

When one *bachur* got up from his seat and left the room, Reb Mendel shook his head and frowned. "I have such pain over him because he's unhappy here, and he's always leaving in the middle of *shiur*. What can we do for him? It is said that when you visit a sick person and share his suffering, you take away one sixtieth of his illness. Maybe if we all suffer over him, Hashem will help."

In later years Reb Mendel's concern for his students began to take a toll on his health. A relative of his once asked him why he took things so much to heart. "If a student doesn't want to listen to you, it's his own problem," the man said. "Forget about it."

Reb Mendel replied, "If they were your own children, would you still say the same thing? I feel they are my children."

He once told a *bachur* who did not take learning seriously, "The *mashgiach* in Slobodka used to fast for students when nothing else helped. I have pity on you; I just can't help you any more. Why am I telling you this? Just to give you aggravation and pain? I'll tell you why. Because I want to get the pain out of my heart. So I'm throwing it on you. I'm an *alter mentsch* (old man) who is weak and has no strength to hold aggravation."

֍ ֍ ֍

Rebbe never rejected a student, and even the weak students in yeshivah enjoyed a special relationship with him. One boy in our class often slept through *Shacharis* and came late to the morning session. The boy's roommate complained to Rebbe about his behavior, and asked if he should make sure to wake his friend up on time. Rebbe realized that the boy was unhappy in yeshivah and told the roommate to leave him alone. "*Nu*, Reuven is built very big," he said. "It's probably difficult for him to get out of bed in the morning."

The same *bachur* once came to *seder* at 10:30 in the morning, red-faced and groggy-eyed. Rebbe began to walk towards him, and we all thought Rebbe was going to let him have it. But he just asked him quietly, "Reuven, have you eaten breakfast yet?"

The *bachur* replied, "That's okay, Rebbe, I don't need to eat."

Reb Mendel took the boy's hand and pointed to some white spots on his fingernails. "Do you see these spots? They come from not drinking enough milk. Go downstairs and have some breakfast, then you can come back up to learn." Although this boy was considered a "bum" by his peers, Rebbe always tried to build up his self-image, and would praise him effusively whenever he asked a good question in class. He even tried to arrange for the boy to remain in his *shiur* for a second year so that he could continue to have an influence on him. This *bachur* is now married and in business. "Although I may no longer remember the *Gemaras* I learned with Reb Mendel," he says, "I will never forget Reb Mendel and his kindness."

§ § §

His respect for every individual — whatever his innate character traits, ability in learning or level of observance — was instrumental in changing the lives of many of his students.

A former student from Chicago recalls that when he was in high school, Reb Mendel once asked him about his summer plans. He told him that he had not made plans for the summer yet. Although Reb Mendel knew that he would probably attend a co-ed camp, Reb Mendel let him save face. "You know what," Reb Mendel said with excitement, "I also didn't make plans for the summer — let's keep in touch."

One day at the beginning of the summer, the boy received a phone call. "Hello, Reb Shmuel, this is Reb Mendel."

"Yes, Rebbe," the boy replied. "What can I do for you?"

"I have a problem and maybe you can help me. I am learning in the *beis midrash* all alone and I find it difficult to concentrate by myself." (Actually, Chicago boasted many scholars who would have loved to learn with Reb Mendel.) "Maybe you can come over, and we can start a *seder* together?"

The boy was elated and rushed to the *beis midrash*. Every day that summer they learned from nine in the morning until three in the afternoon. Afterwards they would take walks in the park, during which Rebbe told him stories about life in Europe and shared with him insights about life in general. Today that student is a successful religious businessman and looks back on that summer as the critical period of his life, a time that changed him completely.

§ § §

One of Reb Mendel's sons-in-law studied for a while with the son of a well-known Torah leader. This boy was generally viewed as the "black sheep" of his family. The son-in-law told Reb Mendel, "The administration here doesn't think much of this *bachur*, but I see in him many good qualities."

Rebbe smiled in approval and told his son-in-law, "The best thing you can do for a person is to hold him in high esteem."

One *bachur* related that for a time after he left the Philadelphia Yeshivah, he had severe problems in many areas and was uncertain whether to continue learning in yeshivah. During this period he made a trip to Philadelphia to speak with Reb Mendel. Before he could say even one word, Reb Mendel asked him to stay over in the yeshivah for a few days to learn together with him and help him prepare his *shiur*. For the next two and a half days, they spent a lot of time learning and doing other things together. Not once did Rebbe give the *bachur* an opportunity to discuss his problem. The *bachur* later said that by treating him as an equal, Rebbe gave him back his self-confidence. By the conclusion of the visit, he felt that all his problems had dissolved and there was no need to discuss them at all.

§▶ §▶ §▶

Reb Mendel did not give "guidance counseling." Sometimes he helped students find solutions to their problems by ignoring the problem and focusing on their positive qualities instead. Other times, he would share with students *his* personal problems and struggles, thereby giving them the strength to fight off their own discouragement.

A student who suffered from depression once broke down in front of Reb Mendel and told him that he didn't know how he would ever be able to live a normal life. Reb Mendel told him, "A young woman, pregnant for the first time, was having a difficult pregnancy. She complained to her mother that she didn't have the strength to continue. Her mother assured her, 'Don't worry, I went through the same experience. And just as I made it, so will you.' And similarly, I'll tell you the same thing. I also suffered greatly from my difficulties in life. Just as I overcame my emotional difficulties, so will you."

An older *bachur* who was having difficulties finding a *shidduch* once came to Reb Mendel in need of encouragement. Reb Mendel related the following story:

When I was learning in Grodno by Reb Shimon Shkop, I suffered from stomach ailments. I went to the local doctor who was unable to find the cause of my ailment. But he did tell me that my diet, which consisted of little more than bread and tea, and lack of exercise could well be the causes. I began swimming regularly in a lake in the area.

While swimming one day, I was suddenly caught in an undertow, which pulled me further and further away from shore. All my frantic swimming was getting me nowhere, and I thought for certain I was going to drown. Then a person on shore caught sight of me and began to scream, "Hang in there! You'll make it! Just one more stroke, just one more stroke!" His constant encouragement gave me the strength to continue with 'just one more stroke' until little by little I finally arrived safely on shore.

FOR REB MENDEL, a rebbe's job did not end with giving a good *shiur*. When a former student was once going through a difficult

The Role of a Rebbe period, Reb Mendel sensed the student's feelings and created opportunities to spend time with him. During lunch break, when Reb Mendel had an errand to do, he took the boy with him. Once he even called the student out of the *beis midrash* during the afternoon learning session. "Would you mind taking a walk with me?" Rebbe asked. "The doctor says I have to take walks." (It was a common tactic of his to act as if it was the other person who was doing *him* the favor.) He talked to the student as a friend and equal and discussed with him world events and sundry other topics.

Sometimes he asked about the student's family and then pointed out various characteristics the boy had inherited from his parents and ancestors. He also spoke about life in general, illustrating his points with observations about his own family and personal life. During one of these walks, Reb Mendel stopped at a wild raspberry bush near the yeshivah and picked a berry in order to show the student how to check it for worms. He asked the student to cup his hands and as he continued to talk, he kept picking berries and placing them in the student's hands. When the boy's hands were finally overflowing with berries, Reb Mendel gave him a big smile and said, "Now go back to your room and enjoy them."

§► §► §►

Reb Mendel often said that a *rosh yeshivah's* job is not only to teach Torah, but also to take care of his students' physical needs. A student once asked Reb Mendel a question that revealed that the boy was allergic to milk. Reb Mendel then discussed with him what foods were important for him to eat, based on his reading of health books, as well as the sayings of *Chazal*. The next morning before *davening*, Reb Mendel handed the boy an article he had clipped from a health journal about alternate foods for people who cannot tolerate milk. In order to impress on the boy the importance of this information, he told the boy, "Read this article three or four times right now, even before *bircas haTorah.*" Reb Mendel also made a point of asking the yeshivah cooks to make special foods for that boy. From that time on, he kept an eye on the boy to make sure he was eating well, and asked others to watch him as well.

Another time, Reb Mendel offered to drive a student to the hospital to get a throat culture. As he dropped the boy off, Reb Mendel told him to call when he was finished so that he could take him back to the yeshivah. Years later, when this student was learning in another yeshivah, he called Reb Mendel at his home and asked if he could come over to speak to him. Reb Mendel responded warmly, "Please! Just tell me a time and I'll be there. My students are the most important thing on my mind, after my wife."

§► §► §►

If a former student came to speak to him either in his house or at the yeshivah, Reb Mendel would personally serve him refreshments and insist that the student eat as they spoke. Before he left, Reb Mendel would prepare a food package for him to eat on the trip back. Whenever a student visited Reb Mendel at his house or at his bungalow during the summer, Reb Mendel would always volunteer to drive him home, as if that were a totally natural thing to do. Once a student rode with Reb Mendel from Philadelphia to Brooklyn on a Friday afternoon. The small station wagon was so filled with people that the student had to sit cramped in the back compartment. Even though Shabbos was only a few hours away and they were behind schedule, Reb Mendel made one last trip into his room after everyone was in the car and came out holding a large pillow for the student to sit on during the trip.

REB MENDEL once advised a young doctor just entering the medical profession, "Every person is a world unto himself. There are

Guide a Youth According to His Way

no set rules and procedures, and you have to treat everyone as unique." Reb Mendel followed this approach in his own work as well and would guide each student according to his own distinctive characteristics. A young and rebellious student was trying to act like a *chassidishe bachur* in a *Litvishe* yeshivah. Reb Mendel encouraged him to learn *chassidishe sefarim*, and thereby channeled his rebelliousness into a strength.

The advice Reb Mendel gave one person often contradicted what he told another. One summer in camp, a student overheard Reb Mendel tell his eleven-year old grandson; "I've learned *Chumash, Gemara* and even a little *Nach,* but I've never seen where it talks about having fun." This remark disturbed the student, and he asked Reb Mendel about it. Reb Mendel replied that there is a danger in camp of making fun into the main goal and relegating Torah to secondary importance. It had to be clear that fun is only secondary. He then said that he would not have told the same thing to another grandson who was more serious by nature. On the contrary, he would have encouraged the second grandson to play more.

Reb Mendel guided each student to develop his individual talents. He recognized in one a gift for bringing non-religious people closer to Torah. During the boy's first week in yeshivah, Rebbe drove him to a gas station near the yeshivah and told him to speak to one of the young Jewish workers there.

At other times, however, he would advise people to put off developing a particular talent. ("Don't worry," he assured them, "you won't lose it.") Although he generally encouraged and admired those who helped others, he discouraged certain individuals from focusing too much of their attention on others. During *shiur*, he once said to a student, "You're so involved with learning with the other boys — why don't you learn with yourself? If you'll feel bad that you can't help others, maybe that's something you'll just have to bear. For that alone you'll get reward."

Another time a student arrived late to *shiur*. After the boy sat down, Rebbe said to the class, "A person finds himself in a good situation and doesn't understand that it won't last forever. What great kindness were you doing now? The years you're in yeshivah are the time to grab learning. There will be plenty of years later on for you to do people favors."

༦ ༦ ༦

Reb Mendel once explained the words of *Chazal*, "*Derech eretz kadmah l'Torah* — Good character comes before Torah," to mean that before you teach someone Torah, you have to make sure he's a *mentsch*. Indeed, Rebbe devoted a lot of time and effort to that end, and guided his students not only in learning and serving Hashem but also towards leading happy, normal lives. At the same time, he tried to weed out any problematic personality traits.

One student was excessively pious and kept himself aloof from the rest of the yeshivah. Occasionally during *shiur* Reb Mendel would send someone to buy him a soda. He would start drinking the soda himself and then give the rest to the "pious" student to finish. Rebbe did not generally drink in *shiur*, but it seemed he wanted to teach that student the importance of being "normal."

One Succos, when some students were visiting Reb Mendel at his home in Brooklyn, the Rebbetzin brought potato chips into the *succah*, but Reb Mendel wouldn't take any. When the students asked him why, he explained, "I don't like to eat potato chips because they make too much noise." The same "pious" student was among those present, and Rebbe noticed that he also did not take any potato chips, so Rebbe took some potato chips and then passed them to the boy. When the boy asked why Reb Mendel wanted him to eat some, Rebbe replied, "*Because* they make noise."

If Reb Mendel ever saw a student acting compulsively zealous, he would gesture to the boy and tell him soothingly, "Take it easy, take it easy. Your temperature is too high." One year, there was a student who had an enormous capacity for work, but who was also tense and impulsive. Once, Rebbe gave a very complex explanation of a certain *Gemara,* and one of the students burst out, "Why?"

A moment later, the impulsive student also cried out, "Yeah, why?"

Rebbe looked very thoughtful, and then said calmly, "What does your 'why' add to his?" That short remark was all that was necessary to get his point across.

ᔆᕈ ᔆᕈ ᔆᕈ

His aim was to build up the self-esteem of every student. One former student recalls that Reb Mendel would at times grab his arm and say, "Pesachya, come with me. I need help figuring out a certain *Gemara.*"

If a student hinted at a good question during *shiur,* Reb Mendel would ask a similar but stronger question and give the student all the credit: "Ah, so that's what you meant to ask."

Even outside the *shiur,* Reb Mendel was attuned to the slightest nuances of his students' behavior. Once, a student started to *daven* with more warmth and concentration than previously. Two weeks later, Reb Mendel called him over to compliment him.

REBUKE IS LIKE A POWERFUL DRUG; it must be administered with care, in precise doses, and only by qualified individuals. Reb

Giving Rebuke
Mendel always exercised extreme caution with criticism. When an elementary grade rebbe hits a troublesome student, he said, he may subconsciously be acting to protect his job, not for the student's benefit, since a student who does poorly reflects badly on the rebbe. He himself always made an effort to view problem cases from an outsider's point of view and to react with logic rather than emotion.

When he saw a student sleeping in *shiur,* he was always careful not to show annoyance. Instead, he would encourage the boy to go lie down for ten minutes, explaining that sometimes a person can sleep for ten minutes and feel as refreshed as if he had slept a few hours. Once he told a boy who was having difficulty staying awake to buy a cold soft drink and hold it in his hand. If someone's hands are cold, he explained, he is more likely to stay awake. He added that the converse was also true: "The *Gemara* says that placing your hand on your forehead makes you sleepy. Similarly, if you want to put a baby to sleep, let the baby hold your fingers in his hands to keep the baby's hands warm."

But he distinguished between laziness and fatigue. Once when a student from Chicago was falling asleep during *shiur*, Rebbe said in his characteristic singsong voice, "My good friend from Chicago, when I was a rebbe in Chicago, I used to give *shiur* to *bachurim* who had a lot of things on their minds. They were going to school at night, studying for *semichah* and also working a little. So when it came time for my *shiur*, what could they do but fall asleep? I took this as a big compliment. Even though these boys had so many concerns, they were able to forget all their problems during my *shiur* and doze off. But *you*, you went into exile to come to this yeshivah to learn, leaving behind your family and friends. When you sleep during *shiur*, I don't take it as a compliment."

Rebbe once said, " '*Midah tovah merubah mi'midas puraniyos chameish meios pe'amim* — Hashem's measure of goodness exceeds that of punishment five hundred times,' and I think the same is true with a rebbe. For every five hundred times I give you a good time, one time I give you a strong piece of *mussar*."

For the most part, Rebbe's *midas hadin* (strictness) was also sweetened with kindness, and even his rebuke was a pleasure to receive. One time, we were studying in pairs in the classroom when a window shade suddenly fell down. One of the boys picked up the shade and began to roll it up sloppily. Reb Mendel called the boy over, took the shade from his hands, and re-rolled it neatly and carefully. As he was doing this he chided the boy, "To roll a shade in a *krum* (crooked) way is more *krum* than saying a *krumma sevara* (a crooked piece of logic)."

He used to say, "One good word is worth ten harsh ones," but he also knew, as *Rambam* says (*Hilchos Talmud Torah* 4:5), that there are situations when a rebbe is obligated to display anger toward his students and shame them with his words. No one in his *shiur* was above reproach, and even the best students sometimes received their fair share of Rebbe's therapeutic rebuke.

Once Rebbe made an observation on a *Rashi*, and one of the quicker students in the class commented in a matter-of-fact tone,

"At first glance, that appears to be exactly what *Rashi* says in such-and-such a place."

Rebbe immediately retorted without any sign of emotion, "This is not a contest to show off your broad knowledge." The boy later admitted that Rebbe's appraisal of his motivation was right on the mark.

ᔈ ᔈ ᔈ

More than anything else, Reb Mendel abhorred conceit, especially when Torah was used as a pretext for intellectual snobbery. A *bachur* once began debating a point with Rebbe, and Rebbe gave him an answer which the *bachur* refused to accept. When the *bachur* then repeated his question, Rebbe angrily put an end to the discussion: "You're like the politicians," he said. "*Zei reddin un reddin un zei herrin gornit* — They talk and talk, and they don't hear a thing."

Reb Mendel's spontaneous remarks and actions often belied the serious considerations that underlay his behavior. One day in *shiur*, a student persisted in asking one inane question after another. Seeing that the boy was asking such questions because he was not using his full capabilities, Reb Mendel made them into a joke. The entire class started chuckling, and one student in particular laughed very hard.

Reb Mendel grew angry and snapped at him, "Why are you laughing? I'm afraid that with every word I say I'm losing my *Olam Haba*. In the World to Come they'll ask me, 'If that student had been your own son, would you have reacted the same way?' I'll answer them, 'Yes,' and still I'm afraid. But for your laughing, there's no question in my mind that you'll lose some *Olam Haba*."

ᔈ ᔈ ᔈ

Rabbi Yaakov Kamenetzky once described Reb Mendel as a *mechanech* par excellence. In speaking of Reb Mendel, Reb Yaakov moved his hands like a baker kneading a large lump of dough and said, "This is exactly what Reb Mendel does with his students. He doesn't only teach them; he molds them."

With all the deftness of a skilled baker, Rebbe knew exactly how much of each ingredient was required. Just as he knew when to draw a student close and when to push him away, he also knew when to concentrate on the words of the *Gemara* and when, in the style of the Talmud itself, to digress into ethical teachings.

Reb Mendel's *shiur* was a form of service in which explaining the *Gemara* was only the beginning. He would frequently interrupt the *shiur* with what he called "*mussar* commercials" — tidbits of wisdom that expanded his students' conception of Torah and the service of Hashem. He was well known for these "*mussar* commercials," which could last anywhere from a few minutes to over an hour, but however long, they were always refreshing and unforgettable.

ᔓ ᔓ ᔓ

"Listen to this now," he once said by way of introducing a *mussar* commercial. "In fifty years this will bear fruit. If *Chazal* tell us that there is a tree that can bear fruit only after growing for seventy years, certainly there can also be such a thing with human beings."

Once, some students complained to the *rosh yeshivah*, Rabbi Elya Svei, that they weren't learning enough Torah in Reb Mendel's *shiur*, since he so often interrupted his *shiur* with stories and insights. The following Friday night during his weekly *mussar shmuess* to the students, Reb Elya related the following story:

> There was one student to whom Reb Chaim Volozhiner often told stories. Being very diligent, this student felt that Reb Chaim was wasting time that could better have been spent learning, and he wanted to leave the yeshivah to learn elsewhere. But Reb Chaim wouldn't let him go. Many years later, when the student had become a great Torah leader, he said, "All the stories I heard from Reb Chaim in my youth helped me in later years to understand deep concepts in *Kabbalah*. To the extent I did not listen to his stories, to that extent I feel that my understanding of *Kabbalah* is lacking."
>
> Here in Philadelphia you also have the opportunity to hear stories. To the extent you listen to Reb Mendel's stories and insights, you will know how to live your entire lives.

CHAPTER THREE

The Greatness of Torah

MORE THAN ANYTHING, Reb Mendel gave us a taste of the preciousness of every word of Torah.

"Some things, like stone and steel, are strong and enduring, but they lack beauty. A flower, on the other hand, is beautiful, but has no permanence and very quickly shrivels up and dies. The Torah has both qualities: it is enduring and beautiful: *strength and beauty are her raiment ... (Mishlei* 31:25).

"People pay thousands of dollars for a diamond the size of a crumb. People have a feeling for diamonds and consider them precious. Every word of Torah is also precious: *If you search for it as for a buried treasure ... (Mishlei* 2:4). Only after you learn Torah a whole lifetime do you really get a feel for what it is."

He used to say that he loved the taste of a *Mishnah*, that it was like poetry. He could show us the beautiful structure and balance in the words of the *Tannaim*. A student who used to learn privately with Reb Mendel recalls how he would repeat a *Mishnah* over and over again, savoring every word with great joy.

Two weeks before Reb Mendel passed away, he called a friend

and asked if he could come over to look at a *sefer*. He stayed until midnight studying the *sefer*, and when he left the friend's home his face radiated the joy of someone who had just found a million dollars.

WHEN STUDENTS ASKED REBBE to help them strengthen their *emunah*, Rebbe would relate a saying of Reb Yeruchem Levovitz:

Torah — Perceiving the Divine

"If someone feels a need to strengthen his faith, he should study *Chumash* with *Rashi*."

"Reb Yeruchem used to say that in his youth he was disturbed by questions of *emunah*. He was a philosopher by nature, and could not stop himself from asking questions. So he went to Reb Naftali Amsterdam, one of Reb Yisrael Salanter's three greatest disciples, and begged him for advice. 'What should I do? It eats me up!' he cried.

"Reb Naftali told him to learn *Chumash* with *Rashi*: 'If you do this regularly, it will build up the foundations of your *emunah* and you won't have any more questions.' Not *Chovos HaLevavos*, not *Moreh haNevuchim*, just *Chumash* with *Rashi*."

At this point, Reb Mendel interjected, "Do you have any idea how many leaves fall off the trees in the fall? So too, our minds are limited and cannot fathom the greatness of Hashem. By studying *Chumash* with *Rashi*, everything becomes second nature to a person."

Reb Yeruchem Levovitz

He continued with the story: "Reb Yeruchem immediately bought himself a set of *Chumashim* that he used for the rest of his life. Even when he became *mashgiach* of the Mirrer Yeshivah, he continued using the same set in yeshivah, although the binding had worn out and the pages were falling apart. When he spoke from it, he had to hold the pages together with both hands.

"Through learning *Chumash* with *Rashi*, one develops into a great person. The fact that the *yetzer hara* doesn't let us find time to learn *Chumash* with *Rashi* is the biggest proof of its greatness. The *yetzer hara* is like a worker on strike at a factory: we want to go to work, but he sits down in the path with picket signs and doesn't let other workers in."

IN WORKS OF *KABBALAH*, the letters of the Hebrew alphabet are called stones, or building blocks. Just as the structure of every living creature is determined by the order of a handful of chemical variables in its DNA, so do the letters of the Torah and their sequence govern the spiritual world.

The Building Blocks of Creation

The letters of the Torah are the structure and life force behind everything in creation. When Hashem brought all the animals before Adam to be given names, it was not an arbitrary exercise in taxonomy. Rather, Adam understood the spiritual makeup of every animal and gave it an appropriate name. The letters *aleph, reish, yud, heh*, in that specific order, *are* the lion — its anatomy and its personality. The *gematria* of the Hebrew word for lion — *aryeh* — is identical to that of the lion's primary characteristic — *gevurah*.

Rebbe was once discussing a passage in *Gittin* which describes the procedure for writing and delivering a *get*. "Just as every tiny part of the eye must be exactly the way it is in order to operate properly," he said, "so too every part of the *get* must be exact to a hairsbreadth. Not only that, the whole of creation has to be exactly the way it is. Every drop of the ocean is counted and so is every particle of dust. And Torah is even more exact.

"To me," he continued, "sight is a miracle like the creation of the world. What is an eye? A ball filled with fluid. One small scratch, and one can no longer see. The same is true with *mitzvos*. There is nothing inconsequential in the Torah — if a person washes his hands, he can do the service in the *Beis HaMikdash,* but if he doesn't wash his hands, he can destroy entire worlds and his own *neshamah.* Just counting days is so serious that if a woman doesn't count her seven clean days, her soul is cut off from the Jewish people. And someone who takes a little pencil outside his doorstep on Shabbos forfeits his right to live."

🙠 🙠 🙠

"We sometimes wonder why the Torah lists at such great length the names of wicked gentile tribes. But the *Zohar* says that those *parshiyos* contain secrets that preceded the creation of the world. We can't ask why the Torah wrote some things openly and other things only through hints. Everything in the Torah contains deep secrets.

"For example, we learn about the *Nisuch HaMayim* ceremony in the *Beis HaMikdash* during Succos from the extra letters *mem, yud, mem* which spell the word *mayim (Taanis* 2b). Why couldn't the Torah write it explicitly? The answer is that Succos connects with the whole of creation; the seventy sacrificial bulls correspond to the seventy nations of the world. But the water libation expresses Hashem's private connection to the Jewish people, and thus is only alluded to in the Torah. So too all hints in the Torah have secrets hidden in them."

🙠 🙠 🙠

"When we learn just one word of Torah it makes us greater. Every word in the Torah is filled with infinite *kedushah* and just saying that word adds *kedushah* to us.[1] *Chassidim* tell a story about a simple woodcutter who didn't know even one word of Torah. One day he learned the word *tamei* and kept repeating it to himself all day, over and over again. Someone noticed this persistency and decided it would be better if the woodcutter said the word *tahor* instead. But when he tried to learn a second word he got so mixed up that he forgot both words. That night the "teacher"was told in a dream to go back and teach the woodcutter to say *tamei* again, because that was his way of serving Hashem, just to say that one word."

🙠 🙠 🙠

---

1. See *Avodah Zara* 19a.

ONCE, REB MENDEL stopped the class in the middle of a line of *Gemara* and declared, "We understand *p'shat* in a *Gemara* like

More than Meets the Eye

we understand a leaf on the tree." A leaf is deceptively simple; it strikes the casual observer as merely a great work of beauty and design. But a scientist sees it as an almost unfathomable mechanism for energy conversion. His greater knowledge gives him the ability to see more deeply the majesty of nature, and it fills him with awe and wonder. So too the great sages were aware of their limited ability to understand the true depths of the Torah.

Rebbe once quoted the Brisker Rav: "We learn a *Tosafos*? We take a small part out of a *Tosafos*!"

§► §► §►

"The great kabbalist Rabbi Moshe Chaim Luzzato said, 'There are more lessons in the letters and vowels of the Torah than in the words themselves. The wonder is that the words also have lessons.' The main meaning in a verse lies in its deeper meanings, *derash, remez* and *sod* (exegesis, hint and secret). When the *Gemara* tells us, '*Ein hamikra yotzei midei pshuto* — A passage does not deviate from its simple meaning,' it's really telling us that the simple meaning is *also* a correct interpretation (*Rashbam* to *Bereishis* 37:2).

"Torah can be understood by each person according to his level. The *Chumash* has a simple explanation that even a first grade student can understand; the *Gemara* is written in the ideal language for a fifth grader, and the *Rambam* has a simple, beautiful style that a child can understand. Yet, the Torah also has infinite depth. Rabbi Shimon Bar Yochai revealed seventy ways just to learn the first word in the Torah, *Bereishis*. And the greatest Torah scholars toil a lifetime to understand the words of the *Gemara*. Even the *Rambam* has hundreds of commentaries on it.

"The *Rambam* writes that even someone with tremendous mental abilities would have to study a passage in the *Gemara* a thousand times to understand all that the Sages put into it. The *Ramban* notes, 'As great as the difference between an ant and the upper spheres, so too is the difference between my understanding of the Torah and what is actually contained in the Torah.'

"Scientists have found separate currents flowing beneath the surface of the oceans. Torah is like an ocean; you can learn the revealed portion, or you can delve deeper into the hidden currents. The Torah isn't merely 'common law' teaching you how to act; it is the basis of creation. The same Torah we learn down here, they learn in the Heavenly academy — even Hashem learns Torah — except that there they comprehend the deepest levels while we only skim the surface."

"SOMETIMES THE *GEMARA* SAYS that a *Mishnah* is incomplete and that something has to be added to understand it correctly. Do

Concentrated Knowledge

you think that even one line of the *Mishnah* was lost? No. The *Tannaim* wrote everything they needed to, but in later generations what they wrote wasn't sufficient, and so to those generations it seemed like something was missing. And the *Amoraim* wrote as much as they needed to write, while the *Rishonim* needed still more and so they added explanations to what they had received, and so on down through the generations."

S➤ S➤ S➤

"See what's in a *Gemara*! The *Beis Yosef* derives countless *halachos* from just a few lines of *Gemara*. In the Vilna Gaon's lifetime, there was a man who hired false witnesses to testify that his wife had been unfaithful to him. The case came before the Gaon and he interrogated each of the witnesses separately. They both told exactly the same story and everyone thought the woman would surely be convicted. Yet the Gaon determined that the witnesses were lying.

"The other members of the court were amazed until he explained: The *Mishnah* that discusses the law of witnesses says, '*V'nimtz'u divreihem mechuvanim* — after examining their testimony the *Beis Din* finds that their words are consistent.' The Sages of the *Mishnah* chose that phrase carefully; they knew that it's normal for two people who witness the same incident to see it with slight variations, and *Beis Din* has to take this into consideration in determining whether their stories match. Since these two witnesses gave *exactly* the same testimony, it is a proof that they were lying.

"You see what treasures the Sages of the *Mishnah* concealed in the phrasing of their words. There is a lot more deep Torah there — even more than the *Gemara* learns from it."

"*CHAZAL* HAD A DEEP UNDERSTANDING of human nature. You know how afraid they were of the sin of adultery, and how

The Greatness of the Sages many decrees they made to protect against it. They were more afraid of it than we are of the atom bomb. Yet they said that if a

woman claims in the presence of her husband that she has previously received a divorce from him, even if the husband denies it, *Beis Din* believes her and writes her a document allowing her to remarry. *Chazal* knew that in their times a woman would not lie about such a matter."

ऽ➤ ऽ➤ ऽ➤

"Can you imagine a human being having the power to bring a dead person back to life? The Vilna Gaon says that every *Tanna* or *Amora* mentioned in the *Gemara* was capable of reviving the dead. Actually this is explicitly stated in *Avodah Zarah* (10b), where the Roman Emperor Antoninus tells Rabbi Yehudah HaNasi, 'I know the smallest among you can revive the dead.' Now you can understand why the *Gemara* calls a certain *Amora*, 'Rabba the son of the son of Chama.' Since his father didn't have any special distinction, the *Gemara* doesn't mention his name. From the way a *Gemara* refers to a person you can tell what kind of person he was. In English you'd call it an exclusive club."

REBBE WAS ONCE EXPLAINING the morning blessings over Torah study to the class: " '*V'haarev na ... es divrei Torascha b'finu*

Understanding the Great Scholars — Please, Hashem, our G-d, sweeten the words of Torah in our mouth.' You see, the *Gemara* can actually be

sweet in your mouth, or else why would the Sages have composed such a prayer?"

Later that day a student happened to meet Rebbe on the street and suggested that the prayer should be understood metaphorically. Just then they happened to be passing two huge chimneys of an abandoned factory, and Rebbe asked him, "There are *gedolei Yisrael* who are as far above us as those chimneys, no?"

"Yes," the boy replied.

"So how do you know the prayer was written for us? Maybe it was written for them?"

The student looked at Rebbe perplexed.

"*Nu*," Rebbe continued, "you understand things on your basic level because that's what's appropriate for you, but another person's more elevated understanding is also true. Most people, however, like to think everything revolves around them."

The Eternal Survival of Torah

"JUST AS THE SURVIVAL OF THE JEWISH PEOPLE through our long history of persecution and exile reveals Hashem's guiding hand constantly at work, so also we can see Divine Providence in the survival of the Torah.

"All the Torah we need is found in the *Gemara*. The Vilna Gaon said *Rabbeinu HaKadosh* (Rabbi Yehudah HaNasi) condensed six hundred Orders of *Mishnayos* into only six. How could he have done such a great thing? Only because of Hashem's promise that the Torah would never be lost from our mouths or from the mouths of our children. We lost the Temple, we've lost our sovereignty, but our greatest possession, our holy Torah, will always remain with us."

ϟ ϟ ϟ

Once the *shiur* was learning a *Gemara* on which very few *Rishonim* had written commentaries. Rebbe said, "How can we learn this *Gemara* correctly if we don't have the *Rishonim* to explain it to us? Without them we could not understand the *Gemaras* on which they comment, so how will we ever understand this one? Yet, the very fact that there are few *Rishonim* here is itself proof that this *Gemara* can be learned correctly without them. If the Creator is taking care of the physical creation, certainly He's also taking care of the spiritual creation."

ϟ ϟ ϟ

"Rabbi Aharon Kotler and Rabbi Avraham Kalmanowitz were dynamic personalities, people who could take the whole world into their hands, yet neither of them was able to build up a large yeshivah in America. On the other hand, their children have built glorious yeshivos, with many hundreds of students. From this we see that Hashem is driving the car; He only puts people in the driver's seat to make it look like nature is taking its course. Our job is to do our best, and Hashem does the rest. The same thing was true during the travels of the *Mishkan*: the *Aron* containing the Torah actually carried those who carried it. The bearers only looked like they were doing the carrying."

"DO YOU THINK THAT *RABBEINU HAKADOSH* made separate volumes for each *masechta* in the Talmud because it would have

What Is a Masechta

been too big to bind together otherwise? Each *masechta* is a world unto itself, and we can't mix them up together. As the *Zohar* says, 'Someone who inherits a *masechta* inherits a world.' That's why Reb Chiya said not to ask a *talmid chacham* a question on a *masechta* that he's not currently studying because it will embarrass him if he can't answer (*Shabbos* 3b).

"When Reb Aharon Kotler asked the Chofetz Chaim whether he should switch *masechtos* at the end of a term, the Chofetz Chaim told him he should first finish the *masechta* he had begun rather than learn a little from one and a little from another.

"A *masechta* has more permanence than real estate. The Torah says concerning the *Ephod* of the *Kohen Gadol* (*Shemos* 28:11), *Inscribe the two stones on the names of the Children of Israel.* You would think it should have said this the other way around: 'Inscribe the names of the Children of Israel on the two stones.' From here we see that the Jewish people has a reality and a permanence that is greater than that of the stones, and the Torah phrases it in that way because the Torah defines reality. Similarly, the *Rambam* mocks those who think that what the Sages of the *Mishnah* and *Gemara* said is less real than cars and books and other physical objects (Introduction to *Seder Zeraim*). A *masechta* has more reality than physical objects.

"You can talk to a *masechta* like you talk to a person. R' Yosi said: 'How fortunate are you, *Masechta Keilim,* because you started with the laws of impurity and you finished with the laws of purity.' During the period of the *Gemara* a *masechta* once came to a person's funeral in the form of a person. Even then, of course, not everyone was on the level to see this.

"You may know that you have to kiss a *Gemara*, but do you know how to kiss the *Gemara*? You look it up and learn it and talk about it — that's how you kiss the *Gemara*. The *Gemara* becomes so happy and pleased it becomes your friend.[1] If you'll look at the *Hadran* (said at the completion of a *mesechta*) you'll see how a *masechta* becomes a person's friend. We 'promise' the tractate, "לא נתנשי מינך" — We will not forget you, and we ask it, נתנשי מינך" "לא — And please do not forget us either."

S➤ S➤ S➤

"The *Gemara* (*Bava Metzia* 85b) tells about a *chassid* (pious person) whom Eliyahu HaNavi used to visit frequently. One day, he was seen walking about with one of his eyes burned out. Someone asked him what had happened, and he answered that he had asked Eliyahu to take him to see the Heavenly Academy. Eliyahu had agreed, but warned him not to look at R' Chiya's throne. He couldn't control himself, however, and when he looked at R' Chiya's throne a fire came out and blinded him in one eye. His friends advised him to go to R' Chiya's grave and pray that R' Chiya intercede on his behalf in the merit of his having learned the *Toseftos* which had been arranged by R' Chiya. He did so and was healed. So you see, by learning someone's Torah you make him your friend. Since we learn many commentaries here, we have lots of friends."

"PEOPLE MIGHT THINK that Jews were thieves, murderers and perverts because they see that the *Gemara* talks so much about

The Protective Power of Torah

murderers and *mamzeirim* (children of illegitimate unions), but the truth is that the cases the *Gemara* spoke of almost never arose. The Jewish people were always far better than the cases discussed in the *Gemara*. For instance, the *Gemara* says there was never an actual case of a "stubborn and rebellious child" (see *Devarim* 21:18-21). Jews learned about such things and saw how severe the transgressions involved were, and therefore took care not to let them happen."

S➤ S➤ S➤

"Someone who has studied the Torah's monetary laws relates to other people's money in an entirely different way. To him there's no difference whether it's a penny that belongs to some-

---

1. See *Rashi* to *Sanhedrin* 99b; see also *Yevamos* 117a.

one else or a hundred dollars, they're both the same. But even a Jew who doesn't study Torah still has these qualities due to all the Torah that has been instilled in his genes by previous generations. One generation can't wipe all that out.

"One who learns Torah is protected from the *yetzer hara*, and if you see that it's not protecting you, that's proof that you're not learning Torah properly."

ᔪ ᔪ ᔪ

The Sages say Torah makes a person healthy and heals him. Rabbi Yitzchak Goldberg, a former student and friend of Reb Mendel's from Chicago, once came to visit him in New York. They met at the Kamenitz Mesivta, which was then located across the street from Maimonides Hospital, and Reb Yitzchak was amazed at the contrast between the small yeshivah building and the enormous hospital, which takes up nearly an entire block. He asked Reb Mendel, "Why is it that hospitals are so big while yeshivos are so small?"

Reb Mendel replied, "If the yeshivos were the size of hospitals, the hospitals would only have to be the size of yeshivos."

"WE SAY EVERY DAY IN *SHEMA,* 'and these words which I command you today,' because the transmission of the Torah from Sinai is constant and continues even today. *Chazal* say that when someone is learning,

Torah Is Current and Alive — Not Ancient History

he should imagine that the Sage who authored the statement he's learning is actually standing in front of him, even more than if he were talking from a television screen. While we learn *Gemara*, all the *Tannaim* and *Amoraim* we learn about are here with us in the room. The Vilna Gaon related that the Patriarch Jacob actually came and kissed him while he was once sitting in his *succah*."

ᔪ ᔪ ᔪ

"I once saw a German *Chumash* which had printed on the top of every page the date on which each of the events on that page occurred. At first I thought this was a good idea, but when I thought about it more, I asked myself, 'If the Torah were interested in dates, why didn't it give dates for all the stories in *Tanach*?' The answer is that the Torah is not a history book that relates stories from the distant past. All the stories are alive today, so dates are inappropriate.

"Until this day we are the children of the Patriarchs and until this day they are still very much involved with us. The Jewish people have no 'history' as such; everything that happens to us is like the sign at the power station, 'live wire.' Hashem views all history periods at once; to Him the past is as real as the present. The Giving of the Torah, Creation and *Mashiach* are all before Him at the same time, and the Torah is as much now as it has ever been. It's not history: Avraham, Yitzchak and Yaakov are now."

ॐ ॐ ॐ

"The *Gemara* (*Succah* 31a) relates the story of a woman who came to Rav Nachman to demand the return of wood that had been stolen from her and had been built into a *succah* (rather than settle for the compensation for the wood). To attract Rav Nachman's attention, she exclaimed, 'A lady whose father owned 318 servants complains, and you don't pay any attention to her!' *Rashi* explains that she was referring to Avraham, who had lived over a thousand years earlier. The fact that her 'father,' Avraham, owned 318 servants made her proud.

"The *Gemara* relates the exact words of her complaint to show us that the Patriarchs are always with us. We possess a father Avraham who helps every Jew — no matter what sins he has committed, he remains a Jew inside. This, says the *Sefas Emes*, is the Shield of Avraham we speak about in *Shemoneh Esrei*. If we also had a Shield of Yitzchak, then every Jew would keep Shabbos, and if we had a shield of Yaakov, every Jew would study Torah all the time.

"Did you ever ride on the Verrazano Bridge from Brooklyn to Staten Island and feel how sturdy it is, how it can support all those cars hanging over the middle of nothing? That's the kind of bridge Avraham built for his children, and we're still riding on it until this very day. We are traveling through our exile on him."

"YOU SHOULD KNOW that earlier generations weren't any '*frummer*' than we are now; it was just that reality was different

Living in the Torah World

to them.

"In the European yeshivos, they used to learn *mussar* before *havdalah* in a mournful melody. That's a sad time, because *Gehinnom* is opened up again after Shabbos, and they were able to feel that. Jews lived in this world and the next simultaneously. It's only in the last one hundred and fifty or two hundred years that the crown of Torah has become so dulled!

"The *Gemara* relates many stories involving the other world because until not so long ago things that went on 'above nature' were present and seen by everyone. Reb Elchonon Wasserman was involved in removing a *dybbuk* (evil spirit). My nephew's wife's grandfather, Rav Elya Dushnitzer, who was a *mashgiach* in Petach Tikva, was one of those present when they removed the *dybbuk*, and there were many other eyewitnesses. Reb Elchonon himself used to tell the whole story every Purim.

"The Torah tells us that a time will come when nothing can be seen except for things within the realm of nature (*Devarim* 31:18). We know that Hashem gives the world everything it needs. Therefore if He has removed these things from the world, it's for our own benefit, since He does not want to tip the scales so as to take away our free will."

"A BABY ACCEPTS as real only those things it can put in its mouth. (That's why little babies are always putting everything

One Reality — Different Perceptions

they can get hold of into their mouths.) When the child gets a little older, it's enough to hold an object in his hand for him to know that it's real. When he grows still older, he realizes that he doesn't have to touch something to know it exists; if he can see it, it's also real.

"But there's an even higher level. Reality is not limited to what can be perceived by the five senses. The more spiritual something is, the more powerful it is; and the more physical something is the less powerful it is. For example, electricity — electricity is not tangible, the wires we see above the railroad tracks behind the yeshivah are just conductors through which electricity passes, and even those wires are so thin that only a squirrel can scramble over them. Yet the electricity that passes through the wires is so powerful that it can pull the massive trains that run on the tracks. Hundreds of oxen couldn't match that feat! And electricity is also physical. Imagine the power of something purely spiritual!

"The other nations only know about the physical world. But

really the spiritual side of a person is his essence; it *is* the person himself. When someone is happy, he begins to dance, but do we say that his feet are happy? Of course not; it's his heart that's happy and he shows it through his feet. If you look at the foot itself, you can't see any emotion on it; only the face shows emotion, because a person's face is the *tzelem Elokim* — the image of Hashem — and it is more spiritual than the rest of his body. The world is like the feet of the happy man. The reality of the world — its soul — is the Torah."

٭ ٭ ٭

"The *Gemara* (*Gittin* 22a) relates an argument among the Sages as to which part of the tree provides its nourishment. You may wonder why it was necessary to argue over such a point; why didn't they simply conduct experiments to determine who was right? But we have to understand that an argument in the *Gemara* over the properties of nature determines how Hashem will establish the workings of the natural world. If we were to decide according to the opinion of Rabban Shimon ben Gamliel, then trees would grow like he says, and if we were to decide like Rebbe, then trees would grow according to his opinion. The physical world is dependent on Hashem's will, which He has revealed through His Torah. Only He is the true reality."

٭ ٭ ٭

"After studying Torah for many years, you come to see that Torah is the reality, and the whole world we see is just an analogy to help us understand deep spiritual concepts. To the Chofetz Chaim, a verse in the Torah was more real than what he saw with his eyes. But not everyone is capable of recognizing the reality of the Torah to this degree. It's just like the *Bas Kol* (Divine Voice) that spoke in the *Mishkan*: the *Bas Kol* was very loud but only Moshe heard it (*Rashi* to *Bamidbar* 7:89). The same is true of certain perceptions in the spiritual domain: some people don't grasp them at all. Each person views the world through his own eyes, and all he can see is what's visible from the level he's on. Reb Elchonon wanted to write a biography of the Chofetz Chaim, but in the end, he concluded that he couldn't write about his teacher because he had no understanding of someone on such a high level."

٭ ٭ ٭

"We only know about the worlds we have experienced. If you ask a child what's going on in the world, he'll tell you about his world. The Sages refer to a child at one stage in his life as a goat because whenever a goat sees a high place it jumps up to it just for fun. I remember that when I was a child I used to run home with all my friends. If we got tired, we rested and then resumed our running. We couldn't understand why the men around us just walked step after step — how could you get anywhere like that? An old man cannot be understood even by the most intelligent youth. That's why I purposely go to an old doctor — he understands me. A young doctor knows only what he's read in his books. You can read all you want but it's not the same as experiencing it."

"ONCE ON THE TRAIN from Chicago to New York, a non-Jewish passenger sitting next to me wanted to discuss 'the Bible.'

Understanding Tanach Properly

I spent two and a half hours discussing the story of 'Adam and the Tree of Knowledge' in order to prove one point: the story doesn't make any sense according to the simple meaning of the words.

"Certain verses make sense only when you look at the deeper meanings of *drash*, *remez* and *sod*. For example, when Shifra and Puah risked their lives to deliver Jewish children (*Shemos* 1:21), how did Hashem reward them? By making houses for them?! That's a joke. It only makes sense if you take the Sages' interpretation that the 'houses' referred to are the house of priesthood and the house of royalty. When someone knows the inner meanings of Torah, then the verses all fit together perfectly."

"YOU PROBABLY WOULD LIKE to have a nice picture of Avraham hanging on your living room wall, wouldn't you? You

Shattering the Myths

probably imagine he was a tall man with a long white beard and a big stick in his hand surrounded by sheep. But how do you know that? Maybe his beard didn't grow nicely? It's all television nonsense. If you ever saw one of the Biblical epics on film, it's nearly impossible to understand these *parshiyos* properly."

Reb Mendel once heard someone speaking disparagingly about a physically unattractive Torah scholar. "Believe me," Reb Mendel told him, "if Moshe Rabbeinu had looked that way it wouldn't lower my opinion of him a single drop."

Viewing a popular portrait of the *Rambam,* he once commented, "From studying the writings of the *Rambam* one can see how he looked. I don't know how he looked, but I can tell you he didn't look like this."

"I ONCE HAD A SMALL WINE BUSINESS in Chicago for which I had to file federal tax returns. Since I couldn't afford a book-

On Biblical Scholars

keeper, I made a number of mistakes, and I was visited frequently by government inspectors. One of them was a nice guy who wanted to help me out so he explained to me: 'Put the same bottom line total on both columns and then work up from that.'

"It's the same thing with the big corporations. From looking at the graphs in the annual reports of banks and corporations, you would think they know exactly what happens to every dollar. What they really do, however, is take the same total figure and put it at the end of every graph and then work backwards to make all the numbers coincide. This is also how "Biblical scholars" work: they start with their own false premises about Judaism, and then work backwards to make everything fit into their twisted principles.

"The Bible critics use their imagination to explain the Torah. They don't know how the Jews traveled in the desert, but they still draw maps depicting their journeys. It's like someone who doesn't know Alaska, but makes a map of it anyhow. Such a person is a lunatic."

"THE HISTORY BOOKS DESCRIBE DAVID HAMELECH as a "brutal" king. Yet the Sages (*Midrash Shmuel* 22:4) tell us that dur-

David HaMelech

ing the time Saul was pursuing him and he was fleeing for his life, he learned more in one night than the greatest Sages of the *Gemara* could learn in one hundred years.

"David suffered such trouble and persecution all his days, and still he wrote *Tehillim*, which is filled with praise and thanks to Hashem. The Sages say that Hashem was satisfied with *Tehillim* alone (*Berachos* 7b). Imagine doing something so great that Hashem says about it, 'It's enough for Me! I don't need or want anything more!' The historians know as much about David HaMelech as I know about the mechanics of an atom bomb."

⌇⌇ ⌇⌇ ⌇⌇

Rebbe was once teaching the *Gemara* (*Kesubos* 9a) that discusses the halachic permissibility of David HaMelech's marriage to Batsheva. Rebbe gave us a new understanding of what his motives were, and the error he made.

"David HaMelech saw that their two *neshamos* were destined for each other from the six days of creation. There are many spiritual worlds in the creation, and in all the worlds except this one — the physical world — it was determined that they should be united. David lived in all of these worlds at the same time, and his sin was that he temporarily forgot which world he was in. If only I could light my Chanukah *menorah* with *kavannos* like those David had when he took Batsheva..."[2]

"TORAH IS NOT A RELIGION, it's the reality of the world. People think there are many types of religions, and Judaism is one

On Rabbis, Religion and Truth

of them, but this is silly! There can only be one truth, and if it is true, then all the others must be false. People think there are three branches of Judaism: there's this, and that and that. Nonsense! There's only one Torah filled with facts."

⌇⌇ ⌇⌇ ⌇⌇

"Everything in this country is money. If you make $90,000 or more a year, you are a Reform rabbi; if you make less, you are a Conservative rabbi; and if you make still less, you are an Orthodox rabbi. Rabbis today feel that the higher their salary, the more they are entitled to uproot the Torah."

In general, Reb Mendel felt that the destructive influence of Reform rabbis stems from their ignorance more than from malicious intent. He once said, "Many of them are nice guys who simply don't know anything, and therefore feel bad for their congregants and want to put them at ease. So they tell them, 'It's okay

---

2. Related by Rabbi Aharon Sonnenshein.

to drive on Shabbos,' or, 'So your son married a gentile woman, that's all right.' "

"THE *AGGADOS* OF THE *GEMARA* are distinguished for their difficulty to learn. Reb Yeruchem Levovitz, the *mashgiach* of the

On Aggadah and Hashkafah

Mirrer Yeshivah in Poland, used to say, 'Not only don't we understand what the *aggadah* is trying to say, we don't even know the meanings of the words themselves.' The words contain so much wisdom that when we read them, we are like someone who overhears a conversation on a subject he has no familiarity with, or a child who overhears his parents talking to each other. He just doesn't understand their language."

Reb Mendel once told a student, "The more you expound on the intricacies of the *Gemara* the better it is, but don't try to express opinions in Torah philosophy and outlook. Only someone thoroughly saturated with a lifetime of Torah is capable of giving an opinion which reflects a true Torah viewpoint, and even then, he is still uncertain if what he's saying was said on Mount Sinai. It is easier to give rulings in *halachah* than in *hashkafah* (philosophy)."

Rebbe once said, "The word *hashkafah* is misleading because it literally means 'viewpoint,' which implies that it's possible to see things from a different viewpoint, and that's not true. Whatever is Torah, be it a verse or a saying of *Chazal*, is the reality of the world. There is truth and falsehood, period, and no in-between. *Hashkafah*, someone's outlook, does not change reality, because there is only one world based on truth, and the Torah shows us what the world is. These things are not outlooks, they're reality! The word *hashkafah* is not to be found anywhere in the classic works and it creates a very wrong image of what the Torah dictates."

CHAPTER FOUR

Torah – A Full-Time Job

"**T**ORAH IS THE LIFE OF THE JEWISH PEOPLE. In earlier times it was as much a part of us as cars are of American society. If the government began

Torah — the Life of the Jewish People

imposing limits on where and how far people would be allowed to drive, there would be a revolution.

So too if Jews had to go without Torah, we'd be lost in depression. Just as today there are very few Americans who don't drive a car, once there were only a few Jewish 'bums' who didn't want to learn Torah."

ら ら ら

"The *Meiri* says in his introduction to *Avos* that the reason we have few writings from the period of the *Geonim* is not that their writings were lost. The reason is that their wisdom was transmitted orally. Jews used to travel to a Gaon to be taught and then go back to

their hometown and relate what they had learned. There was no necessity to write things down, except for those scholars who needed to judge cases. Certain things were written down to guide the weaker ones, but for the multitudes no writings were needed.

"Did you need a dictionary to teach you how to speak English, or a book to tell you how to play baseball? Jews generally didn't need books to know how to learn. It was, *l'havdil*, like learning baseball: a friend gives you a few lessons, and you watch what everyone else is doing and follow along. That's how Torah used to be among Jews. They learned it like a girl learns to cook — by watching her mother. That is why they needed few books."

⁂ ⁂ ⁂

"Did you ever see anyone not playing ball because it was too hot, or someone who got tired from idle talk? That's how much David HaMelech loved Torah: *How much I love Your Torah, all day long it is my conversation* (*Tehillim* 119:97).

"In Shanghai, I once saw someone I knew lying on the floor learning. He was relaxing with his feet up on a mattress, almost as if he was watching T.V. At first I thought, 'How could some-one learn Torah like that?' But then I realized that Torah was his life, and just as someone can lie on the floor and chat idly, so too you can learn lying down. Someone who views learning as some-thing formal, as a kind of work, will get tired easily when learning, but someone to whom learning is natural can just lie down on the floor and learn."

One night around midnight, there were only a few boys left in the *beis mdrash* learning. One *bachur* sat down on top of his *shten-der* in the middle of a debate with his *chavrusa*. Suddenly Reb Mendel walked in and the embarrassed *bachur* quickly tried to get down from his *shtender*. But Rebbe motioned that he should stay where he was. He smiled and nodded his head in approval as he walked by.

⁂ ⁂ ⁂

"In previous generations, people found pleasure in learning. I once saw a child in Baranovich sitting on the steps learning *Chumash* after the *cheder* closed for the day. When Reb Nochum Partzovitz, *rosh yeshivah* of the Mirrer Yeshivah in Jerusalem, was a boy in Troki, he had such a desire to learn that he couldn't wait to run to *cheder* in the morning. He would go barefoot because it took him too long to put on his shoes. I was told by a close relative of Rabbi Chaim Ozer Grodzenski that when Reb Chaim Brisker's *sefer* on the *Rambam* arrived in the house, Reb Chaim Ozer got so excited he actually began dancing with joy."

§ § §

"You have to look at the *Gemara* in the same way you look at a new model car, or at least in the way you listen to a piece of good news. Only then will it make a permanent impression on you. The *Pri Megadim* called one of his works *Shoshanas HaAmakim* ("Rose of the Valleys"). Isn't that a beautiful name? He didn't just pick the name out of a hat — it shows what an excitement he must have had in its words. You can develop such a taste for a page of *Gemara*. Not an *Olam Haba* taste, but a real *Olam Hazeh* taste.

Reb Mendel with Rav Shimon Schwab

"We once had a *bachur* here in yeshivah who had such a taste and desire for the *Gemara*. He had the same relish in learning Torah that a lowlife has in profanities. You may wonder how I could make such a comparison, but you find such things in *Chazal* also.[1] By looking at the extreme on the side of evil you can see what the extreme on the side of good should be."

Once after finishing a *Rashi*, Reb Mendel rubbed the tips of his fingers together and asked the class, "*Nu,* do you hear the music of *Rashi*?" Another time he said to the class, "When someone hears the name of an expensive car mentioned, his eyes light up; and when he gets to drive one, he is elated. When I hear the name of a *sefer*, I become happy; and looking into a *sefer* is to me like riding in a fancy car."

§ § §

---

1. See *Bereishis Rabbah* 80:6, *Rosh Hashanah* 4a.

"When someone learns a lot, he develops an appetite for it like for food. When Reb Aharon Kotler returned from collecting for the yeshivah, he would sit down to learn like a hungry man. Reb Yisrael Yaakov, the *mashgiach* in Baranovich, had such a love for Torah that he didn't have the heart to give the signal at the end of *seder* to go on to *mussar seder*. He just couldn't do it. One Friday, I saw him reviewing the *parashah* with such gusto, like a famished person eating a frankfurter with a Coke.

"Rabbi Shimon Shkop would toil in Torah with so much energy that he had barely any strength left for anything else. If someone tried to discuss a topic not related to learning, his eyes would slowly shut and he would fall asleep. When I studied under him in Grodno, I always knew if my questions were good or not — if I asked a weak question, he would fall asleep on me.

"The *Tzemach David*, a *rosh yeshivah* in Baranovich, was known for his great involvement in learning. He became so engrossed in learning that while walking in the street he used to bump into walls and posts. As a result he could often be seen with bruises."

Rabbi David Rappaport,
the Tzemach David

Rebbe would sometimes ask students to read to him from the *Gemara* while he was driving, but he always cautioned them not to delve too deeply into a topic since it would impair his concentration on the road. Once, a student disregarded this warning and said something that agitated him so much that he sped up to fifty miles an hour on the sharp approach ramp of the Verrazano Bridge. He quickly slowed down and rebuked him, "Now you see why I can't learn while I drive!"

ᔊ ᔊ ᔊ

Reb Mendel used to say in the name of his rebbe, Reb Elchonon Wasserman: "Learning is very hard, but without learning, *living* is very hard."

To a former *talmid* who was having severe personal problems, Reb Mendel offered the following advice: "People in Europe had the custom of drinking a little whiskey in the morning and that gave them the strength to get through a rough day. Learning Torah is like drinking whiskey."

No Business like Torah Business

REB MENDEL LIVED IN WILLIAMSBURG for a time in a house that was nearly one hundred years old. Once, when he needed a part for a very old fixture in the house, he went to a large supply store in the neighborhood and showed the owner the part. The storekeeper immediately climbed up a ladder and took a small dusty box from one of the upper shelves. He gave Reb Mendel the part he needed and said, "Rabbi, I haven't been asked for this part in thirty years."

Reb Mendel asked him how many different parts he had in the store and the owner answered, "Over thirty thousand." When he related this story, Reb Mendel would ask, "Do you think he has such a brilliant mind because he can remember every part he sells? It's his business. If it's your business, you know it. You don't have to have a head like Reb Chaim Ozer to know where everything is in *Shas*. Torah just has to be your business.

"You see how thick Rav Moshe Feinstein's *sefarim* are. Do you know how that came about? Because Torah is his business. I hear businessmen talking like they have nothing on their minds except their business. Torah is our business. Just like a business needs Divine assistance and businessmen say the blessing *Mevarech*

HaShanim (for sustenance) with intense concentration, so Torah is our business and we have to say the blessing *Ahavah Rabbah* (for understanding in Torah) with intense concentration."

ᔓ ᔓ ᔓ

A *bachur* once asked Reb Mendel why he should remain in yeshivah if he knew that he would not become a *rosh yeshivah* in any event. Rebbe told him, "People go into business even though they know they won't become Rockefellers. They know that in business, even if you don't become a Rockefeller, you can still get rich. In business no one stops trying after a certain point, they always keep striving to go higher. So, too, in learning you can never be satisfied and say, 'I know enough.' "

The Torah has its own set of marketing strategies. "If you want Divine help," Reb Mendel used to say, "Hashem has to see that you really want to learn. If He sees that you learn even at times when it's hard, you get the Divine assistance you need. Also, you should try to think about your learning when you're away from the *Gemara* — when you're walking down the hall or waiting on line for food. Another tip is that when you have to leave the *Gemara*, you should feel a longing to return to it. If you do that, then the *Gemara* waits for you to return as well. But the desire has to be true because you can't fool the *Gemara*.

"If a person hurries back from breakfast to start learning, the angels wait at the door to bring him help from Heaven, but if he takes his time and stands around chatting before beginning to learn, they go home."

"IF SOMEONE IS PREVENTED FROM LEARNING Torah but wishes he were able to, that's also a big thing. *Teshuvos HaRosh*

Torah — Always Close to the Heart

(4:2) says that Torah is considered to be someone's calling if he constantly thinks, 'When will I be able to return to my learning?' each time he is prevented from learning.

"If someone has to leave the *Gemara*, it should hurt him. The *Chayei Adam* was a businessman. He writes in the introduction to his *sefer* that he remembered what he had learned because while working he constantly thought about returning to his learning. The *Gemara* says that a woman who doesn't marry for ten years becomes infertile, but if she always intends to get married she remains fertile. The same is true of Torah."

During his years in Shanghai, Reb Mendel often had to care for sick members of his family, and many times spent most of the day away from the yeshivah. But as soon as he entered the *beis midrash* he was able to resume his learning exactly where he had left off, as if he had been learning the entire day. Rabbi Ephraim Mordechai Ginsberg, later *rosh yeshivah* of the Mirrer Yeshivah in New York, asked Reb Mendel what his secret was. Reb Mendel replied, "All day I walk around with the feeling that I can't wait to learn."

"EVERY DAY YOU WAKE UP to a new sunrise because Hashem renews the creation every day. That constant renewal is one of

Waking Up to a Fresh Start

Hashem's great kindnesses. Otherwise we would fall into depression from all our troubles. But this way, a person wakes up each day with the feeling that he has a new chance. *Chassidim* immerse themselves in the *mikveh* every day, since each day they are able to do *teshuvah* and start over, like a new person. For this reason, too, a convert needs to immerse in a *mikveh* when he starts his new life as a Jew."

ᔥ ᔥ ᔥ

Once, as a *bachur* was on his way across the *beis midrash* to chat with a friend before morning *seder* began, Rebbe called to him, "Hey, Boddy! Boddy! That's how you call a good friend in English, no?"

"Buddy," said the boy.

"Buddy," said Rebbe, "why do you start off morning *seder* like that? You should start *seder* with learning, not with foolishness. The *Avudraham* (a *Rishon* who wrote about prayer) cites an opinion that the blessing that precedes *Elokai neshamah* is not *Asher Yatzar*, as we think, but rather the *Hamapil* blessing that we said when going to sleep the night before! If you approach sleep in the right way, even your sleep becomes a service to Hashem rather than an interruption. If you wake up in the right way, eat in the right way and start learning in the right way, each of the activities of your daily life becomes different."

ᔥ ᔥ ᔥ

"ACCORDING TO THE CLOCK IN HEAVEN, each hour is divided into 1,080 parts. The Vilna Gaon says that each part brings

Making the Most of the Time a new judgment; every second is a renewal, a new opportunity to make yourself better. If you didn't learn well during the first half of *seder*, you can still strengthen yourself and learn well in the second half.

"The *Mishnah* (*Avos* 4:25) compares the Torah one learns in his youth to ink written on fresh paper. Torah studied in old age is likened to ink written on smudged paper. The Alter of Kelm says that when the *Mishnah* talks about the Torah one learns in his youth, it means you should learn right now instead of waiting a few minutes to learn (when you will already be that much older).

"Every minute is precious. There is a building in Chicago, the Wrigley Building, which was built with the profits from selling millions of pieces of chewing gum at a penny each. From this we see that every small thing is precious.

"The author of the *Yonas Aylem* was a prized student of Reb Boruch Ber. He didn't write very much, but whatever he wrote is extremely clear. He used to say: 'If someone is a *masmid*, he has time for everything — even for *batalah*. But someone who is a *batlan* doesn't have time for anything, not even for *batalah*.' That is a holy saying which hopefully you'll understand now, or maybe when you get older. This one saying really sums up how clear he was. When I was in the Mirrer Yeshivah he was half-rebbe, half-*chavrusa* to me. He didn't leave Europe with us and was later killed by the Nazis. He was still only a *bachur*, but from his wisdom you can see how mature he was. Today, even many married people are like children.

"I once walked into the home of a *talmid chacham* in Jerusalem and found him examining building plans spread out on the floor. That's how it is: when you are a *masmid*, you are a *masmid* in everything, and when you are a *batlan*, you're a *batlan* in everything."

§➤ §➤ §➤

Rebbe valued every moment of Torah study, and did not hesitate to ask those less advanced than he to learn with him. During Pesach break, just a week before he passed away, he approached a former student after *Shacharis* and asked him to sit down and learn with him for a while. He said he was wrapped up in helping "this person and that relative," and had a lot of things on his mind. "But what's it all worth if I don't have a settled mind to sit down to a *Gemara* for a few minutes to learn?"

₰ ₰ ₰

Rebbe placed great value on maintaining an uncluttered head. His concept of idle speech included not only matters that had no connection to Torah, but even Torah-related subjects he considered to be of a political nature or of no great concern to students, whose concentration should be on the basic, time-tested curriculum. Once a student was riding with Rebbe in his car before Tishah B'Av and started to discuss differing opinions about saying *kinos* written to commemorate the Holocaust. Rebbe grew uncharacteristically annoyed and snapped, "Ah! This discussion is *devarim beteilim!*" and immediately switched the discussion to a topic in learning. On another occasion, a young *talmid* new to yeshivah was riding with Reb Mendel and asked him what the Torah's opinion is regarding life on other planets. Reb Mendel responded immediately: "To me it makes as much difference as knowing about the life of the man driving the next car ahead of us."

In a similar vein, he was upset when someone once put up a public notice, issued by one of the *gedolim* in *Eretz Yisrael*, which was not relevant to the yeshivah. As soon as Reb Mendel noticed the sign he tore it down, saying, "A yeshivah is just for Torah — it's not a public thoroughfare; nor is the head of a *ben Torah* a public thoroughfare in which all can enter. That is not the way to raise a generation to Torah."

ONCE THE ENTIRE YESHIVAH went to New York to attend a public assembly to uphold the honor of Torah. Upon returning,

True Honor for Torah Reb Mendel addressed the class: "Allow me to think out loud. We're making a public demonstration of the honor we have for Torah. Can you imagine how much more care we must take not to disgrace it through our private actions? The *Gemara* (*Sanhedrin* 69b) says that the verse *And the word of Hashem he disgraced* (*Bamidbar* 15:31) refers to anyone who is able to study Torah and does not. We're worried about honoring the Torah, but our problem is to avoid disgracing it! Do you think honoring the Torah means going to an assembly? We have to get it through our heads that honoring the Torah is not just something they write about in the newspapers. I ask myself: How can I go and demonstrate for the honor of the Torah if I'm disgracing the Torah so much? That bothers me because it's hypocrisy."

Rebbe would relate how *bitul Torah* was a constant concern in Europe. Even *cheder* children would scream, "*Bitul Torah!*" at their friends when they were annoyed with them and didn't want to listen to them any longer. He recalled that he had an older friend in *cheder* named Avraham Mordechai who would sleep in the *beis midrash* on a hard bench in order to learn longer. During *mussar seder* Avraham Mordechai used to read *sefarim* that spoke of the severe punishment for *bitul Torah* over and over again, in a loud voice that everyone around him could hear.

S➤ S➤ S➤

He who commits adultery with a woman lacks heart (*Mishlei* 6:32). *Chazal* say this refers to someone who learns Torah with interruptions (*Sanhedrin* 99a). Torah is like a woman and is acquired the way a wife is acquired. The *Gemara* doesn't like to be with just anybody — for instance, with conceited people. You can't throw Torah around and come back to it when you feel like it, just as you wouldn't treat a wife that way. And if you don't show an interest in the Torah, she won't look out for you, either.[1]

"*Chazal* say all beginnings are difficult. That explains why it's hard to start learning. But why is it still hard for us even after we've started? The reason is that we're always getting distracted in the middle and so we're always having to begin again, and all beginnings are difficult."

S➤ S➤ S➤

Once Rebbe saw a boy whispering a joke to the boy next to him. "Why are you talking in the middle of *shiur*? Didn't you ever hear of something called *bitul Torah*? *Chalav Yisrael* you've heard of, wearing a *yarmulka* you've heard of, but not *bitul Torah*! That's what *Yiddishkeit* has become in the street — *chalav Yisroel* and

---

1. See *Rashi, Sanhedrin* 99b.

yarmulkas. Do you know how severe the sin of *bitul Torah* is? I'm afraid even to say."

Reb Mendel's son was once walking with his father when he stopped to watch some construction workers digging a tunnel. Reb Mendel asked, "Why don't you ever see them stopping to watch what you're doing? They must be so totally wrapped up in their work that they don't have time for it. And you, why aren't you so wrapped in the Torah you're supposed to be learning?"

IT IS THE CUSTOM FOR A RABBI to address his congregation on the Shabbos between Rosh Hashanah and Yom Kippur to arouse

Rebbe's Shabbos Shuvah Drashah

them to repent. This was Rebbe's *erev Shabbos Shuvah drashah* to his class one year:

"The easiest and most necessary *teshuvah* for *bnei Torah* is not to speak *devarim beteilim* and to learn with greater determination. *Chazal* say that the sin of *bitul Torah* is equivalent to all the sins enumerated in the confession we say on Yom Kippur. A big problem is the *devarim beteilim* that *bachurim* speak at meals. Shlomo HaMelech, the great doctor, prescribed for us to stop our mouths from talking too much and thereby save ourselves a lot of trouble. There should be a big sign in the dining room saying, 'It is forbidden to speak *devarim beteilim* during meals.'

"Why don't *bachurim* speak words of Torah while they're eating — who says that meals have to be a time for idleness? I know what the root of the problem is: it's the mentality that carries over from secular schools where they give a recess to let you forget what you've learned up till that point. Please don't be college students here. Here there are no passing marks of 60% or 70%; in yeshivah, success is 100%. If you accustom yourself to show love and honor for the Torah and hurry back to learn after eating, you'll succeed more than from having a good head."

Rebbe was once unable to find the English word for something. He turned to a *bachur* and said, "You probably think that when someone doesn't know a word in English it's embarrassing. But when he doesn't know a word from our Torah, do you feel that's an embarrassment? Shouldn't a Jew know the words in his Torah?"

"IN AMERICA, people run to open doors for their rabbis, but that's not honoring the Torah, that's a joke. In Europe we didn't

Honor for Torah Scholars

do that, but we learned from our rabbis and accepted what they taught us in all ways."

Reb Mendel once described the great reverence and respect the students in Baranovich had for their mentors. "A boy in the yeshivah once came over to Reb Elchonon to ask him a question, holding his *Gemara*. While he was standing there, the boy's opened *Gemara* began shaking up and down from his fear of Reb Elchonon. Finally it shook so much that it fell from his hands. And Reb Elchonon was not a scary man; the boy's fear came solely from the awe he felt standing in the presence of his rebbe."

$\;$ ⑊ ⑊ ⑊ $\;$

If Torah is akin to royalty, then a Torah scholar is the king who wears the crown of glory. As *Chazal* say, "Who are the kings? The rabbis" (*Gittin* 62a). Reb Mendel would never take honor for the crown of Torah he himself wore, but he always showed the utmost honor to the crown worn by others.

Rebbe once asked a question in *shiur* to which a *bachur* replied, "The *Nachalas Moshe* (a contemporary *sefer* that focuses on basic *p'shat* problems) answers this and says..." Rebbe gave a warm smile and said, "Ahhh! If I ever meet that Jew I'll kiss him. He is a straight person and his Torah is very reliable." Although Rebbe often presented more complex approaches to the topics he discussed, each time that particular work was mentioned he always expressed great respect for it.

In the presence of a great Torah sage, Reb Mendel always conducted himself with total self-abasement. Rabbi Moshe Feinstein spent some summers in Ellenville, New York, a ten-minute walk from Reb Mendel's bungalow. One morning Reb Mendel walked over to *daven* there and Rabbi Gershon Weiss asked him to sit in an honored place on the eastern wall. Reb Mendel declined because he could not bring himself to pray at the same eastern wall with Reb Moshe.

He later confessed to the class, "What could I do? To me Reb Moshe *is* the Torah, so how could I just sit there next to him? To me he's Torah personified. Do you have any idea how great Reb

Moshe is? For all his simplicity with people and his good-heart-edness, he knows the entire Torah. Maybe you'll tell me he has a good memory and a quick mind — but the entire Torah! He's writ-ten thick works on many *masechtos*, and the Torah flows like music, it just pours out. And in *sevara* — his *sevaros* are endless! I just could not bring myself to *daven* right next to him."

Reb Mendel gave honor to all Torah scholars regardless of their affiliation. He once told the class, "Some *talmidim* call the *rosh yeshivah* of a certain place by his initials. What they are doing is terrible. They should call him *HaRav HaGaon* and so forth. He knows a world of Torah." Reb Mendel did not agree with all of the views of that *rosh yeshivah*. Nevertheless, he felt that since that *rosh yeshivah* is a great *talmid chacham*, he must be recognized as such and referred to by his proper title.

He once told the Satmar Rebbe's *gabbai*, Reb Yosef Ashkenazi, "I'm more of a *chassid* of the Rebbe than you are. Thirty-two years ago the Rebbe came to Chicago and I became his *chassid*."

ᔐ ᔐ ᔐ

One day after *shiur*, Reb Mendel abruptly stopped his usual question-and-answer session with *bachurim* who gathered around his desk, and rose to speak with a visitor who had come to see him. After the visitor left, Rebbe said, "I had to interrupt our dis-cussion because he's a *talmid chacham* and honoring Torah comes before learning Torah" (*Megillah* 3b).

Reb Mendel then related the following story: "Once a halachic question came to the Mirrer Yeshivah from a small town that could no longer continue to support both its *rav* and its small yeshivah. Reb Yeruchem said that the yeshivah had to go. The cost and inconvenience for the boys to relocate would not be so great. They are only boys. But to make the *rav* pick himself up and leave would be degrading his Torah."

ᔐ ᔐ ᔐ

Honor for Torah takes many forms. Rebbe once told us the story about an *Amora* who noticed that there was a *sefer Torah* lying on the bench on which he was sitting, and he jumped up as if he had been bitten by a snake. This shows, he said, how strongly *Chazal* felt about the honor of Torah.

"I myself," he added, "feel the disrespect when I see a *sefer* turned over on its face. You might think you're justified in leaving a *sefer* open like that to save time when you're going away just for a moment, but it's only American laziness."

S❧ S❧ S❧

At one yeshivah where Reb Mendel *davened* on Shabbos, he was disturbed that students left their private *sefarim* in boxes on the floor. He would bring in milk boxes to raise the *sefarim* the required *tefach* from the floor.

The yeshivah at which Reb Mendel taught in Chicago once moved into new quarters, temporarily storing many of its *sefarim* in an old building scheduled to be demolished. While the *sefarim* were there, the building was set afire by vandals, resulting in severe damage to many *sefarim*. The remnants of the *sefarim* and other holy objects lay strewn around. Reb Mendel asked Yitzchok Goldberg, a former student, to borrow a car. As soon as the young man had done so, Reb Mendel stopped *shiur* — something he almost never did — and took a few boys with him to the old building.

Once there, he realized that the damaged *sefarim* would not all fit into their car, so he rented a trailer which they hooked to the back of the car. They carted all the boxes to a Jewish cemetery and with shovels and picks proceeded to dig a grave in which to bury them (as prescribed by Torah law).

CHAPTER FIVE

Learning Torah

"IMAGINE A DOCTOR who comes on a house call and brings forty-eight instruments to cure the patient. It sounds pretty serious, right? The more instruments he needs, the more complicated the ailment must be and the harder it's going to be to treat. Well, the *Mishnah* (*Avos* 6:6) says that to acquire Torah you need forty-eight different tools. This shows us how demanding learning Torah is.

How to Acquire Torah

"The Alter of Kelm said that study alone is not sufficient to acquire Torah. Since the Torah is spiritual, it can be retained only by someone who is also spiritual. The whole purpose of these forty-eight "tools" is to raise the physical side of man onto a higher spiritual level so that he can connect with the Torah."

❧ ❧ ❧

Reb Mendel once told us that in his eyes the model of a "spiritual" person was his Rebbe, Reb Elchonon, whom he called *"hakadosh v'hatahor"* — the holy and pure one. Once Reb Elchonon wanted one of his sons to give a *shiur* in his yeshivah. But first he went to Reb Yisrael Yaakov, the *mashgiach,* to ask his opinion. Reb

Yisrael Yaakov said nothing, but made a slight gesture of disapproval. Reb Elchonon walked away and never brought up the subject again. "That," said Reb Mendel, "is what it means to be a *kadosh v'tahor*."

৯৯ ৯৯ ৯৯

The *Mishnah* (*Avos* 6:1) says, "Anyone who studies Torah *lishmah* merits many things." One of these things is that "people will benefit from his counsel." Reb Mendel explained that in order to give someone good advice, you have to put yourself totally in his position, to see what the world looks like from his perspective. Studying Torah *lishmah* gives one that ability.[1]

In *shiur*, Reb Mendel once gave us a barometer for gauging the purity of our Torah study. "To learn Torah *lishmah* means thinking not only of your own learning, but also of that of others. If your *chavrusa* doesn't benefit from the way you learn, it shows that you're selfish. And if someone doesn't get along with his *chavrusa*, the chances are he won't be happily married either, unless he shapes up in time."

Humility

AMONG THE *MISHNAH'S* FORTY-EIGHT "TOOLS" for acquiring Torah is "humility." Reb Mendel exemplified that trait to the highest degree. Once when we were preparing for *shiur*, a *talmid* took his *Gemara* to ask Rebbe a question. As soon as the boy showed Rebbe the place in *Tosafos* where he was having difficulty, Rebbe nodded and asked the very question the boy was about to ask. He added, "I don't know the answer. Maybe in Heaven they'll have mercy on me..."

Each year when a new group of students arrived in the *shiur*, Reb Mendel would deliberately explain the *Gemara* incorrectly during the first day or two. Then, as he watched the students studiously writing down what he had just said, he would say, "Oy, I made a mistake! What, you're writing down everything I say? Why do you have to write down my mistakes?" Not only did he

---

1. The quality of viewing a situation objectively is useful in other areas of life as well. Reb Mendel was once asked by a student for help in deciding which of several *mitzvah* projects to undertake. Reb Mendel told him to look at the situation as an outsider, and make a decision without letting his emotions get involved. "Look at yourself the way you look at your car," he said.

thus teach us that he could make mistakes, but also that we had to think independently about everything he said.

Rebbe once explained why he said his own *chiddushim* in *shiur*. "I like the things I say myself more than things I see in other places. Not because I think I'm any better or what I say is any better, but because what I say is clearer to me and I understand it better."

REB MENDEL had the greatest possible reverence for the work of earlier generations. He used to say, "A *Rishon* thought about more things while he was dipping his feather in the inkwell than we think about in a whole year of learning."

Awe of His Predecessors

In *shiur*, Reb Mendel sometimes quoted from a famous work of one of the early *Acharonim* which makes light of the explanations of the *Rishonim* in numerous places. The attitude of this author visibly annoyed him, and he told the class he had always wanted to write a critique of this work in the style of the *Hasagas HaRaavad*. It gave him great pleasure whenever a student could find support for the opinions of the *Rishonim*.

Even regarding latter-day commentators, Rebbe held that the best way to arrive at the truth was to defer to their opinions and to try to understand what they meant. He once cited a question asked by Rabbi Akiva Eiger and proposed his own answer. Having done so, he added, "I don't understand why I can't say this, it seems like such a simple thing. But since Rabbi Akiva Eiger is our master in straight thinking and he doesn't say it, we have to accept that our solution is wrong."

On another occasion Rebbe attempted to answer an unresolved question of Rabbi Akiva Eiger. With the greatest humility, he excused himself several times before saying the answer, and again several times afterwards. Although it was a brilliant answer, he insisted that no one record it or repeat it during the review period later that night.

৯০ ৯০ ৯০

Reb Mendel felt it was better to remain with an incomplete understanding of a topic than to embrace solutions of dubious validity. Someone once asked him how to understand a certain difficult concept. Rebbe answered, "Not everything is meant for us to understand. We have to learn how to accept things as they are. In a letter to his son, the *Rambam* stresses that if he has learned a point one way and later sees something that seems to contradict the first approach, he should not abandon his previous approach just because there is room to question it. That's wrong. The reason the *Rambam* stressed this is because it's the nature of a person to question, and to allow his questions to interfere with what he has learned previously. Uprooting this tendency requires work."

At the end of *shiur* one day, Rebbe left us with an unresolved question. "*Nu,* so there's a question and I don't have the answer. It's no big deal; you have to learn how to say 'I don't know' and that's that. You don't have to know everything, and it's better to say you don't know something than to try to squeeze in your own contortions to make everything fit perfectly. A good question is as good as a good answer. Just because you don't know one thing doesn't mean you can't say over a thought you've had."

Reb Mendel had little regard for modern commentators who consider themselves competent to challenge the opinions of their predecessors. Once in *shiur* he mentioned a question of Rabbi Akiva Eiger which Rabbi Akiva Eiger leaves unresolved. After class, a *bachur* showed Rebbe a *sefer* by a young scholar who offered a solution to that question. Rebbe looked at the answer and began to laugh, prompting the student to ask Rebbe what he found so funny. Rebbe replied, " 'Kids say the darndest things.' Do you know what this author is comparable to? To a kid standing on a railroad track who boasts that he is going to give the locomotive one good punch and stop the whole train in its tracks."

"THE FIRST CONDITION FOR LEARNING TORAH is to strive to find the truth. I once heard a *shiur* given by Reb Boruch Ber at

To Search for the Truth

which he stood on a large platform in front of hundreds of people. Suddenly in the middle of the *shiur* he stopped, walked to the back of the platform, and silently thought out what he was going to say for the rest of his *shiur*. He had just thought of a problem and would not continue until he was sure that all his ideas were absolutely true."

Reb Mendel typified this quality. Rabbi Leib Lopian, *zt"l, rosh*

*Reb Leib Gurewitz (L)
and Reb Leib Lopian (R),
Roshei Yeshivah of
Gateshead Yeshivah
(England)*

yeshivah of Gateshead, said, "I have never met *aza rainem lamdan* (such a pure Torah scholar) as Reb Mendel."

To Listen and to Hear

"A PERSON HAS TO PRAY that his pride not prevent him from listening to the Torah. In the blessing *Ahavah Rabbah* we ask for the ability to hear even before we ask to be able to learn.

"The *Rambam* says that losing an argument in *Gemara* is better than winning, since if you win you don't know any more than you knew before, but if you lose, then you know the truth.

"A *chaburah* (a seminar in which students present and discuss dissertations on *Gemara* topics at an advanced level) is not like a ball game in which you have to fight constantly. Hearing what your colleague has to say is better than fighting against it. After you 'hear' it, then you can fight it. If you fight all the time you are no better than the boxers you see in the pictures with their fists up; on the other hand, though, it's a *chaburah*, not a rabbi's sermon, and you don't have to just listen and then give a compliment for nothing."

ᔰ ᔰ ᔰ

"People used to be so great that they were able to listen. In those days not everyone *davened* for himself; instead, one person would *daven* for the whole congregation and everyone else would listen to him. It's not easy to listen; a person has to acquire the ability. As it says (*Devarim* 27:9) '*Haskeis u'shma* — prepare yourself and hear.'

"In Yiddish they say that there's *herren* (listening) and there's *derherren* (absorbing the inner meaning). *Chazal* say that there's a level of hearing that enters the heart like venom — it fills the body and everything's affected. For example, when Yisro heard of the Splitting of the Sea he changed his whole life. The Torah emphasizes that Yisro *heard*, because the main thing is to hear."

ᔰ ᔰ ᔰ

Reb Mendel said his *shiur* in a mixture of English and Yiddish. Some of the students did not understand Yiddish before they entered the *shiur*, but Rebbe explained things in such a way that the language barrier was no problem. "When we were in Japan, there was a small Jewish community there that didn't understand Yiddish, which made it difficult to buy groceries and the like. Rabbi Michel Birnbaum, now *mashgiach* at Mesivtha Tifereth Jerusalem, was the one person who was successful in buying food. He would enter the grocery and take out his wallet, and the grocer immediately understood everything. Here too, the rebbe has Torah in his pocket, so even if you don't understand Yiddish, you can still understand him. If you want Torah like that grocer wanted money, you'll look at the rebbe's hands, at his face, and little by little you'll understand."

To Hear and to Accept

"I ONCE ASKED A GREAT *CHASSIDISHE* SCHOLAR what *sefarim* he had written and he told me, 'They're inscribed on the hearts of my *Chassidim*.'

"In the secular world, a *talmid* is called a 'student,' meaning a poor guy who can't wait to open up his own office. *Talmid* to us is a very distinguished title, someone who is willing to learn from others. We do not refer to great scholars as *chachamim* but as *talmidei chachamim*. The only time we use the term *chachamim* is when we review their *chachmah*. Then we call them *chachamim*.

"If only we could merit the title *talmidim* all our lives... Some people go to a rebbe to get a rubber stamp of approval for whatever they want to do, but a *talmid* goes to find out what to do. The *Mishnah* (*Rosh Hashanah* 2:9) recounts that although Rabbi Yehoshua disagreed with the calculation of Rabban Gamliel and concluded that a particular day was Yom Kippur, he nevertheless submitted to Rabban Gamliel's order and appeared before him on that day carrying his staff and money purse. Rabban Gamliel then called him, 'my rebbe and my *talmid* — my rebbe in wisdom and my student in that you accept my words.' Now that's a *talmid*. The ability to accept something that is opposed to one's whole understanding is the greatest quality a person can have."

s➤ s➤ s➤

Once we encountered an uncommon word in the *Gemara* and Rebbe pronounced it for the class and added, "That's how I heard it from my rebbe, who heard it from *his* rebbe, and so on all the way back. Shmayah and Avtalyon were converts who could not pronounce a certain letter in the *Aleph Beis*. Their students pronounced it the same way they did, even though they knew how to pronounce the letter correctly (*Rambam* to *Eduyos* 1:3). The way the rebbe said it is the right way for his student to say it."

Reb Mendel's notes of a shmuess by Reb Yeruchem Levovitz

ALTHOUGH REB MENDEL explained the *Gemara* as clearly and simply as possible, he trained his students to develop into true

To Make It on Your Own *talmidei chachamim* in their own right. There are no simple solutions or shortcuts to that end; success can come only through diligent study and total involvement.

One day, before *shiur,* two boys approached rebbe's desk in the *beis midrash* to ask a question, but he refused to answer. "Don't just come to me for a nice hot shower. Do the *Rishonim* yourself. Go through *Shita Mekubetzes* (an anthology of *Rishonim*), and find the answer to your question."

In *shiur* once when a student asked Reb Mendel to repeat something he had just explained, Rebbe realized that the student hadn't been paying attention. "If you want to hear the *Gemara* over, I'll say it for you," he said. "But you first have to put some money in this envelope. If you know you're paying for it, then you'll listen." He had learned this method from Reb Yeruchem's teacher, the Alter of Kelm.

"What's wrong with everyone?" he exclaimed to the class one day. "Why aren't you paying attention? You're acting like my son did in Shanghai. He never liked to eat the cereal, he just had no taste for it. I'd tell him, 'Hurry, eat it up, your mother is coming!' And he'd ask me nicely, '*Tatte,* please help me. Eat some cereal for me.'

"You're thinking just like my son: 'Oh, good! Rebbe is learning a lot of *Tosafos* for us; let him have some more.' I can't learn for you. You have to pay attention for yourselves."

"PRAYER IS CALLED THE SERVICE OF THE HEART, while *Gemara* is called the service of the mind. Even though it's impos-

Torah — Heart and Mind sible to put your heart into something without your head being involved, it is possible to put your head into something without your heart being there. The early *Chassidim* used to prepare themselves before *davening,* and we can prepare our hearts before studying Torah.

"There's no comparison between someone who has only his head in learning and someone who also feels a desire to learn —

it's the heart that gives you the drive to learn. When Hashem sees that someone is putting his heart into learning, He helps him understand, like a mother who sends her children packages of good things. As we know, Torah knowledge is completely dependent on how much of Hashem's wisdom He chooses to send us. That is why we pray in *Shemoneh Esrei*, 'Endow us graciously from Yourself with wisdom.' "

ᔖ ᔖ ᔖ

"Sometimes we're so involved in preparing a *chaburah* that we can't sleep at night. One time in Chicago, I was staying in a businessman's home, and I woke up in the middle of the night. I went down to the living room, and there I found my host lying on the floor with plans spread out all around him. His mind was so involved with his business that he just couldn't sleep.

"It used to be that people didn't need an alarm clock to wake up to say *Tikkun Chatzos*. They thought so much about the exile that they couldn't sleep at night, so what could they do but get up and cry over the destruction and say *Tikkun Chatzos*. It's wonderful not to be able to fall asleep at night like my businessman host because you can't get your mind off what you're learning. Ah, if you can do that, then you'll get a special gift of insight from Heaven."

"CHAZAL SAY THAT TORAH is as hard to acquire as golden vessels and as easy to lose as glass ones (*Chagigah* 15a). It's easier to

Breaking the Barrier

jump into a freezing *mikveh* than to learn a page of *Gemara*. Even for an easy thing such as reviewing the weekly Torah portion, the *yetzer hara* tries its hardest to stop you. Reb Elchonon used to say in the name of the Chofetz Chaim that the *yetzer hara* allows someone to do all the *mitzvos* in the world as long as he can stop him from learning Torah."

ᔖ ᔖ ᔖ

"The *Gemara* is on the stove but it's not ready to be served yet; you have to cook it for yourself. Why do we naturally shake when we learn Torah but not when we learn secular subjects? The *Kuzari* says it's because Torah boils inside us. That is why a *talmid chacham* is called a *tzurba merabnon*. The word *tzurba* means to cook. When someone boils with Torah, even his bad character traits are sterilized by the process."

٭ ٭ ٭

"*Chazal* say that Torah remains only with someone who 'kills himself' over it (*Berachos* 63b). Reb Yisrael Salanter explains that 'killing yourself' means breaking down your selfishness and uprooting all thoughts of your own needs and desires. Learning when you're feeling tired and lazy is 'killing yourself.' Someone who begins to do these things will feel immediate reward in terms of his ability to better understand what he learns.

"The more you accept the Torah as your yoke, the better you'll learn. If you can learn Torah even when it's hard, you'll excel far more than you would by learning in conditions of comfort and pleasure. I can tell you from experience that this is particularly true at times when you don't want to learn and you have to say to yourself, "NO! I WILL LEARN!" and fight off all your other desires. I have the greatest successes when I am stubborn or push myself. If you can learn with stubbornness, you'll see for yourself that you'll immediately start to learn better, and the time you spend learning will be the best part of your day. If you learn only because it's a nice way to spend the day, then it's nothing more than a hobby, and you won't have any success in it.

"If someone claims he has found success in learning without toil, '*al taamin* — do not believe him' (*Megillah* 6b). The word *emunah* also connotes permanence, because if you don't get excited about the Torah you learn, then the lessons it teaches you won't stay with you for long. It's like a driver who slows down and drives more carefully after he sees an accident. A few minutes later though, he forgets all about the accident and speeds up again. The lesson he learned didn't last because it was only happenstance: he just happened to see an accident, but he didn't work to make it part of himself."

٭ ٭ ٭

"The *K'tzos HaChoshen* was so poor that he couldn't heat his home and had to spend all day during the winter under heavy blankets to keep from freezing. While he was writing the *K'tzos*, the ink would freeze in his inkwell and he had to write under the blankets to keep it warm. It's because he sacrificed himself so much for Torah that his Torah is so sweet and has merited to be studied by so many generations."

ᔈ ᔈ ᔈ

"If someone breaks himself in trying to understand Torah, Hashem will reveal the Torah to him in a way that goes beyond the laws of nature. The *Gemara* (*Taanis* 23a) tells about a *Tanna* who did not understand the verse (*Tehillim* 126:1), *When Hashem will return the captivity of Zion* (a period of seventy years), *we will be like dreamers*. He couldn't understand how someone could sleep for seventy years. So Hashem performed a miracle for him, and he slept for seventy years. This teaches us that it is worthwhile for Hashem to perform a miracle, and for someone to sleep for seventy years, in order to understand one verse in *Tehillim*."

Reb Mendel once showed his class another meaning of toil in Torah. One day they were having difficulty comprehending a concept. "So what if you don't understand it," he said. "When you learn Torah, you grow greater even though you don't understand it. I'm just as happy when I don't understand a *Gemara* I'm learning as when I do. When you learn diligently for the sake of finding the truth, without sticking your own preconceived notions into the *Gemara*, and you still can't understand it, then you've learned it. Every drop, every crumb, every little piece you manage to get plants a seed that keeps on growing even when you go away from it. Then when you come back to it again, what you learned the first time will help you come to the true understanding. If you *toil* now, even without understanding, then later on you'll *find* it. It will be given to you from Heaven.

"I want you to know that you'll get more reward for believing in a *Gemara* that you don't understand. You might not agree with me because you want to become a big scholar, but I'm interested in the reward!"

"DID YOU KNOW that it's possible to get a headache from concentrating? *Baruch Hashem*, I once had the merit to get a headache from concentrating in learning.

Great People — Breaking Greater Barriers

"Just like your feet can become tired from too much walking, your head can also become tired from too much thinking. Take Reb ____, he uses all his concentration in learning. I've never seen anyone like him anywhere. People should be asking him for *berachos*. And do you think that the *Rishonim* learned like we do? From Reb _____ you can see how much more the *Rishonim* must have strained their minds and pained themselves to think, with headaches and all.

"Reb Elchonon used to give his *shiur* until his strength gave out; when he was no longer able to stand up straight, he would begin to wobble holding onto the *shtender*. He would then excuse himself and lay his head down on his arm for about two minutes until he'd gathered enough strength to go a bit further. When someone exhausts his resources to the very last drop, then even a few minutes' rest can keep his eyes open and clear his mind. Sometimes when Reb Elchonon was learning with a younger study partner and got tired, he would go lie down and ask the young man to knock on his door in a few minutes to wake him up. If someone's really tired, he can even sleep standing, resting just his eyes and head. That's how we slept on the crowded trains when we were escaping from Europe. I've heard that when soldiers get very tired from marching constantly, they can even rest their eyes and their heads while they're marching and gain strength like that.

"Hashem counts the pain we suffer on His computer. The *Midrash* says that if someone toils in Torah until he needs his last bit of strength to drop onto his bed and fall asleep, then when saliva begins to drip from his mouth, Hashem cherishes it like the incense offering in the *Beis HaMikdash*."

Reb Mendel himself regularly learned until he had used up his last bit of energy and concentration. One night after *Maariv* a student asked to speak to him concerning something unrelated to learning. Reb Mendel excused himself saying he was very tired and planned to go to sleep immediately. As the student was walking away, several other boys approached Reb Mendel to speak about Torah subjects. Immediately he perked up and conversed with them for over half an hour with his usual enthusiasm and excitement. After they left, the first student saw Reb Mendel's strength ebb visibly and followed him as he slowly made his way back to his room. At the foot of the staircase, he had to stop for several moments to gather his strength, and even then he was so weak that each step required great effort.

ONE DAY A NUMBER OF BOYS were late for *shiur*. Rebbe blocked the door shut from the inside with an old air conditioner

Overcoming Obstacles for Torah

which had been lying in the corner of the room. The latecomers waited outside for a while, until Reb Mendel finally moved the air conditioner away and lamented, "Alas for those who are gone and are seen no more (*Sanhedrin* 11a)!" In Chicago they would get ladders and climb in through the second-story windows when I locked them out. Why didn't you push the door open and come in anyway, what could I possibly have done to you? The *Shela* says that when the Heavenly voice told *Acheir* that *teshuvah* was possible for everyone besides him (*Chagigah* 15a), he should still have tried to push his way back to Hashem. 'You have to listen to whatever the host says except to leave ... (*Pesachim* 86b).' "

"FROM GOLD NOTHING GROWS, but from the earth grow beautiful flowers."

To Struggle in Learning — A Cause for Pride

Reb Mendel felt especially close to those students who had to struggle with difficulties in learning. He once said that when someone gets wounded in battle or hurt on a baseball field, his bandage is as much a badge of honor as a diploma. Similarly, when someone falls while trying to learn, it is to his credit. He trained us not to be discouraged by failure and not to be afraid of making mistakes.

Once a *bachur* was arguing adamantly with Rebbe in defense of his interpretation of a *Gemara*. Finally Rebbe told him, "Don't feel bad. Sometimes you have to be a sport and lose the game. Do you think you have to come out with great honors every time, like a general in the army?"

"Don't be afraid to make mistakes," he said. "I make mistakes many times. You don't succeed in Torah from getting honors — only from humiliation. You should act in *shiur* like on the basketball court: Don't be afraid to shoot the ball because you might miss. *Chazal* say that any student who keeps quiet when his Rebbe screams at him will merit to understand important portions of the Torah (*Berachos* 63b). You have to accept embarrassment for Torah.

❧ ❧ ❧

"When Reb Elchonon came to Chicago, he would stay at my brother's house. He kept nickels for his personal phone calls separate from the ones he used for yeshivah calls. Though he was in Chicago only on the yeshivah's behalf, he still used separate nickels. He was so poor that one of his hats had a hole in the top. The books showed that Reb Elchonon's official salary from the yeshivah was thirty dollars a week, but in reality it was much less.

"Once, in Chicago, Reb Elchonon went out collecting with a *bachur*. They traveled a long distance to see a wealthy junkyard owner who promised them a hundred-dollar donation if they would find him at home. When they finally reached his house, the maid who opened the door said that the owner was not home. It was a very hot day so the boy asked for a glass of water for the *rosh yeshivah*. The maid brought out a glass of water, gave it to the boy, and then shut the door, leaving them in the heat.

"At this the *bachur* was heartbroken: they had traveled such a long way, in such heat, and didn't even get invited in to drink a glass of water. Reb Elchonon took the cup and sat down on a big rock nearby to drink. When the *bachur* saw what disgrace the *rosh yeshivah* had to endure, he broke down in tears. Reb Elchonon looked up at him and said, '*Voss veint ir?* — Why are you crying? Do you think it was for nothing that the prophet was called Yechezkel ben Buzi? He was given the title of Buzi because he humiliated (Hebrew: *buz*) himself for Torah. The name was a mark of respect.'"

Reb Mendel continued, "My father-in-law, Reb Hirsch Gutman, worked for the Baranovich Yeshivah and was also supposed to receive a salary equivalent to thirty dollars a week. By the time I was married, the yeshivah owed him three thousand dollars — almost two years' pay! I tell this so you'll know that the best deal you can make is to give yourself away for Torah. By nature, honor feels good and it might even make you stronger, but it's a *segulah* to humiliate yourself for Torah. When you prepare something to say in a *chaburah*, you have to struggle over Torah and may well end up embarrassing yourself; it's a big business proposition where the rewards are very great."

CHAPTER SIX

Learning Skills

TORAH STUDY is a science with its own structure, techniques and tricks of the trade. Reb Mendel shared with us the

Learning Skills

tips and insights he had gleaned over a lifetime of experiences and observations.

"You have to look for ways to learn better in the same way people look for ways to get their car out of the snow," he told us. "You keep trying one thing and then another until you discover whatever it is that works."

৯৯ ৯৯ ৯৯

One morning at the beginning of a study session, a boy asked Reb Mendel why the *Gemara* asks a certain question. Rebbe told him, "Why ask why the *Gemara* asks what it does? The *Gemara* says that when someone first enters a *beis midrash*, all the arguments he hears

seem to be the opposite of the truth. But after he's been there long enough and his mind draws closer to the logic of the *Gemara*, he begins to see that everything makes sense. Consider the difference between when we first started *Bava Kama* and when we finished it. Once we finished, it was tasty and juicy because we'd developed a feel for it. Every *masechta* is a different world; after you get into it, your mind is different. So for someone to come from breakfast and ask a question on the *Gemara* is wrong — he has nothing to ask.

"You don't have to 'learn' how to drive, you just have to get used to it. After you've been driving for two years, you feel like the car is an extension of yourself and it becomes as easy and as natural as walking. The same is true with learning — you just have to let the learning become part of you, and then you'll start to understand things automatically.

"Learning a *Gemara* is like acquiring a field; once you establish your rights on one corner of it, the rest of it becomes yours. Knowing even some *Gemara* in a *masechta* is very different from not knowing the *masechta* at all."

Although having some knowledge in many different *masechtos* is a good thing, Reb Mendel cautioned us against spreading our learning program too thinly. "It's not advisable to learn more than two different *masechtos* a day. If you learn more than that in one day it scatters your mind too much and takes away from your taste for learning your primary *masechtos* properly."

§⟶ §⟶ §⟶

To the novice, the style and structure of the *Gemara* can seem strange and confusing. Sometimes the *Gemara* may digress for pages on a subject totally unrelated to the main one, or it may repeat an entire passage from the page before. To the outsider all this may seem chaotic, but the experienced scholar can grasp the wisdom and order in it all.

Reb Mendel told us, "Every piece of *Gemara* has its own characteristics and no two pages are the same, just as no two days have the same set of clouds or the same temperature and sunshine. Even when the *Gemara* repeats the exact same passage in two different places, each time is different, because the context in which it appears is different. Every piece has its own taste.

"The reason the *mishnayos* of *Zeraim* and *Taharos* don't have *Gemara* written on them is because *Chazal* saw that people wouldn't learn them because the subjects they deal with are for the most part not relevant in our day. Therefore, they scattered their discussions of those topics throughout *Shas* so that they would be learned along with other relevant *Gemaras*. Similarly, the *Rishonim* sometimes digress at great length on obscure topics in the popular *masechtos* because they want students to be familiar with those topics as well."

Torah for Everyone

THE TORAH IS NOT THE EXCLUSIVE DOMAIN of an elite few; it is the inheritance of the whole Jewish nation. It does not require exceptional acumen or ability: *It is not in the heaven, that you should say: "Who shall ascend for us to heaven, and take it for us ..." Neither is it beyond the sea, that you should say: "Who shall go over for us to the other side of the sea and take it for us, and make us hear it ..." But rather, the matter is very close to you, in your mouth and in your heart, that you may do it* (*Devarim* 30:12-14).

"There was a saying in the old country, 'It's better to have a good seat than a good head.' The *Mishnah* (*Avos* 2:8) says, 'The more one sits (to study), the more wisdom one acquires.' It's not your head that brings you wisdom, it's simply the act of sitting — nothing else, just sitting and learning the whole day.

"Reb Elchonon used to say that a *bachur* with average abilities who is very diligent can become a great Torah scholar. Once, he told a young man who had become discouraged with his learning, '*Yeh kishron, nit kishron, ob men lernt ken men lernen* — Whether or not you have innate ability, if you learn, you'll be able to learn' — and Reb Elchonon added, 'I'm the proof of this!' " Reb Mendel added, "That was Reb Elchonon. Who else in the world would say such a thing about himself!"

≈ ≈ ≈

Once Reb Mendel remarked to a particular student with whom he was studying a complex topic, "It's really a wonder that we can learn and understand a *Gemara* in America. In previous generations, someone would first have to know the whole *Shas* before he could start to reason analytically in learning. Reb Isser Zalman Meltzer was eleven years old when he came to the

Volozhiner Yeshivah, and he already knew by heart *Bava Kama*, *Bava Metzia* and *Bava Basra*, as well as part of *Chullin*."

At that point Reb Mendel noticed a look of astonishment on the student's face and commented, "That's nothing to wonder about," he said. "The children in America fill themselves up with a *'Shas'* of foolishness, but in Europe there wasn't such foolishness, so naturally they could learn *Shas* in their childhood."

REB MENDEL STRESSED that good results depend on good beginnings.

Gold Nuggets of Advice "When you first sit down to learn with your *chavrusa*, take care not to start off with idle talk. When the Torah commands us to sanctify every first-born (*Shemos* 13:12), it also means that we have to make the first part of whatever we do into something holy."

S➤ S➤ S➤

Reb Mendel once saw a student straining over the wording of a *Gemara* and asked him, "Why are you concentrating so hard on the words of the *Gemara*? Take it easy, relax and sing while you learn. Don't spend so much effort on the words; instead try to work through the ideas. After you learn the *Gemara*, speak out the main ideas on that page — what Abaye says, what Rava says and what *Rashi* and *Tosafos* say about it. We should talk about *Gemara* the same way we talk about trivialities, like it's something enjoyable that we won't get tired of talking about. True success comes from this way of learning, speaking out the questions and answers of the *Gemara*, but in the way that's most comfortable to you."

S➤ S➤ S➤

"Learn what the common expressions in the *Gemara* and the Torah mean so that you know how to translate them, and you'll have a rich world. Without that you're forever lacking. Chinese women used to have small feet because when they were little, their feet were bound into small shoes. Learn the basic vocabulary or else your world becomes boxed in."

ֿֿֿֿ ֿֿֿֿ ֿֿֿֿ

"Coming to a new *Gemara* is like coming to a new yeshivah; at first everything feels strange and uncomfortable, and you don't know where to turn or what to do. We should familiarize ourselves with a *Gemara* by going over it four or five times before approaching *Tosafos*."

ֿֿֿֿ ֿֿֿֿ ֿֿֿֿ

"Usually we understand the other *Gemara*s cited in *Tosafos* as much as we know what goes on inside the house across the street. Nevertheless, our brief encounter with those *Gemara*s pays off, since when you eventually learn them, you'll feel like you're meeting an old friend."

ֿֿֿֿ ֿֿֿֿ ֿֿֿֿ

The *Gemara* must be learned with *Rashi* and *Tosafos*; they are the essentials.

"Without *Tosafos* we'd rip the *Gemara* apart, but *Tosafos* makes all the *Gemara*s come out without contradictions and problems. To learn just *Gemara* and *Rashi* is acceptable if you review it ten times."

ֿֿֿֿ ֿֿֿֿ ֿֿֿֿ

While he was learning, Reb Mendel would point with his finger to the place in the *sefer*. He once explained to the class the benefits of this practice: "Did you know that you can learn with your hands? Moshe Rabbeinu lifted his hands toward heaven and the heavens shook. Your finger can connect your thoughts to the *Gemara* like an antenna connects the airwaves to a radio. Hook yourself up to the *Gemara* by pointing to it. A finger that points, that's used in learning, gets reward and gains holiness. If you do this, you'll also save that finger from suffering."

ֿֿֿֿ ֿֿֿֿ ֿֿֿֿ

"Many times *Rashi* uses the phrase, 'my heart tells me.' Each person has his own feeling whether an explanation is true or not, but he's only right if he is a truthful person."

ֿֿֿֿ ֿֿֿֿ ֿֿֿֿ

"If you have an 'itch' of a question, it's a gift from heaven and you mustn't let it simply slip by you. You have to develop your understanding of the problem and express it in thoughts and words. We say, 'I labored and I found' — the creative thoughts that come from toiling in learning are a gift from heaven."

ᔆ᠄ ᔆ᠄ ᔆ᠄

"Great scholars have said we should look back at the *Gemara* after we've learned *Rashi* and *Tosafos* to see how we would have explained the *Gemara* ourselves, and to understand why the *Rishonim* differ. [Reb Mendel did not recommended this approach for all students.] Similarly, it's good to learn the *Gemara* and then look back into the *Mishnah* to see how it all fits in."

ᔆ᠄ ᔆ᠄ ᔆ᠄

"It's always good to look over an argument between the *Rambam* and the *Raavad* because there's always something even for ordinary people to think about there."

ᔆ᠄ ᔆ᠄ ᔆ᠄

"The best time to learn and to innovate is on Shabbos, because then you have a restful attitude."

"*SHAS* IS LIKE A PUZZLE. When you know all of it, then everything fits together.

Learning to Move On

"You have to learn to move on. Learning is like carpentry. You'll never learn how to make anything except by cutting up a lot of new wood. The *Shach* had the *Rishonim* at his fingertips, like a maestro at the keys of a piano, and he could play many of them together at the same time and combine them in different ways. But we're living on the bare essentials."

ᔆ᠄ ᔆ᠄ ᔆ᠄

"In the yeshivah world, some people are still on *daf daled* (the third page of a *masechta*)," Reb Mendel once said several months into a term. "Learning so slowly is nothing to be proud of. From learning *Gemaras*, people like Reb

Reb Leib Malin

Chaim Brisker were produced, but from learning Reb Chaim Brisker, *Amoraim* are not produced. Reb Leib Malin, the *Rosh Yeshivah* of Beis HaTalmud, knew 500 *blatt Gemara* by heart when he was a *bachur* in the Mir.

"If someone doesn't learn a lot of *Gemaras*, it's like the best businessman stuck without money;[1] all his talent is worthless. To do business you need to have start-up capital. Of course it would be nice to learn the *Gemara* with all the commentaries; but we need to learn a lot of *Gemara*. I say this in the name of my teachers, and if it was like that in Europe, it's certainly like that here. If you learn the *Gemara* ten or fifteen times over, it's just as good as delving into all the fine points, and in later years it pays off. Rabbi Lazer Plachinsky[2] went very fast and we wondered about it then, but later we saw how his approach paid off.

"In earlier times a student would have to learn the whole Talmud before he started a close analytical approach to learning. The *Maharal* complained when they first printed *Tosafos* on the same page as the *Gemara*; he felt that only *Rashi* should appear on the page. If you learn the *Gemara* with only *Rashi* it goes much faster and lighter; the toil required increases many times once you start learning *Tosafos*. Still, the *Maharal* felt you should first learn just *Gemara* and *Rashi*, and only afterwards begin *Tosafos*. The problem with our generation is that we don't learn enough *Gemaras*."

৯ ৯ ৯

Nonetheless, on another occasion Rebbe said in *shiur*, "Let's look at *Tosafos* before the *Rosh*; that's why they put *Tosafos* on the page — they didn't do it for nothing. The *Maharal* was upset that they put *Tosafos* on the same page with the *Gemara* because he felt that it would keep people from finishing all of *Shas*. Still, you see that it's there, so it must be that we need to have it there. You can be sure that it wasn't just the printers who decided to put it there."

৯ ৯ ৯

Rebbe once passed by a student studying *Birchas Shmuel* of

---

1. See Introduction to Sefer *Chayei Adam.*

2. The author of *Shalom Yehudah,* who was known in the Mirrer Yeshivah in Poland for the breadth and depth of his knowledge. He corresponded with the *Chazon Ish* on *halachah* topics. The latter related that it was a challenge to argue with him because he knew everything so clearly.

Rabbi Boruch Ber Leibowitz and commented, "Wouldn't it be better to have a look into the *shiurim* of Abaye and Rava?"

Another time he was overheard saying to one of the *roshei yeshivah* as they walked away together after *Maariv*, "We have *Gemaras* and *Rishonim* — so why do we need such a big library?"

$ ▸ $ ▸ $ ▸

Reb Mendel frowned upon teachers whose lectures reached beyond the capacity of their students. He once told a tenth-grade rebbe from a yeshivah for exceptional students, "When I was the age of the *bachurim* in your *shiur*, I was more advanced than any of them. And if Reb Elchonon's Torah was good enough for me, then it's good enough for them." (Reb Elchonon's approach emphasized elementary analytical reasoning far less complicated than what that rebbe employed in classes for that age group.)

"It's too much to squeeze material for forty *chaburos* out of three pages of *Gemara*. Today, everyone goes after that style, like when a wind blows through a forest and all the trees bend. A person should plan his learning schedule so that he'll know all of *Shas* in the course of his lifetime.

"*Chiddushim* are like cake — if you eat just cake, you'll have only fat and no muscles. Getting the simple meaning down is the bread and meat, that's what you need the most of. It's like a skyscraper — the foundation is the least glamorous part, but it's also the most important."

One day, after we spent a long time discussing later commentators, Rebbe said: "Enough entertainment — let's get on with the *Gemara*."

"IF YOU WANT TO GET A *GESHMAK* in learning a *Gemara*, you have to review it many times. We say in *Krias Shema*: *V'shinantam*

On Chazarah *l'vanecha* — *You shall repeat them to your children* (*Devarim* 6:7), but this can also mean, 'You shall *sharpen* them for your children.' Studying Torah is like a sharpening wheel that spins around and around to make the knife sharp. You have to review a *Gemara* many, many times, to make it sharp in your mouth.

"Reviewing Torah is like polishing a shoe: You go over it once, twice, three times and th-e-e-en," he practically sang the word, "it begins to shine.

"We shouldn't learn Torah just to know it; we should learn it until it becomes part of us and rings in our ears. *He gave us the Torah of truth and implanted eternal life within us (Shacharis).* Review the *Gemara* until it's 'implanted within us,' then it's not just in the *Gemara*, it's in you. The *Maharal* says that the Written Torah is in the scroll, but the Oral Torah is engraved in the hearts of the Jewish people."

ᔕ ᔕ ᔕ

"*If you hear the old Torah, you'll hear the new one, too (Berachos 40a).* The way to make new discoveries in the *Gemara* isn't by creasing your forehead and racking your brains; it's by learning one *Gemara* on a subject, and then others on the same subject, and then talking about them and looking at them from this angle and then that angle," Rebbe said, tilting his head and motioning his hands as if he were examining a large diamond. "That's how to come up with new interpretations. That's the meaning of the adage, *If you hear the old Torah, you'll hear the new one, too* — if you pay close attention to what you've learned already, then you'll hear new interpretations in it as well."

ᔕ ᔕ ᔕ

"To a businessman, the prettiest music in the world is money going into a cash register. Well, each word of Torah we hear is the same thing. It's possible to repeat an easy saying of the Torah a hundred times while you wait in line in the dining room. It may sound easy to do, but once you try it, you'll see how hard the *yetzer hara* works to stop you from doing it. From this alone you can see how important it is."

ᔕ ᔕ ᔕ

"The only way to know something is to review it many times; there are no shortcuts. Whatever I know comes from persistent reviewing. Even the *Amoraim* needed to review a simple statement forty times (*Megillah* 7b). You must review everything over and over again, five times at the very least, and you can even skip a regular learning period just to review. In Europe, we saw more Divine assistance in our learning because we reviewed so much.

"The foolishness a person thinks about pushes Torah out of his mind. But if you review a lot, you can push out all the idle words that have accumulated in you since you were a year old."

S➤ S➤ S➤

"Whatever you learn in Torah is for the good, even the easy things. It's even a big accomplishment just looking over a *Gemara* a few times to get a picture in your mind of how the page looks, because even the shape of the page is something."

S➤ S➤ S➤

Someone once asked Rebbe where would be a good place to begin reviewing. He answered, "Many Sages wrote books just on the alphabet. Even though they only finished the first few letters, all of them started from the beginning. So you should start from the beginning, unless you're particularly weak in a certain subject."

The Many Facets of Torah

"THE *HALACHAH* IS LIKE A HIGHWAY that everyone drives on, but there are six hundred thousand paths in learning to suit the taste of every individual. Each one of them is an exit to some particular destination."

S➤ S➤ S➤

"There is no single proper approach to learning Torah. The One Who made our fingers also created the Torah, and just as He designed the fingers as a tool to perform thousands of different jobs, so too each verse can be learned in many ways.

"Some people think that only their Torah is the true Torah, and any other style is not Torah, but in reality there are many types of Torah. I used to be a bit of a *chazzan* for the *Yamim Noraim* in Vilna and Shanghai. Years later, I was riding in a car together with a friend of mine who was a *chazzan*. He sang several different versions of *HaYom Haras Olam*, and then asked me to sing my version. I was completely dumbfounded! How could he keep so many different melodic twists for *HaYom Haras Olam* in his mind, while I barely know one version! The *Rambam* pondered whether to write *Mishneh Torah* in the language of the *Gemara*, or of the Torah itself. So you see, there are many different approaches to the same subject."

S➤ S➤ S➤

"Some people here feel that a *shiur* is good only if it includes a *chiddush* from Reb Chaim. You don't have to worry just because you don't learn each topic like the Briskers do; there are also other ways to learn Torah. Reb Elchonon, Reb Shimon and Reb Aharon were big *lamdanim* who didn't follow the Brisker approach. The Torah was studied for thousands of years since Mount Sinai without the Brisker approach.

"But still, it's worthwhile to learn Brisker Torah since it gives you a taste in the *Gemara*, like an appetizer. I was in Vilna for a short time, and I learned *Menachos* with the Brisker Rav. I had already learned that *Gemara* in the Mirrer Yeshivah, but the Brisker Rav's Torah was so sweet that I can still taste it today. As a young man, Reb Chaim Brisker said a *chiddush* in the presence of Reb Yisrael Salanter, who was a genius in everything, not just in *mussar*. Reb Yisrael said to Reb Chaim's father, the *Beis HaLevi*, "There will be a time when his analytical approach will help students by giving them a desire for learning."

AFTER REB MENDEL HAD BEEN LEARNING in the Mirrer Yeshivah for a term, he approached the *mashgiach*, Reb Yeruchem **Pure** Levovitz, with a request: "Naftoli [Reb Naftoli Wasserman, Reb Elchonon's son and a close friend **Jealousy** of Reb Mendel's] had a good *chavrusa* and he grew as a result of it; I would also like to have such a study partner." The *mashgiach* stared at Reb Mendel intently for several minutes but said nothing. Reb Mendel explained to us why he gave him that prolonged stare: "He wanted to make sure that what he saw was true *kinas sofrim*.[3]

"Make no mistake," Reb Mendel told us, "true *kinas sofrim* I have not yet seen. What you see nowadays is only personal competition, not *kinas sofrim*. Unfortunately, we often fall into the trap of envying the person who possesses a good quality rather than the quality itself, and that's an impure motivation. It's not easy — you have to be a good 'chemist' to separate the elements and realize what is true *kinas sofrim* and what is ordinary envy."

---

3. *Kinas sofrim,* literally, jealousy among young scholars, is praised by the Sages as a motivation for increasing knowledge.

"A PERSON MISTAKENLY THINKS he can hide those parts of his personality he doesn't want the world to see, and reveal only

Fooling Yourself

the parts he's willing to let others know about. But the truth is that even the deepest parts of a personality stand out on the tip of your nose for everyone to see — everyone except yourself.

"A person thinks he knows himself, but even that he doesn't know. Similarly, a person thinks he knows how his voice sounds, but when he hears himself on a tape recorder he sounds strange. He can't believe it's really him while others recognize his voice right away. This is also true of our drives and motivations; we deceive ourselves as to what we really think, while to an outsider it's obvious."

On another occasion he said, "If a hot-tempered person could see a movie of how he behaves when he's angry, it would be the best cure for his anger."

"HASHEM HAS ONLY the four cubits of *halachah* in His world — everything else is just a big headache to Him. It's only in places

The Yeshivah Years

like this, in the yeshivos, that He gets a bit of *nachas*."

Sも. Sも. Sも.

"The trials the Jewish people have gone through under dictators were no harder than the spiritual trials we're exposed to in a liberal place like America. The reason that we're fortunate enough to learn in yeshivah is probably due to the merits of ancestors who were big *tzaddikim*. A yeshivah is like Noah's Ark in that it saves one from the rest of society. You have to prepare yourself in yeshivah before you go out into the world."

Sも. Sも. Sも.

"When a large number of people learn together, they can sometimes understand a *Gemara* better than one of the really great sages. The *Yerushalmi* says that if the Sages are in doubt regarding the law, they should look at how the masses conduct themselves (*Yerushalmi Peah* 7:5), because Hashem doesn't allow the masses to err."

Sも. Sも. Sも.

"In later years you'll say that the best period in your life was the time you spent in yeshivah. Even if you become a *rosh yeshivah*, you'll have the trial of honor to worry about, and you'll also have a lot of burdens unrelated to learning.

"Yeshivah boys have nothing to worry about. They don't have to worry about money, children, or health; they can just sit and learn. You are already in *Gan Eden.*

"As long as you're in yeshivah, you should grab as much Torah as you can, because in yeshivah you're a different person. It's like when we went up to Jerusalem three times a year for the *Yamim Tovim. From Zion comes forth Torah and the word of Hashem from Jerusalem* (*Yeshayahu* 2:3) — when the Jews came to Zion, they saw real holiness and it changed them."

s➤ s➤ s➤

Rebbe once said of a successful professional who lived near the yeshivah, "I have pity on that poor guy who comes to *daven* in yeshivah occasionally. He's a very nice man, and if he'd come all the time he'd be a different person. But the truth is that even if you *daven* in yeshivah only once in a while, you become a different person.

"You have to treat each day you spend in yeshivah with honor, because the spiritual acquisitions you get in yeshivah will have to sustain you for the rest of your seventy years. In Europe, working people used to go to yeshivah for the month of Elul to get a boost for the coming year. Do you want to hear what an old Jew says? Not only do you have to live for seventy years on the strength of your yeshivah days, you have to live much longer — you have to live eternally."

Rebbe then looked at one student. "You are aware, aren't you, that you will be around forever? Because the soul comes from His Throne of Glory. I'm not just telling stories for your entertainment. I'm saying this because I hope it'll build your faith — which is in itself a lifetime's work."

s➤ s➤ s➤

It used to please Reb Mendel when students thought of the yeshivah as their home. In Chicago there was a boy who always left his belongings scattered all over the yeshivah. The administration wanted to take drastic measures to curb his sloppy habits, but Reb Mendel defended him and said that it was to his credit that he felt so much at home.

On the other hand, Rebbe also got upset at boys who threw their clothing around carelessly. He once told the class, "It bothers me to see so many things just thrown around and left in disarray in the yeshivah. I have no rest from this. You must be careful with your parents' money. First you have to take responsibility for yourself. Then you have the responsibility of dealing with your parents' money properly. Afterwards you'll be able to bear the responsibility of a wife and family. Only then will you be able to really carry the yoke of your responsibility to Heaven. This country is built on the idea that everyone is free from any kind of responsibility. Go to skid row and see what happens to people who can't bear the yoke of responsibility."

"LEARNED PEOPLE are compared to flowers. Yeshivah *bachurim* are like flowers which have not yet blossomed. I'll tell you some-

The Holy Yeshivah Bachur thing. You hear so much about Mir and Baranovich, you probably won't believe me when I tell you that the boys in this yeshivah are just as good as they were. If you value the time available here to learn and don't waste it with idle talk, you will merit the same distinction that was known in the European yeshivos.

"Do you remember the feeling you had while you were dancing and rejoicing on Simchas Torah? Well, if someone learns the way he should, he can make himself into a *sefer Torah,* or something even greater. Each one of you has a *sefer Torah* inside. It may be only one percent, with the rest filled with foolishness, but hopefully all of you have more than that. You have to keep that realization inside you always and conduct yourself accordingly."

❧ ❧ ❧

Reb Mendel considered yeshivah *bachurim* to be *tzaddikim.* "They're straight and simple," he said, "and they don't have to worry about any sins except for slighting Torah study." He would tell us, "Through you, I hope to merit to learn and grow more myself, since if you grow, I will too. The Sages say that the world rests on the merit of the breath that comes out of the mouths of little schoolchildren (*Shabbos* 119b). As long as you're not twenty years old yet, you still count as little children."

A student about to go to *Eretz Yisrael* once asked Reb Mendel which places there he should visit and which outstanding people he should be sure to meet. Reb Mendel told him, "Go to the yeshivos and speak in learning with the *bachurim*. They're our truly great ones."

s➤ s➤ s➤

"There was once a *rosh yeshivah* who used to scream at his students, 'Better to leave the yeshivah than to just stay around and rot.' When you're young you think years are nothing — 'So I wasted this year, so what?' You care as little about time as you do about the rubbers and umbrellas lying around the yeshivah. The years aren't precious to you and you think you have a lot of time left. But when you get older and see how you spent your younger years on nothing, then you'll start to treat every second as precious."

CHAPTER SEVEN

The Greatness of Man

The Greatness of Man

"YOU DON'T HAVE TO BE A *TZADDIK*, you have to be a *mentsch*!" was Reb Mendel's motto. Someone in *shiur* once referred to Avraham as a *tzaddik*, but Reb Mendel corrected him: "Nowhere do we find that the Torah calls Avraham a *tzaddik*.[1] He was simply a *mentsch*. He was what a person is supposed to be."

§➤ §➤ §➤

Reb Mendel often spoke about man's unlimited potential. "You see how marvelously the mind operates! And what is it? A handful of flesh and gel. Yet its complexity is nearly unfathomable. There are over 1,000,000 fibers connecting the eyeball to the brain. And this is all just the physical side of a person; the spiritual is infinite. And man is the switchboard of the whole of creation; everything in the world, up till the Almighty Himself, rests in his hands."

"In Hashem's eyes there is no such thing as a failure," he once said to the class. "To speak of someone as a 'failure' is a secular thing, and we should totally eradicate that thought from our

1. See Introduction of *Ha'amek Davar* to *Chumash Bereishis*.

minds. G-d forbid, how could a human being, who has so great a purpose, be a failure? And it's also silly to label every wealthy person as 'successful.' We must be careful not to use these incorrect English expressions when we talk. Language shows mentality.

"The *Gemara* (*Chagigah* 13b) notes a contradiction in the prophet Yechezkel's account of his vision of Hashem's 'chariot.' One verse says that on the four sides of the chariot are an eagle, a lion, a person and an ox, while another verse lists a *keruv* instead of an ox. The *Gemara* explains that when Yechezkel saw the ox it reminded him of the Golden Calf and he wondered how an ox could be on the chariot since it would remind Hashem of the sin of the Golden Calf! Hashem agreed with him and therefore changed the ox to a *keruv*! Can you imagine that? The thoughts of a flesh-and-blood human being had the power to change Hashem's chariot! From here you can see the greatness of man. The whole world is made just for him.

"These aren't new ideas, they are fundamental principles which the holy books speak about. A human being is the switchboard of creation, though usually we have as little awareness of this as the small children who run around in the yeshivah have of what's going on in our *shiur*. The Torah says, *The angels of G-d were ascending and descending on it [Jacob's ladder]* (*Bereishis* 28:12). The verse can also be read to mean that the angels were ascending and descending on *him*. Man is the vehicle on which the ascent and descent of all the angels depend. The celestial creations wait in anticipation of his every movement.

"Whatever exists here in the world below exists also in the world above. Man encompasses both worlds: one end of the soul is connected to the uppermost part of the person and the other end is hooked up to Heaven. Did you ever see the toy they have where a magnet hidden underneath moves a metal piece on top of a piece of paper, so that it looks like the piece of metal is moving by itself? So also our actions cause movements in the upper world that we don't see."

৯ ৯ ৯

Although Rebbe wanted us to have some understanding of the ramifications of our actions, at the same time he did not want us to live in the clouds. After learning a section of *Nefesh HaChaim* that discusses these concepts, he concluded, "We're only expected to drive the car, to do what the Torah requires of us; we are not required to know the mechanics of what goes on under the hood."

REB MENDEL FELT THE SPARK OF HOLINESS in every human being. During the time he spent in Japan and China, he could not

Appreciating the Worth of Every Human Being

bring himself to ride in a rickshaw and be pulled by another human being. Later in life, when he drove a car, he would use the horn only for safety purposes, never as a way of venting annoyance. He explained, "You don't speak to a person with a horn!" When he drove into a gas station he always drove to the pump nearest the attendant so the worker would not have to walk any further than necessary.

Reb Mendel never treated anyone with disdain. A young gentile janitor who worked at the yeshivah was generally considered foolish by the boys in yeshivah, and they often made fun of him. Reb Mendel, however, always spoke to him seriously and patiently, asking him the reasons for his strange actions and attempting to help him. Once Reb Mendel told the class, "Don't laugh at him; I have such pity for this *tzelem Elokim*. If it were fitting for me to do so, I would take the broom from his hand and help him sweep the floor."

One morning before Rebbe arrived, this janitor came into the class with a picture and asked if anyone wanted to buy a portrait he had drawn of himself. The entire *shiur* burst into laughter at the picture, which depicted a strong, handsome man — just the opposite of the janitor. Just then, Reb Mendel walked in and immediately assessed the situation. He said to the janitor, "Don't feel bad. These boys have no appreciation for art." He then took a great interest in the picture and inquired how much it cost.

One hot summer day, Reb Mendel was driving with a *talmid* on the highway and got lost. Seeing construction in progress at the side of the road, he pulled over to ask the workers for directions. The student got out of the car to talk to the workers, and was greeted with curses. "Can't you read the signs!" they screamed. "You can't come here!" Reb Mendel got out to help the student, and a big, bare-chested worker came towards him speaking in a disrespectful manner.

Reb Mendel just walked up to him, put his arm over the man's sweaty, grimy shoulder, and said, "You know, you should have respect for me because I'm old enough to be your father. I can understand your getting upset like this — I don't see how you can even work on such a hot day — but let me tell you something that will make you happy even on a hot day like today. Because of your work, people will be able to travel easily for years to come; old people, people with children and people with old broken cars like mine. And they'll be able to do it only because of your work." The worker's face lit up, and he gave Reb Mendel elaborate directions to his destination.

For a time in the early sixties, Reb Mendel used to spend his summer vacation at a bungalow that was located next to an egg farm in upstate New York. Every morning around five or six o'clock, trucks used to come to pick up deliveries from this farm. Many times Reb Mendel would interrupt his early morning learning to bring coffee and sandwiches to the hungry truckers.

S➤ S➤ S➤

Reb Mendel appreciated good qualities, whether in Jew or gentile, ever mindful of Hashem's declaration: "I [Hashem] testify before heaven and earth that upon both Jew and gentile, man and woman, slave and maidservant, the Divine spirit shall rest in accordance with their actions" (*Tanna d'vei Eliyahu* ch. 9). At the summer camp we attended, there was a very old handyman named Earl, who had been born on the campgrounds not long after the Civil War. In fact, he was raised in the very bungalow where Reb Mendel slept. Although he was then in his nineties, he still believed in doing a good day's work — something Reb Mendel greatly admired. When Reb Mendel saw Earl again the second summer we were there, the two men embraced each other with great warmth. At the end of the summer, Reb Mendel bid him farewell and added, "We should both be around together next year as well."

Reb Mendel's warm feelings for others were always reciprocated. There was an Italian who used to do a lot of woodwork in the yeshivah. We knew him simply as Mike the carpenter. But Rebbe had a friendly relationship with him, and it was said that they sent each other greeting cards on special occasions. A week after Rebbe passed away, Rabbi Leib Taub, a Maggid Shiur in the yeshivah, walked into the yeshivah's workshop and found Mike crying. Rabbi Taub thought he must have just suffered some personal tragedy and asked him what was the matter.

"Didn't you hear?" Mike answered in a choking voice. "Rabbi Kaplan died!"

Soon after Reb Mendel passed away, someone brought his car to his regular auto shop for repairs. One of the gentile workers recognized the car and asked, "Where's the Rabbi?" When he heard that Reb Mendel had passed away, he sat down and began to cry. "I know all I am is a simple mechanic, but the Rabbi treated me like I was a special human being," he explained. "He used to take an interest in my life and that made me feel like a million dollars. No one in the world made me feel as good as the Rabbi did."

REB MENDEL TAUGHT US to respect everyone's property as well.

Respect for Another's Property

"Even though we're permitted to keep certain things that come into our hands, a smart person knows not to take anything that isn't his. I'll tell you a story that happened to me a long time ago. One day I bought something at the post office and by mistake the clerk gave me too much change. All that day, I debated with myself whether or not to return it, but in the end I didn't. The next day I also didn't have a chance to get back there.

"That day, I went to a grocery store and accidentally paid too much money. When I came home and realized my mistake, I returned to the store but the owner didn't want to return my money. He was a nice person, and honest as well, but I was so embarrassed that he didn't believe me that I didn't press the issue. What I gained at the post office I lost at the grocery store, and had no benefit from the extra money.[1]

"Another story took place in Chicago. I found an expensive gold watch in the street and didn't know exactly what to do with it, so I did nothing and it just sat in my house. Not long afterwards, my wife lost the watch I had given her as a wedding present. It wasn't so expensive, but when you lose something like that, it leaves you with a hurt feeling."

---

1. See *Be'er Hagolah Choshen Mishpat* 348:50.

"MAN IS GREATER than even the angels, which explains why only Adam was able to give names to all the animals. *Rabbeinu*

The Dichotomy of Man

Tam observes that man's superiority vis-a-vis animals can be seen from the fact that animals walk on all fours, since their essence is close to the ground. Only man walks erect since his soul comes from heaven. The *Radak* points out that while an animal's brain tells it to do things, it can only think about things that are within its power to do. An ant, for instance, never thinks about flying. Only man can think about whatever he wishes.

"Conversely, the body of a man is inferior to that of any animal. An animal looks nice without clothing, but not a person. During *davening* you don't have to distance yourself four cubits from the waste of an animal as you do from human waste. Physically the body of a person is the poorest of all mammals. What kind of match was this: to give man the greatest spiritual qualities and the worst body?

"When Hashem asked Adam what he himself should be called, he answered, 'Adam — because I was created from the ground (*adamah*).' Now, why didn't he say *neshamah*, since man also possesses a portion of Hashem from Above? The answer is that man's soul was created already perfect; his purpose in life is to improve the earthly side of himself. Hashem created man with an inferior body to constantly remind him of his need to perfect it — not through body building, but spiritually, by making it holy through the performance of *mitzvos*."

"Hashem is referred to by many names in the Torah [corresponding to the different attributes through which we perceive Him]. But the name Adam gave the Creator was 'Lord,' which describes the essence of our relationship with the Creator: He is the Boss. Our whole purpose in life is to accept Hashem as our boss and to refine our earthly side during our stay on earth."

"WHEN YOU SEE A CHAIR, you know that its purpose is to be sat on. In the same way, man's purpose is to work. To toil and

Man Is Created for Toil

work, even for a livelihood, perfects a person. Carrying a yoke is what makes someone into a man both in this world and in the next. Reb Yeruchem said that during the time he's working, a worker is the 'holiest of holies,' since he's so totally involved with his work that he doesn't have anything else on his mind.

"Did you ever see how hard the gentile worker in the kitchen works all day long? By doing his work, he is carrying the yoke meant for him. People can't change the way Hashem made the creation; there is no escaping the fact that there is no life without toil. Everyone has to work, and woe unto those who are without work.

"Retirement is a terrible and bitter curse. The *Rishonim* write that if a father hires a rebbe for his son, he has to pay the rebbe even when the son is unavailable to learn, because if the rebbe ceases to learn it ruins him. If you don't work or learn, the inevitable result is that you get rusty.

"Since our life is the Torah, we must accept on ourselves the yoke of Torah. Our toil in Torah saves us (*Avos* 3:5); but only if we learn Torah the way a worker works. A person's mind is like the wind: it blows in every direction and makes it hard to concentrate. Learning to concentrate is also part of accepting the yoke of Torah."

᧥ ᧥ ᧥

"This whole country is built on having fun. They used to say that a person's goal in this world is to have fun, but you just have to make money first. But now they say, 'Let's have fun now and let our parents give us the money!'

"Belief in evolution makes them throw off their yoke. It causes people to think that life has no higher purpose than enjoyment, just like the dog who walks back and forth on the carpet. The schools where they teach evolution are really teaching kids to become criminals. They are at a loss to understand why there's so much crime in the country, and they make commissions to study the question. They don't realize that they themselves cause it. When *Mashiach* comes, it will be a kindness not only for us but for them as well."

᧥ ᧥ ᧥

"Earning a living is a very hard thing.[1] There is no easy way to make a living; no one makes money from having fun. People

---

1. On this Reb Mendel said, "Money is called *damim* (a word which can mean either money or blood) because it is acquired with one's own blood. 'Tzedakah saves from death' (*Mishlei* 10:2) because giving away money is like giving away a piece of your own soul. After someone works so hard to acquire money, it's not easy for him to give it away, since he earned it with *midas hadin* (through being strict with himself). Giving charity has the ability to reverse Hashem's attribute of strictness and turn it into mercy."

think comedians have fun, but really it's just as hard for them to make up their routines as it is for us to learn a *Gemara*. In any case, the comedian himself isn't laughing, because he's too busy worrying about whether the audience will laugh at his jokes. Jokes can be the destruction of life. In all of Torah you don't find one joke. Life is not a joke, and those who think it is only do so because they have nothing else."

REB MENDEL OFTEN CONTRASTED the life-styles and philosophies of America and Japan. He used them as metaphors to distinguish between the markedly

Japan and America

different results of following a lifestyle that accords with the plan of the Creator and one totally removed from His will.

"Americans don't want to work; they want everything to be easy. They want gimmicks and more gimmicks, and they'll pay all kinds of money to avoid having to use their brains or their bodies at all. Every house has so many special machines that the house needs a special room to fix them, and if you have to walk three steps to go somewhere, you take your car instead. You can press a button and the garage door opens by itself, and this gives Americans the greatest pleasure in the world.

"On the other hand, the Japanese work like oxen carrying a burden, and the whole world is buying up their products. The Creator made miracles so that this country, together with England, was able to win the war against the Japanese, but our debts keep getting bigger and bigger. We won the war, but they won the business."

s➤ s➤ s➤

"*It is good for a man to accept a yoke in his youth* (*Eichah* 3:27). This is the exact opposite of American philosophy. People today don't want to accept responsibility and think working is anti-American. The Government did a test and sent out blood samples to 140 labs and more than half came back with the wrong results. If they don't even care about matters of life and death, how can you expect them to care about anything else?

"When I first came to America, I saw a mother ask a child to do something and the child refused. The child said, 'Do you know why I'm not doing this? Because I don't *want* to.' At first it seemed strange to me that 'I don't want to' was a good enough reason not to do something. But then I came to realize that this is the way it is in America.

"The two things America stands on are half-mistakes and half-fun. The whole country is so messed up. There are so many ways it could be improved. In Japan the people were so clean, they washed the sidewalks. The trains rode through gardens, and right up to the tracks it was completely covered with green growth. Here, some of the things you pass on the trains can make you sick just looking at them. Why can't they draft all the bums and give them room and board and put them to work improving it? Instead of drafting people to kill others and get killed, that's what they should be doing.

"During the war, in Shanghai, I saw a Japanese propaganda poster poking fun at American soldiers running away from the front to eat ice cream. The same ad that they used to make fun of our army, we use as an advertisement for the army!"

S▶ S▶ S▶

"People think democracy is an improvement, and that monarchies are archaic. The history books don't know what the world and people used to be like. Rule by a king is the true nature of creation, and if there's a good king who truly cares for the welfare of his country, then it's much better than democracy. Since Americans don't want to be burdened with any kind of yoke, they also won't accept a monarchy.

"In Japan the people were united and there was no crime problem because there was so much respect for the emperor. The storekeeper we went to rationed food without any special papers and rules; he was just told to ration it and he did. Once a policeman caught him selling us more than he was supposed to because we were bribing him. The policeman slapped him and his son as if they were in school and that was all.

"Here it's just the opposite — people are interested only in themselves. That's why they have slogans like STUDENT POWER and all kinds of councils to give themselves rights. In Japan, people respected each other; they would greet each other by bending their heads in humility. Today in America there is no respect; they just wave their hands and say 'Hi!' "

S▶ S▶ S▶

Reb Mendel illustrated how a person who truly lives up to the title "man" feels his intrinsic self-worth and acts in a manner befitting his exalted title. Once we were learning a *Gemara* that speaks of the embarrassment one suffers by going uncovered (*Bava Kama* 86b). "It's more dignified for a person to be covered up," Reb Mendel said. "In Shanghai I saw the Amishnover Rebbe, who wore a *bekeshe* that covered even his knuckles. That was his mark of distinction. The gentiles in Japan were also dignified to a certain extent, until the U.S. came and 'civilized,' or, rather, demoralized them. The Japanese wore long clothing, in spite of the terribly hot and humid climate, and they looked more distinguished because

Rabbi Shimon Kalish (Amshinover Rebbe) and Rabbi Moshe Shatzkes in Shanghai. Note the sleeves.

of it; they had an air of importance about them. From the *Gemara* (*Bava Kama* 91b) we see that there is such a thing as clothing that honors a person, something we don't see any longer in this country."

"AMERICANS STAY BABIES their whole lives, with their soda and ice cream and other childish pleasures. Small children play

The "Ice Cream" Mentality

with small marbles, big children play with big marbles [bowling]. No one is capable of carrying a yoke anymore, everyone has to have fun: television and more television, vacations and more vacations. They think that you have to enjoy everything, and have fun and more fun until you wind up in the old-age home."

ঌ ঌ ঌ

Rebbe always impressed upon us the importance of not being babies any longer: "If you don't remove the baby from yourself, it will stay with you. To come to the cream of Torah one must first wash away the taste of the 'mother's milk' he had as a child" (*Berachos* 63b). Reb Mendel always used ice cream as a symbol for the childish mentality of constant pleasure-seeking. When a student could not accept a criticism, Rebbe would say that he didn't have to stay for the lecture, he could go outside and eat ice cream.

He once raised his voice at the class on a hot summer day when no one was attentive: "You are ruining future generations! You can't take a little humidity?! You need the ice cream of cool air...?" Even in learning, Rebbe employed the metaphor of ice cream to describe an enticing approach to Torah study: "After Reb Yisrael Salanter heard something from Reb Chaim, he said that there would be generations that would need to be fed Reb Chaim's Torah in order to learn. This is our generation. It's not that we are greater students, but we need to be fed ice cream."

When Men Were "Mentschen"

"WE SEE FROM THE *GEMARA* that gentiles once had the power of witchcraft, and *Amoraim* were able to bring the dead back to life. Don't think it was like the history books say: once upon a time people were savages who lived in caves and today they are civilized and travel in space. No! Once people were *mentschen*, real people, and now they are not real people. Do you think the *Amoraim* had the power to bring back the dead because they were greater *tzaddikim*? No, it was because they were greater people.

"Don't think that the problem with today's society is that people used to be religious and now they're irreligious. No! The problem is that years ago people were *mentschen* and now they're not *mentschen*, that's the problem. You know how afraid the Sages were of the sin of adultery and how many precautions they made to protect people from it. But still they ruled that if a woman says she's divorced, you can believe her because she wouldn't say such a thing if it weren't true. Today, however, halachic authorities no longer rule like this, because people are no longer *mentschen*."

On Accepting Suffering

"AVRAHAM WAS IN TERRIBLE PAIN after his circumcision and he had to wrap up his wound in bandages. Still he managed to take care of his guests. If he couldn't do kindness any more, life wasn't worth living to him. But this country is just the opposite: you can only do things that give you pleasure — that's the ultimate goal. This is why we are so much weaker than we were before.

"A *mentsch* knows how to bear suffering. The Marines used to advertise on their recruiting posters, 'We'll make you into a man,' because they worked you hard. The schools today don't punish children. Children used to bear pain and punishment, and they grew better from it. The *Kohanim* in the *Beis HaMikdash* used to get beaten if they fell asleep at their posts; they screamed so loud that you could hear their screams from afar. Regarding this Rabbi Yochanan said, 'How fortunate were the early generations — even for accidentally falling asleep, physical punishment was meted out to them' (*Tamid* 28a)."

ֱֱֱֱ ֱֱֱ ֱֱֱ

"I once stayed with a family in Europe where one of the young boys was having problems with his eyes. They didn't drain well, and the ducts got stuffed up. One night he woke up in the middle of the night, and I told him to tell his sister that we were going to the doctor. But he didn't want to tell her since she knew that the doctor used a painful needle, and he didn't want her to suffer from thinking about his pain. So he went without telling her! It didn't even enter my head to think of saving the sister from pain.

"Twenty years later, when I was in this country already, I had a problem with kidney stones. They caused me great pain and I was about to tell my daughter I was going to the doctor. Then I remembered what that little boy had done. So I didn't tell anyone I was going to the doctor. The problem hasn't recurred, and I have a feeling that Hashem let me off lightly because I kept quiet to spare others from anguish.

"Years ago, people used to be able to accept suffering. I once saw a parade in China involving a dragon. In the middle of the parade was a man who walked with his hand straight out carrying a very heavy cement flowerpot on a hook which was piercing into his flesh. You could clearly see the suffering etched on his face.

"Similarly, I once happened to be in my landlord's house in Chicago when he was watching a boxing match on television. I saw one man pounding another until he fell down on the floor. But then he jumped up and started to punch his opponent back. That's the strength even common people used to have ... but now there's almost nothing."

(Another time, Reb Mendel commented on the same experience in a way that revealed his deep sensitivity for other human beings. "Television is the cause of the inhumanity you find in America. Once I happened to see a boxing match on television and it made me nauseous. I felt such a bad taste in my mouth that I had to run away and spit from disgust.")

🙶 🙶 🙶

Reb Mendel talked about Reb Elchonon Wasserman's son Reb Dovid. Reb Dovid suffered greatly throughout his life, and yet always acted as if he were oblivious to his pain. After he developed cancer, Reb Mendel used to ask him about his condition. "He talked about his illness as if he were talking about his car," said Reb Mendel with great admiration.

Not long before his passing, Reb Dovid spoke at a *sheva berachos* for his son, and praised Hashem publicly for the constant and abundant kindness He had shown him throughout his life, and for permitting him to be present at his son's wedding. Reb Mendel confessed that he was overwhelmed by Reb Dovid's simple and heartfelt acceptance of all the hardships he had endured in a manner that even great Torah scholars could learn from.

Reb Dovid Wasserman, zt"l

Rule of the Intellect

REB YERUCHEM LEVOVITZ discusses the "rule of the intellect" — control by the mind over the emotions. Reb Mendel once described the extent to which Reb Elchonon possessed this trait: "Reb Elchonon never got excited during *shiur* and never acted in an extreme fashion. He always functioned on one frequency."[2]

🙶 🙶 🙶

---

2. See also *Reb Elchonon* (Mesorah Publications, New York 1982) pages 409-410 for an eyewitness account of how Reb Elchonon went to his death at the hands of the savage Lithuanian nationals with absolute calm.

"*Menuchah*," Rebbe said, "is a gift that includes many things, and one of them is control over one's thoughts and emotions. To possess *menuchah* means not to have anything pushing you. This is a hard trait to attain, but we can merit it through prayer. Indeed, we should pray for it all the time, as David HaMelech did: *A pure heart create for me, G-d* (*Tehillim* 51:12). The *Rambam* writes that one fulfills the positive commandment of prayer by crying out to Hashem for something he needs, so when you say this verse, you are fulfilling this *mitzvah* as well." Rebbe added that only someone who has no desires can truly be said to have a pure heart; otherwise one is always subject to pressures and cannot be truly objective and calm.

The acquisition of this trait was one of the primary goals of the *mussar* yeshivos. Reb Mendel once described how the students of those schools showed great calmness in everything they did: "Calmness was such an important trait at Kelm, that if someone turned around to see if his bus was coming, his action was considered bewildering. It wasn't like things are here, where people are always running and speeding. (And for what? To watch television!) There was a great calmness there, like David HaMelech's description of the righteous, *Like a tree deeply rooted alongside brooks of water* (*Tehillim* 1:3). Did you ever see a tree growing by a riverside? It leaves such an impression of quiet and calm on you. I've never been privileged to achieve such a thing, but you're young; you can still have it. Do you see the *baal teshuvah* who learns in the yeshivah? He has a calmness in learning that I've never seen. There are no problems in the world while he's sitting and learning."

℘ ℘ ℘

The great *mussar* works teach one how to acquire the trait of *menuchas hanefesh*, but internalizing those teachings and putting them into practice is another story. Reb Mendel once explained the difficulty of *mussar* study: "The Alter of Kelm was a *baal mussar*; he *absorbed* all the lessons of *mussar* and had full control over himself. The Alter's son said that he *learned mussar*, and Reb Yeruchem said of himself that he read *mussar*, like he read *Ein Yaakov* (a collection of the aggadic portions of the *Gemara*). I myself have no connection to *mussar*; I read it, *l'havdil*, like I read *The Times*, and if I would ever think I *do* have a connection to *mussar*, I'd just be fooling myself."

Yet in spite of Reb Mendel's claims to the contrary, he too possessed great reserves of calm. His family relates that even on his most difficult and trying days he remained as calm and as fully in control of his words and actions as at any other time. Even in times of danger he would always say to those around him, "There is nothing for a person to fear — except Hashem."

Reb Mendel was once driving with a car full of *talmidim* when the car spun out of control. As the car went off the highway and down a steep hill, he turned to the *talmidim* and told them reassuringly, "Don't worry, it'll be all right." And it was.

Reb Mendel was fearless and to an extent daring as well. The neighborhood where he lived in Chicago had changed. Yet Reb Mendel was not afraid to walk anywhere, even in the dark alleys late at night. His children were astonished by his seemingly reckless behavior, but Reb Mendel would tell them, "What do you think a bum is thinking when he sees me walking in the alley at two in the morning? 'This man must be a real gangster if he's not afraid to walk here in middle of the night. I'd better not start up with him.' So I'm not afraid of him — he's afraid of me!"

Reb Mendel's citizenship photo, c. 1957

S➤ S➤ S➤

One winter day in Chicago Reb Mendel took his young son to buy a pair of shoes. Suddenly three thugs appeared from out of nowhere. One of them put a knife to Reb Mendel's face and said, "Rabbi, this beard is coming off!" Reb Mendel quickly picked up his son and threw him several feet away onto a nearby snowbank. His assailants were momentarily bewildered, and Reb Mendel seized the opportunity to smash the heads of two of them against each other. When they fell to the ground unconscious, the third one cried out, "Holy Moses!" and fled. Rebbe quickly brushed the snow off his son, took the boy by the hand, and continued with him to the store. He admonished his son never to tell anyone what had happened, and indeed, the son never did until after his father had passed away.

"WHEN THE SUBJECT OF MONEY was raised in the course of discussions over a *shidduch*, my mother commented, 'What does

True Strength money have to do with a *shidduch*? A *shidduch* is for eternity and money is only for a short time.' How did she come to think in such a noble way? It was by fasting on Yom Kippur and working *erev* Shabbos until she was on the verge of collapse. When a mother washes the floors for Pesach, she gets as much *mussar* as a yeshivah *bachur* gets from learning a whole term in yeshivah. But if a person runs after the pleasures of this world, he won't achieve anything in spiritual matters."[3]

S✦ S✦ S✦

Reb Mendel encouraged us to develop this kind of inner strength in ourselves. When a *bachur* once came into *shiur* coughing, Rebbe told him, "There's nothing wrong in trying to suppress the cough. You don't have to give in to every whim of the *guf*. The *guf* is no *yachsan* (privileged character), since it comes from the word *niguf*, which means 'beaten up.' This tells us that a person's body goes through a lot of hard knocks and bumps in his life. Did you ever see a junkyard? That's how a *guf* looks, even with a nice suit and tie."

In his later years, Reb Mendel suffered from a medical problem, and he went to a nutritionist who claimed he could cure the ailment through diet. The diet was extremely limiting, and Reb Mendel — who was always eager for an opportunity to exercise control over himself — enjoyed the challenge of the regimen, even though the diet often left him without energy. (One fast day he told a tired student an old European saying: "When you go to sleep hungry, you wake up tired.") His diet did not allow him to eat even bread, and without bread, he said, a person is always hungry.

Even on Shabbos he kept busy learning — often with people whose learning was on a much lower level — and found very

---

3. Reb Yeruchem Levovitz once said, "The same spiritual levels one attains through Torah study can be attained through suffering." See also *Toras Avraham* by Reb Avraham Grozinsky, *zt"l*, p. 44.

little time to rest during the day. Not long before his passing he even wanted to add an additional session, and offered to learn with the author for a while before *Shacharis*. However, after a short time he found it necessary to discontinue the session, saying, "I simply don't have the strength for it."

His last year was the hardest. The travel to and from New York often drained him of all energy the following day, and he had great difficulty sleeping. Yet he never showed any outward signs of strain, and continued to exemplify the verse, "Man is created for toil."

❧ ❧ ❧

To Reb Mendel, effort counted more than results, both in doing *mitzvos* and in learning Torah. He used to comfort boys who tried very hard but still did not excel in their studies by telling them that their toil would help their future descendants to become great scholars. As a source for this assertion, he cited a story in *Pirkei D'Rabbi Eliezer* (Chap. 1): when Rabbi Eliezer HaGadol decided to study Torah at a late age, his father told him that his children would learn Torah. "How did his father know that his children would learn?" Rebbe would ask. "Because he saw that Rabbi Eliezer had such a strong desire to learn Torah, he knew that even if he was not successful, he would still bequeath the ability to learn to his children."

Rebbe once told a student who was very dear to him, who was having difficulties in learning despite his trying his utmost, "Either you yourself will be a *talmid chacham* or you'll attach yourself to one, which is just as good. Do you think you need the degree? This isn't school — you don't need titles."

"Reb Chaim Volozhiner once asked a dying rich man, who was unlearned but supported Torah scholars, to ask certain questions for him in the Heavenly Academy. Soon after the man passed away, he appeared to Reb Chaim in a dream and gave him the answers to the questions he had posed. Reb Chaim later said that it was no wonder to him that this man was able to learn in Heaven together with some of the greatest Sages. Since the man supported scholars in this world, he deserved to be with them in the next. What did surprise him, though, was that he was able to learn so much in such a short period of time."

REB MENDEL GREATLY ADMIRED genuineness. But his criterion for assessing this quality was uniquely his own. Actions

Great Mitzvos

others saw as representing great piety, Reb Mendel dismissed as an American version of the "pious fool." But actions to which others didn't give a second thought, Reb Mendel admired tremendously.

One summer a boy arrived at summer camp in the middle of the season. The camp had accepted him despite his special problems, which included persistent bed-wetting. Yossi Kirsch, a close *talmid* of Reb Mendel, and the author were asked to take him into their room and to take personal charge of him. They took turns waking the boy twice each night to send him to the bathroom. When Reb Mendel found out about this, he publicly praised them, saying, "This is as great a merit as the Water Libation in the *Beis HaMikdash*!" Later he told us in private, "What you're doing is really a father's job and because you're doing it now, your own children won't have this problem." For a while afterwards we often noticed Rebbe looking at us with pride and admiration.

The responsibilities for the boy increased until finally Yossi approached Reb Mendel to say that it was becoming too difficult to continue attending to all his needs. Reb Mendel told him that when a difficult *mitzvah* comes along it is a special opportunity to earn great rewards.

He then related a story he had once heard from Rabbi Mordechai Rogow in Chicago. Reb Akiva Eiger was once interrupted from his learning during a snowstorm by a knock at the door. Opening the door, Reb Akiva Eiger found a poor man who had walked a long way and was almost frozen from the cold. He ran to gather some snow, which he rubbed on one of the man's legs to restore his circulation. After he finished the first leg, he turned to a guest who was staying with him and offered to let him rub the second one! The opportunity to do that great *mitzvah* was such an honor that he did not feel right hoarding it just for himself.

꙳ ꙳ ꙳

Reb Mendel also felt great pleasure and honor when he was able to help poor people. Once he returned to camp from a trip to the city with a heavy box, which he started to carry from his car up the hill toward his bungalow. Yossi Kirsch was disturbed at the sight of his rebbe straining from the great effort and immediately ran to take the box from him, and carried it up to the bungalow, where he placed it on the porch. Rebbe then said, "Bring a knife to cut the rope, and then have some bananas."

Once the box was opened, Rebbe pointed to the bananas inside, which were a bit overripe but edible, and said, "Sit down and eat a banana; these are *mitzvah* bananas. After you eat one, I'll tell you what makes them *mitzvah* bananas."

As Yossi started to eat, Reb Mendel began happily offering bananas to everyone in the vicinity: "Please come and eat some bananas. They're healthy, they're delicious. Eat as many as you want; just come and eat." Soon a crowd had gathered and someone asked how much they had cost. Answered Rebbe, "These things I can't tell." After the boy tasted one and remarked how much he liked it, Reb Mendel assured him, "They were such a bargain; if you knew how much they cost you'd like them even more."

After everyone had finished eating and left, Rebbe explained to Yossi what made them "*mitzvah* bananas": "When I was in the city earlier today, I saw a Russian Jew selling fruit on the corner and I noticed that most of his bananas were beginning to turn brown, and no one was buying them. By tomorrow he would have had to throw them all out. Even though they weren't so nice looking, and weren't so cheap either, I bought them all. Therefore, they're *mitzvah* bananas!"

s► s► s►

Chazal say: "Any *talmid chacham* who is not as strong as iron is not a *talmid chacham*" (*Taanis* 4a). Elsewhere, however, they say, "A person should always be as soft as a reed" (ibid. 20a). Reb Mendel resolved the contradiction as follows: Internally one must be as strong as steel, but in one's relationship with others one must be as pliant and yielding as a reed. Reb Mendel used to express this idea in his own typically down-to-earth fashion: "A person has to be like a subway door; the door itself is made of steel, but the part that comes in contact with people is rubber."

Once Reb Mendel hired someone to install locks on the windows of his winery in Chicago, but the worker installed the latches in such a way that they did not close properly. A family member noticed the shoddy workmanship while the man was still at work and pointed it out to Reb Mendel. Reb Mendel gestured to him as if to say, "I know, I know, but don't you dare say a word." Reb Mendel saw that the worker had "two left hands" and was simply not capable of doing a better job. Although he did not have much money, he paid the worker in full without saying a word. Then he redid the entire job himself since he could not afford to hire another worker.[4]

Following in the Footsteps of Hashem

"THE SAGES SAY that when the Jewish people perform the thirteen attributes of Hashem's mercy, they will not leave empty-handed (*Rosh Hashanah* 17b). They don't say when they 'pray' or 'recite' the thirteen attributes, but rather when they *do* them. A person has to follow the ways of Hashem.

"When a baby kicks his father's hands, the father holds him anyway, and the same is true of Hashem in His relationship with us. When we sin, Hashem should shut down the world, but He's a loving Father and even though His children rebel He still allows them to live, and continues to sustain them. Rabbi Moshe Cordovero wrote the entire *Tomer Devorah* to explain how we may emulate Hashem's traits of mercy."

Reb Mendel once brought his car to a Jewish mechanic in New York for repairs. Before long the problem reappeared and he took the car back again. When he took it in a third time, Reb Mendel remarked that perhaps the repair had not dealt with the real cause of the problem. At this, the mechanic hurled a tirade of curses at Reb Mendel. Reb Mendel's son, who was with him at the time, grew very agitated and attempted to remind the mechanic that he was speaking to a Torah scholar, but Reb Mendel calmed his son, saying, "Believe me, it doesn't bother me in the least."

Early the next morning Rebbe called up his son to ask if they could go together to his son's regular mechanic rather than the one he had used until then. When they arrived there Rebbe explained, "I feel that the reason the mechanic lashed out at us so bitterly yesterday is that he was under a lot of stress. He must not have enough competent mechanics working for him to do his work

---

4. See *Bava Metzia* 83a.

well. Therefore I would like you to ask the owner of this garage if he can lend out a good mechanic for a month to the other station."

His son hesitated, feeling uncomfortable about presenting such an unusual request. Reb Mendel said, "If you don't want to do it, I'll ask him myself," and immediately walked over to the owner to ask if he had any good help he could spare. It was obvious that the owner, an Italian, also thought Reb Mendel's behavior was out of the ordinary. He looked at Reb Mendel inquisitively for several moments and then replied, "Rabbi, I'm short of good help myself!"

*≫ *≫ *≫

When Reb Mendel performed an act of kindness, it was without any thought of his own personal interests and entirely for the benefit of the other party involved. One winter, Reb Mendel spent much time every *Motzaei Shabbos* (which should have been a time for him to rest and prepare for the coming week) in conversation with a person who needed a great deal of help. These conversations were taxing and seemingly unproductive, as the person was obviously uninterested in Reb Mendel's involvement.

A family member asked Rebbe why he put so much effort into helping someone who was so unappreciative, and Reb Mendel answered, "When you do someone a favor, you have to be prepared to do it even though he might have grievances against you, just like a father acts to help his son. Does the father take into consideration that his son might later have complaints? If he knows it's for his son's benefit, he does it anyway and pays no attention to whether or not his son appreciates it."

CHAPTER EIGHT

Dealing with Our Fellow Man

What makes a person great? Someone is considered great if he includes within himself the entire Jewish people. But how can one person include so many people? — By feeling for others and thinking about them all the time. What makes someone into a true person is that he works for others with no desire for money, flattery or honor. Love of self is nothing more than falsehood and idolatry. David HaMelech said (Tehillim 81:10), There shall not be in you false idols, meaning that one should not have any false idols within himself (cf. Shabbos 105b).

...Since the Torah is true, only someone who himself is true can comprehend it. Forcing oneself to be concerned for the needs of others leads him to love them more and himself less, and thereby uproots the falsehood within him and makes him into a true person. Only then can one come to understand Torah (from Chochmah U'Mussar by the Alter of Kelm).

GADOL HAMESHAMESH — someone who serves is great. Noach was great enough to serve all forms of life. The

Helping Others with Their Burdens

bigger a person is, the bigger the yoke he accepts upon himself, and the more Hashem helps him to bear that yoke. A *rosh yeshivah* can accomplish things that ten other people couldn't do. One person can carry not only his own yoke but also that of the whole world.

"The *groisser sefer* (Reb Mendel's term for *Chochmah U'Mussar*, which he considered the greatest *mussar* work of modern times) says that the quality of serving others is the beginning of what makes someone into a *mentsch*. No one in the Torah merits a special introduction about his youth except for Moshe Rabbeinu. The Torah tells us that he was raised in the king's palace, and even so he went out to bear his brothers' burdens and share in their suffering. It was this merit, says the Alter of Kelm, that caused him to be chosen to lead the Jewish people."

Reb Mendel once observed that a *bachur* in another *shiur*, who was blessed with a good mind, distinguished lineage and good looks, was not showing proper respect for a weaker *chavrusa*. Reb Mendel told the boy's rebbe that for all his advantages, he might not merit to become a leader, citing Moshe Rabbeinu as proof that a leader must be humble and concerned with the needs of others.

‰ ‰ ‰

"Taking on other people's problems and extending them help is what makes a person great," said Reb Mendel. "Even today we find people who worry about others and try to help them. The Wiesel family is famous in Jerusalem for raising money to distribute food to poor people. Once they didn't have enough money to buy eggs for these families, and Rabbi and Rebbetzin Wiesel could not bring themselves to eat eggs for a few weeks. A pious Jew named Rav Dan recently came to America from *Eretz Yisrael*. When he heard of someone who was sick, he couldn't sleep all night and spent the time in tearful prayer.

"I once saw several women who went to consult with Rav Moshe (Feinstein) concerning a problem they were having. He sat listening to them, bent over to share in their woe, with such a look of concentration and concern etched on his face. It wasn't as if he were sitting back in a cushioned chair handing out advice to anyone who came.

"Look at Reb Elya (Svei) — you can feel how he walks around with a yoke on his back at all times. If he were to receive a salary for everything he does for the Jewish people, he'd get at least a million dollars a year.

"A great man has all of the concerns of the Jewish people on his mind. Once, in the middle of a meeting with the *rabbanim* of Vilna, Reb Chaim Ozer was told that there was a young girl outside waiting to speak with him. He interrupted the meeting right then and there to ask her what she needed. When she said that she needed to see a certain doctor in Vilna, Reb Chaim Ozer spoke with her and then gave her exact directions to the doctor's office. About five years later, he happened to meet her again and asked her if his directions had made it easier for her to find the doctor. From this you can see how much he cared about each and every individual."

S➤ S➤ S➤

"*Rashi* did not write his commentaries just to get his name on a *sefer;* he did it to take the Jewish people by the hand and show them what each piece of *Gemara* means. My teachers said that every word in *Rashi* shows you his kindness. The Chofetz Chaim was also like a father to Israel. He gave a two-hour *shiur* each day in the *Kodashim* Kollel and wrote many learned books, but he only wrote what he saw was required to help his generation. He wrote *Machaneh Yisrael* to guide Jewish soldiers forced to serve in gentile armies and a book on *Kodashim* to bring *Mashiach* closer. His *Mishnah Berurah* is such an important work for the Jewish people that the Satan tried everything to prevent him from writing it. While he was in the middle of writing it, his son died, and he said that the Satan did it so he wouldn't be able to continue writing. But nothing the Satan could do would stop him."

S➤ S➤ S➤

Reb Mendel felt sympathy for all Jews, both the religious and the non-religious. A student once told him about a wedding which the *chasan's* irreligious parents refused to attend because his sister's gentile husband had not been invited. The student asked Rebbe, "Can you imagine the pain and embarrassment the son felt because his parents didn't show up at his wedding?"

At this Rebbe grew sad and said, "That's the wrong way to look at it. You just can't fathom the pain the parents must have felt that they couldn't be at their son's wedding. They were brought up to think that religious Jews are like a cult; they really think their son is marrying into a cult. Where the parents genuinely don't know better, it's not so easy to write them off and disregard their feelings."

S▶ S▶ S▶

Mesillas Yesharim writes that whenever someone does a *mitzvah* the entire world is also elevated. Reb Mendel once mentioned that idea with reference to an article he had recently read on the *baal teshuvah* movement in *Eretz Yisrael*. The article described how the movement had grown so large that non-religious parents of *baalei teshuvah* had formed a coalition against *baalei teshuvah*. The article related the story of two mothers who met at the airport to meet their children returning from the front lines. One said to the other, "Your son is coming back to you, but I'll never have my son back — because he became a *baal teshuvah*."

Reb Mendel commented, "The tone of the article was, 'Hooray! We're making the non-religious rip the hair out of their heads!' " At that point tears came to his eyes as he continued, "Can you imagine the sorrow a mother has thinking she's lost her son? When we serve Hashem, we must try to do it in a way that's good for everyone, in a way that the whole world benefits."

S▶ S▶ S▶

Reb Mendel's heart had room for the whole world. There was a Russian carpenter at the yeshivah named Yossele who spent a good portion of the day working in the woodshed. Reb Mendel often ate his lunch out in the woodshed to keep Yossele company. Once a student wanted to hear what words of wisdom Reb Mendel had to say to Yossele and eavesdropped on their conversation. The student was surprised to hear Yossele doing most of the talking. Yossele described in great detail his life story, philosophy and daily concerns. Reb Mendel listened to everything he said in total fascination, interrupting only with an occasional, "Yeah? You don't say?" and other friendly comments.

Reb Mendel was once seen at 6:30 a.m. helping Yossele with his work, and another time Reb Mendel drove Yossele to a lumberyard to pick up some wood he needed. Later that day, Yossele came in sheepishly during *shiur* — he had forgotten his lunch in Reb Mendel's car. Rebbe quickly interrupted him, "Oy, no, it's my fault!" and stood up to take his car keys out of his pocket.[1]

ꜱ➤ ꜱ➤ ꜱ➤

It hurt Reb Mendel to see any human being in discomfort, whether Jew or gentile. Once he arrived at the train station near the yeshivah together with a disoriented elderly black man. The man asked Reb Mendel for directions to Maple Avenue, a twenty-minute walk away. Seeing that he was in no condition to walk so far on his own, Reb Mendel took him by the arm and escorted him all the way to his destination.

A student once was driving with Reb Mendel when they stopped at a highway rest station near Harrisburg. For some reason, the guard at the rest station showed them an old silver coin he had recently found and asked if they knew its origin. Reb Mendel examined the coin intently and then asked the guard for paper and pencil. The guard watched in bewilderment as Reb Mendel placed the paper over the coin and scraped an image of it onto the paper. "I think it's a Persian coin," he said. "I have a student in the school where I teach who just came from Iran. If you'll give me your phone number, I'll show him the paper and ask him what he knows about it and get back to you."

After they left, the student asked Reb Mendel why he was taking such an interest in a gentile. Reb Mendel said, "About an *Amora*, the *Gemara* asked, 'How was Rav able to do what he did?' About me you can't ask such questions." As they walked further he added on a more serious note, "The angels were not allowed to enter the Holy of Holies, but humans were. From this we see the greatness of every *tzelem Elokim*, like that guard. Furthermore,

---

1. Cf. *Piskei Tosafos* (*Taanis* §8): תלמידי חכמים כל אחד מודה לחבירו בין על האמת בין על השקר, *Talmidei chachamim* admit that they have wronged their fellows, whether truly or falsely.

he spends all day all by himself just to protect us; for that alone you have to feel gratitude.'[2]

The following Purim Reb Mendel showed the student a passage in which the *Ramban* says that one of the attributes of Hashem which Avraham strove to emulate was the ability to bestow kindness on good and bad people alike (*Bereishis* 24:1). This attribute is known as *bakol*.

THE FOLLOWING WAS SAID IN *SHIUR* in Sivan 5742 (June 1982), when Reb Shneur Kotler, zt"l, the Lakewood *rosh yeshivah*,

Bearing Others' Burdens — To What Extent

was critically ill and the war in Lebanon was in progress.

The troubles of the Jewish people have to be a part of you. Just *davening* for someone doesn't help so much by itself. For your prayers to have power, you have to *feel* his suffering, you have to literally put yourself in his situation. That's the way we have to pray for a sick person, as it says in regard to Moshe's prayer, '*Vayechal Moshe*' — it started to burn in him like an illness (*Berachos* 12b). If you cry and scream as if you yourself were the sick person, then you can accomplish something. This is what it means to be 'a great man,' not to be selfish but to open your coat to enfold everyone within.

Early one winter morning, a *bachur* saw Reb Mendel shoveling snow to make a safe path for the boys to go to *Shacharis*. The *bachur* insisted on doing this job himself, so Reb Mendel gave him the shovel and walked away. Later, however, someone else noticed that Reb Mendel had found another shovel and had continued shoveling in a different area. It was not uncommon to see him fixing a stuck window or banging a protruding nail in the hallway.

Once a *bachur* saw Reb Mendel enter one of the dormitory buildings late at night holding a hammer. He asked if the Rebbe needed any help. Reb Mendel replied that he had noticed a

---

2. See *Tanna d'vei Eliyahu Zuta* 15: "One should always make himself humble to do Torah and good deeds, even ones he does for a gentile in the street."

broken window in the building and was worried that the boys would be cold the next morning, so he was looking for something to put over the hole.

∽∽∽

A former *talmid*, who is now a lawyer, relates the following incidents: "I was once involved in a serious accident and had to undergo major surgery at Bellevue Hospital. For a time afterwards I had an intravenous drip and was semi-delirious, but I remember Rebbe standing at my bedside holding an ice cube in my mouth. (He obviously knew that after surgery a person's mouth gets very dry.) I knew that this was against doctors' orders, but he kept saying gently, 'Don't worry — it'll be good.'

"When my first child was born eleven weeks prematurely and had to have emergency surgery, Reb Mendel gave me strength to cope with the situation. As soon as he heard what was happening, he came immediately and stayed throughout the entire operation. Amazingly, he arrived still wearing his *tefillin*! He had gotten the message during *Shacharis* and didn't want to delay the extra few minutes it would have taken to remove them."

An old scholar whom Reb Mendel knew from Europe once underwent a serious operation. When the man returned home from the hospital, Reb Mendel moved into his apartment and lived there for the next several days to help cheer him up and to be constantly available to attend to his needs.

REB MENDEL ONCE EXPLAINED the term *HaKadosh Baruch Hu*: *HaKadosh* — because He is removed from all physical matters;

Minding Another's Business

Baruch Hu — we bless Him because He is still involved in all earthly matters, constantly creating and sustaining.

Even when Reb Mendel was not directly involved in a situation, he still made other people's concerns his own. In a camp where he once stayed as a guest, he always managed to be around when he was needed. One night the campers were all gathered in the gym when suddenly the lights went out. A few minutes later, a car drove up in front of the large entrance to direct its headlights into the room. It was none other than Reb Mendel lighting the room for us. He had been concerned that someone might panic and be injured in the darkness.

Another time the camp went on a canoeing trip, and one boy accidentally caused another boy's expensive glasses to break. The boy who caused the mishap did not want to pay. Reb Mendel did not know either boy personally, but when he heard the story he contacted an eyeglass wholesaler he knew personally and arranged to have the glasses replaced.

One summer, a family from Tennessee drove to Philadelphia to visit their son in yeshivah. Reb Mendel happened to be watching from a distance as they pulled into the yeshivah yard. He gave a student standing near him money to buy sodas for the whole family, who looked thirsty after their long journey.

S➤ S➤ S➤

Reb Mendel took an interest in the boys in the building where he had his room, although *rebbeim* from higher *shiurim* didn't usually have much to do with the boys from the younger grades. Once, there was a boy from Philadelphia who dormed in the same building as Reb Mendel. He was a freshman who had become ill and was forced to spend a lot of time in bed. Reb Mendel made a trip to a fruit store, bought a few boxes of strawberries and brought them to the boy in a huge bowl. The boy was stunned and tears came to his eyes.

Reb Mendel cared even about those he did not know. It bothered him that clothing and shoes were so expensive and that large families had to spend a small fortune to keep their children clothed. Once he learned of a close-out sale at a shoe store on the outskirts of Philadelphia. He went to the store and bought cases upon cases of children's shoes and boots. Then he contacted a former student learning in Lakewood, and asked him to help make arrangements to sell the shoes at four dollars a pair to *kollel* families.[3] When that student showed reluctance to take on such a responsibility, Reb Mendel did not rest but kept asking people in the community until he found someone willing to undertake the *mitzvah*.

---

3. The price was determined with exactitude. One summer in the early '80s, Reb Mendel discovered another close-out sale for men's shoes. He bought several cases and asked a *bachur* to sell them to yeshivah boys and *kollel* men for six dollars a pair. After seeing how well they were selling, the enterprising boy decided to raise the price to ten dollars a pair to make more money. When Reb Mendel learned of his plan, he told the boy, "Don't make such deals. You sell them for only six dollars and don't worry, I'll give you an extra dollar for every pair you sell."

When someone expressed amazement that Reb Mendel should concern himself with such a mundane item as children's shoes, he told him, "It wasn't my own idea. I picked it up from a shoemaker in Baranovich who used to fix shoes for the yeshivah *bachurim* free of charge."

WHEN REB MENDEL WENT TO *ERETZ YISRAEL* or took a summer break, it was no "vacation" for him. Wherever he was, he

Making the Most of a Vacation

found ways to help others. He once noticed that the awnings that covered the vegetable markets in the Meah Shearim section of Jerusalem were ripped, and some stalls were left without protection against the winter rains and the intense heat of the summer. Upon his return to New York, he made arrangements with the father of one of his students who sold canvas products to provide material to repair the leaking awnings of Jerusalem.

One Friday afternoon as he passed by a small hovel in Jerusalem, he overheard a woman complaining to her husband that they still had no food for Shabbos. The husband tried to reassure her, with great faith, that there was still time before Shabbos and Hashem would surely provide for their needs. Rebbe felt that he had been sent as a special messenger from Hashem and quickly gathered a considerable sum of money which he presented to the family before Shabbos. From then on, he often sent money to support that family.

S◆ S◆ S◆

During all his trips to *Eretz Yisrael* he made a point of locating poor people, for whom he would raise money upon his return to America. Each year he collected thousands of dollars for the needy of *Eretz Yisrael*. Over the summer, he went around to bungalow colonies in the Catskills soliciting funds. He said that these outings left him with so little strength that sometimes he could not even get out of his chair.

On one such expedition, he met an old friend who asked him why a distinguished *rosh yeshivah* would go door to door collecting money. Reb Mendel confided to him, "It embarrasses me a lot to do this, but what can I do — the poor people need the money."

For several summers, carloads of *bachurim* would leave camp for a day to go around to bungalow colonies raising money to lighten Reb Mendel's burden. When the *bachurim* returned, sometimes as late as midnight, he would be sitting outside his bungalow waiting to serve them a meal he had prepared. Still, he was not entirely pleased. "You shouldn't have stayed out so late," he chided them. "You have young boys in the car with you. Didn't you know I'd worry?"

Those moments were very special for the *bachurim*; they felt like troops returning to their commander after completing a successful mission. They never counted the money while they were collecting and only after they returned would they place it all in one large pile on the table and watch Reb Mendel count it joyfully. They would also recount all their adventures and mishaps on the way, which Rebbe would listen to with great interest. Once one boy told him that a man had almost punched him in the nose when he came to ask for a donation. Rebbe smiled and told the group that it reminded him of the story of a *chassid* who dressed up as a poor person to collect *tzedakah* for others. Someone got angry at him and slapped him in the face. Said the collector, "Fine, that's for me. But why are you punishing the poor people? What'll they have?"

Even on the evening that he passed away, despite the fact that his strength was failing rapidly, he prepared Pesach packages for poor people in New York and personally delivered a package to one woman who claimed she had not received her package the year before.

S➤ S➤ S➤

The *Gemara* (*Yoma* 71a) praises "*talmidei chachamim* who are as weak as women [*Rashi*: humble and of feeble strength] and yet perform the mighty actions of men." This is an apt description of Reb Mendel's fund-raising activities. One relative observed: "We could not understand how he was able to go to people to raise money for the poor. He had such a delicate nature that he would not ask or take anything from another person, even for the smallest personal matter. He would give to everybody, but never would impose on another in the slightest. It was certainly very difficult for him to ask people for money, but he overcame his nature in order to do things for others. Once he saw what a person needed, he couldn't take his mind off it."

When Reb Mendel took money from someone, he did his best either to honor or to entertain the donor in order to give him some tangible benefit in exchange for his generosity.

" THE *CHOCHMAH U'MUSSAR* TEACHES US to use our imaginations and not be constrained by our physical senses. For

Dealing with the Poor

example, a member of our *shiur* hurt his foot at his sister's wedding and must walk around on crutches for a while. Who here imagines his friend's pain and *feels* it? The power of imagination is the key to the art of advertising in America. A new model car is merely an old model car with sheet metal bent into a different shape. They make the 'new' car look so beautiful, and the person in the sign looks so happy, that the customer imagines that if he had that car, he'd also be happy and well off.

"In giving *tzedakah*, the Torah speaks of 'the poor person *together* with you' (*Shemos* 22:24) to tell you that you have to feel as if *you* too are a poor person in exactly the same position as he. My mother once told us, 'You don't know who you are and you don't know who this beggar is. Maybe he is someone who did not sympathize with the pain of a poor person in a previous life, so he was sent down to this world again as a beggar so that he would feel it.'

"What about Yankele, the beggar who comes here? You don't care, you laugh at him and enjoy making fun of him. Can you imagine the pain he has in life? Do you think it couldn't possibly happen to you? No one is safe from anything in this world. Once I sat near Yankele in *shul* and he smelled so foul that I wasn't sure I was allowed to *daven* near him. Then after *davening*, I saw Doctor Askovitz[4] greet him and embrace him with open arms like an old friend! Later that morning I had to stop at Dr. Askovitz's house to pick up a pair of glasses, and who did I find there but Yankele. He was sitting at the table and Dr. Askovitz was serving him a

---

4. Dr. Shimon Askovitz, zt"l, an ophthalmologist, was a hidden *tzaddik* who *davened* at the yeshivah. He was held in awe by all the *gedolim* of his time and Reb Mendel admired him to no end. After Dr. Askovitz passed away, Reb Mendel strongly encouraged this author to write an article about his life. A brief article appeared in The Jewish Observer of Sept. 1981.

meal like a distinguished guest! Dr. Askovitz was a great man, a true *tzaddik.*"

∾ ∾ ∾

When Reb Mendel lived in Williamsburg, he did not hesitate to take beggars into his house. Many smelled terrible because they had nowhere to bathe or wash their clothes. Reb Mendel's children used to ask him how he could stand the smell and he would reply, "Do we look any better in Hashem's eyes? You have to heartily absorb the smell of a poor person. The bird offered by a poor person in the *Beis HaMikdash* was burned together with its feathers even though it gave off a terrible smell because Hashem loves the smell of a poor man. In Hashem's eyes no one is privileged — there are no upper and lower classes; with Him the big and the small are all equal."

Once Reb Mendel saw a poor old tramp picking up cigarette butts from the sidewalk. As soon as he saw this, he quickly ran into a store and bought the man a pack of cigarettes. He was always eager to meet this fellow so that he could give him a few dollars for his needs. The day before he passed away he happened to see the man passing his house, and ran out and gave him a sizable donation.

REB MENDEL ONCE EXPLAINED how the blessings of great people work: "It's not easy to give a *berachah*; it's like writing out

Chesed — Beyond the Laws of Nature

checks from your own bank account. In his later years the Chofetz Chaim was once approached by someone for a *berachah*, and the Chofetz Chaim told him, 'I can't give everything away; I have to leave a little for myself.' In order to fulfill a blessing, Hashem has to rearrange His previous plan for the benefit of the person being blessed, which is almost like making a change in the Creation itself. Such a feat requires great merit.

"If, however, someone relies totally on Hashem and lives without making his own plans, then when he gives a *berachah*, it's different. Most people live their lives according to a certain pattern: a time for eating, a time for sleeping, and so on. When someone entirely ignores his own personal needs and serves Hashem with no personal plans, then in return Hashem overrides the natural order of the universe, so to speak, and grants this person's requests. Such a person's blessings are fulfilled without taking anything away from his 'account.'

"That is why the Chofetz Chaim used to send people to Reb Yisrael Yaakov for blessings. Reb Yisrael Yaakov was a person who lived without making any calculations — everything he did, even if it embarrassed him or put his health in danger, was for Hashem's sake. A blessing given by someone like that has a power far beyond the natural order of creation. That's what the *Gemara* (*Berachos* 20a) means when it says, 'What's the difference between former times, when miracles were done, and our times, when they are not? In former times, people served Hashem with total dedication, so He did miracles for them.' When Rabbi Yehudah HaNasi did *mitzvos*, he didn't take his personal interests or his own safety into account."

"WHEN KORACH AND HIS ASSEMBLY came before Moshe to contest Aharon's appointment as *Kohen Gadol*, Moshe told them,

No Limit for Chesed

'*Rav lachem bnei Levi* — the position you have is enough for you, children of Levi' (*Bamidbar* 16:7). Years later, at the end of the forty years in the Wilderness, Moshe pleaded with Hashem to be allowed to enter *Eretz Yisrael*. Hashem denied his request with the same expression (*Devarim* 3:26): '*Rav lecha...* — The reward waiting for you in the World to Come is enough for you; do not speak to Me any more about this matter.' The *Midrash* (*Bamidbar Rabbah* 18:18) comments that Hashem deliberately used the same expression Moshe had used in speaking to Korach and his followers.

"This *Midrash* teaches us the lengths to which we're required to go in order to accommodate others. When Korach approached Moshe to ask for the High Priesthood, Moshe did not have to respond as he did. He could have said, 'Let me go to Hashem and see what I can do. Maybe He'll allow us to have two High Priests, or come up with some other solution.' But since Moshe pushed him away curtly — 'You have enough' — Hashem pushed away his request with the same expression."

§∻ §∻ §∻

Reb Mendel made every effort to accommodate other people's needs even when they seemed eccentric to the rest of the world.

In Chicago he knew a man who was so obsessed with collecting newspapers that the man's landlord wanted to throw him out together with his collection. When Reb Mendel became aware of the situation, he rented a garage for the man's newspapers, and then rented a U-Haul and transported everything to the garage. Other people found it strange that Reb Mendel spent so much time and expense on such an idiosyncratic fellow, but Reb Mendel explained, "How can we make light of his feelings? His newspapers are as important to him as our furniture is to us!"

Another time in Chicago Reb Mendel was awakened late one night by a phone call from a friend he had known in Shanghai. The friend apologized for calling so late, but said his car was stuck fifty miles from Chicago, and he had no one to call. Did Reb Mendel know of a trustworthy garage he could contact? Reb Mendel said, "Wait right there — I'll be right over!" and immediately went out with his old car and a chain and spent the whole night towing the friend's car back to a garage in Chicago.

But Reb Mendel's willingness to help others was not limited to his friends and acquaintances. He once received a call from someone who described himself as a friend of a former student of Reb Mendel's from Chicago. Although the young man himself had never met Reb Mendel, he had heard so much about him from his friend that he wanted to come to discuss a personal problem.

Reb Mendel asked him, "Where are you now?" "Well... I am calling from the Lakewood Minyan in Boro Park." Reb Mendel said, "Wait! Wait! I'll come to see you!" Reb Mendel, who lived in Bensonhurst, a different neighborhood, immediately drove over to meet this person whom he had never met before, but who needed him.

Reb Mendel's sensitivity to other people's needs was matched by remarkable perseverance. He once noticed that a certain student's shoes were torn. He did not say anything at the time, but the next time there was an "off" Shabbos, and both Reb Mendel and the boy were in New York, Reb Mendel asked the student to come with him to buy shoes. Reb Mendel picked the student up in his car and took him to a shoe store in Williamsburg. The shoes there were unsatisfactory, however, and the two of them spent four hours going to shoe stores in Brooklyn and Manhattan until Reb Mendel finally found a pair of shoes to the student's liking.

In the Torah, Hashem's attribute of kindness is immediately followed by His attribute of truth. True kindness is not an unchecked expression of emotion. Rather, it is only after the emotion is meaured by the yardstick of truth that true *chessed* can be achieved.

Once, in Shanghai, Reb Mendel invited a distinguished *bachur* from the Mirrer Yeshivah to eat supper at his home. Shortly before the *bachur* arrived, however, a poor man came to his house in search of food. In wartime Shanghai, food was very scarce and it was rare to see any more food at a meal than was needed. So when the *bachur* arrived Reb Mendel quietly drew him aside and said, "Please forgive me, but this person has nowhere else to go, while you can eat wherever you usually eat." With this, Reb Mendel escorted the *bachur* to the door and served his portion to the uninvited guest.

Our Sages describe a person favored by Hashem as having drawn "a thread of *chesed*" (*Chagigah* 12b). Reb Mendel once explained this expression: "What is a thread? Something very thin and unnoticeable. Nevertheless, a whole garment is made up of these small and unnoticeable threads." In a similar vein, Reb Mendel once observed as he walked by a construction site near the yeshivah, "Do you see how a building is built? A person is built the same way: one small brick, then another and another, until finally all the small actions join together and a great structure comes into being."

CHAPTER NINE

Family Relationships

Role Models for Life

NE DAY, Reb Mendel told the *shiur*, "Take out the *groisser sefer* [*Chochmah U'Mussar*] and I'll give you a treat." There were not enough *sefarim* for everyone, so some of the boys had to share with others. When Rebbe noticed two boys sitting next to each other, each with his own *sefer*, he asked, "Why are you keeping yours if your neighbor has one too? There are others who don't have a *sefer* to use at all. The very foundation on which this *sefer* is built — at least the first ten chapters — is to share the yoke of your friend. Not sharing a *sefer* with your friend is just as selfish as wanting to keep a whole piece of cake for yourself.

"This *sefer* explains that the Creator made the world

The Kaplan family before leaving Shanghai (L-R): Cyril, Rebbetzin Kaplan, Rochel, Shimon, Reb Mendel, Yeruchem

in such a way that people have to live in relationships with others, so that they will learn how to treat others. People want to get married, for instance, and through marriage you learn to get rid of a little of your selfishness. You can't understand this now, but wait twenty or thirty years, and you'll see it. Life in a family — learning how to treat your wife and children — helps you develop the qualities you need to use with everyone."

"WE ARE SUPPOSED TO EMULATE Hashem's traits. He needs nothing and He gives everything just for the sake of bestowing goodness on His creations. Parents are like that;

Fear and Honor of Parents

they give of themselves to their children without thought of reward. They're chips of the Creator.

"Did you ever think about the pain your mother suffered at your birth? You can't begin to understand such a thing as caring for a child from reading a book about human psychology because it's totally beyond all limits of understanding — it's a piece of the *Shechinah*. The *Gemara* (*Kiddushin* 31b) says of a particular *Amora* that whenever he saw his mother he saw the *Shechinah* coming towards him. You can see the *Shechinah* in a mother's concern. Did you ever see how your mother works until her last bit of energy is gone, or till the last minute on *erev* Shabbos? If Shabbos didn't come, she'd keep on working more and more — that's a piece of the *Shechinah*.

"The same thing applies to a father as well. We call Hashem *Avinu Malkeinu* — our Father and our King. Every father works without rest for his family. A father is more like a likeness of *Elokeinu* (the name that represents Hashem's strict justice). Have you ever seen such a father, a chip of *Elokeinu*? Probably in Brisk you could have seen such a father. When Reb Chaim saw his son momentarily hesitate to move a lamp for a sick person on Shabbos, he rebuked him in the strongest terms. Now that's a father!

"The honor of a rebbe comes before that of a father only when the rebbe learns with his student without charge, but if the father pays the rebbe to teach his son, then the honor of the father takes precedence.

"Hashem says that if you honor your parents, then He knows that if He were there you would honor Him too. If you do not honor your parents, He knows you would not honor Him either

(*Kiddushin* 31a). Many people today have no feeling for their parents. When their parents get older, they plan on putting them in an old-age home. They don't realize that putting someone in an old-age home can be just like putting him in the cemetery!

"This country is all messed up. The reason there is so much crime and drugs in America is because children aren't trained to have any fear. If a child has no one to play ball with, his father has to play with him or teach him to ride a bike. Otherwise he's considered a poor father.[1] Since the father teaches his son how to have fun and takes him places to have fun, the child thinks that everything in the world was put there for his pleasure.

"In Shanghai the water was unhealthy and had to be boiled before we could drink it. It was hard for individuals to gather wood and make a fire, so there was a store that sold boiled water. The store we bought from was a family business in which everyone helped out. Once the mother told her fifteen-year-old son to do something for the baby. When the boy didn't listen, she gave him a few good slaps. The boy just stood there without making a sound; he lowered his head in shame, accepted it and went away. But this country is filled with people who aren't *mentschen.* If a mother did that today in America, she'd be put in jail."

s➤ s➤ s➤

"In Shanghai, I once saw a young girl holding an elderly woman by the hand to guide her just to show respect for the elderly.

"The *Gemara* (*Kiddushin* 31) relates many cases of gentiles who honored their parents. Why did the *Gemara* tell such stories about gentiles but not about Jews? Firstly, we learn from them that even if the Torah did not command us to honor our parents, our intelligence would obligate us. Secondly, when we honor our parents, it must be truly from our hearts, not like the Arabs who show someone great honor when he comes to their home as

---

1. Reb Mendel did not reject these activities in and of themselves. When his daughter, for instance, needed to learn how to drive, he taught her himself. His objection was to the father becoming a slave to his child's demands. "If the father can do it, fine," he said. "But a parent is not obligated to do anything for a child except feed him until a certain age. And even that is not in the Torah; it was instituted by the Sages."

a guest, but who wouldn't hesitate to kill the same person on the road. Honoring parents has to come from feelings, not from tradition.

"Just honoring parents in order to do a *mitzvah* is not enough because the only way you can fulfill this special *mitzvah* is when it comes from the heart. In the first chapter of *Kiddushin* a *Tanna* said that he felt himself inferior to Eisav in honoring his parents because Eisav used to put on fancy clothes before he served his father. The obvious question is: Why didn't this *Tanna* also put on such clothes to serve his father? Because he knew that without the same feeling of respect that Eisav had, the mere action was insufficient."

ৎ৯ ৎ৯ ৎ৯

Reb Mendel once told a recent *baal teshuvah*, who was about to return home to visit his parents, that he had only one *mitzvah* to perform when he went home: honoring his parents. Rebbe told him to constantly seek out things to do for his parents, such as washing and waxing his father's car.

Reb Yisrael Yaakov, the *mashgiach* of the Baranovich Yeshivah, would beg his mother to give him things to do for her, but she always refused because she did not want to take such a great Torah scholar away from Torah study.

An alumnus of the Philadelphia Yeshivah returned there one year when his own yeshivah had already begun its Pesach break. Reb Mendel saw him and asked him why he was there. The *bachur* told him proudly that he had returned to put in an extra week of learning. Reb Mendel told him, "Pack your bags and go straight home; your parents need your help getting ready for Pesach."

That same student once had a difference of opinion with his parents as to whether he should return home for Shabbos or spend Shabbos in yeshivah where he could learn more. Reb Mendel advised him to spend Shabbos with his family. The *bachur* pointed out that the *Shulchan Aruch* rules that one does not have to listen to his parents if they want to keep him from going to a place where he will be able to learn Torah better. Reb Mendel answered that this ruling applied only in former times, when a father's advice was like that of a rebbe and the father did not take it as a personal affront if the son did not listen to him. Today, however, if a son does not follow his father's advice, the father suffers a lot of pain and distress.[2]

"*CHAZAL* SAY that all the songs in the Torah are holy and *Shir HaShirim* is holy of holies (*Yadayim* Ch. 3). *Shir HaShirim* is a para-

The Greatness of Women ble based on the relationship between a man and a woman. A woman is holy of holies because her whole nature is to do for others.[3] A woman gives of herself completely for her home and husband, and all she asks in return is a little recognition.

"Reb Yeruchem Levovitz said that man is like someone who plants seeds: he doesn't expect to eat fruits immediately, but he knows that he'll reap sweet fruits later. We just plant seeds in this world that will bear fruits in the next. That is what *Iyov* meant when he said, *Man is created for toil* (5:7). 'Toil' is working without seeing any fruits from one's labors.

"Women exemplify such toil. Everything they do seems like servitude, and they don't see any immediate fruits: housework — cleaning, cooking and raising children — is work without imme-diate fruits. Women say the blessing, 'Who made me according to His will,' to express, 'I am happy to serve as Hashem's example of how the world should be. Men must learn from me the lesson of what it means to toil.'

"From the fact that women are not required to study Torah and are absolved from many *mitzvos*, we see that women are nat-urally good and don't need Torah study and all the *mitzvos* to mold their characters. A man without Torah is lost; his good qual-ities will fade away in the course of time."

THE PRESIDENT OF ZEIREI AGUDATH ISRAEL, a national movement of *bnei Torah*, once asked Reb Mendel's advice con-

On Shidduchim and Marriage cerning which projects the organization should undertake. Reb Mendel told him, "The most important thing your organization can do is make *shidduchim*. Reb Yeruchem Levovitz once said about himself, 'What's my job in the yeshivah? Making *shidduchim*.' Reb Yeruchem even tried to find *shidduchim* for the

---

2. See *S'dei Chemed* 20:147.
3. Reb Mendel said this in the name of R' Leizer Horedzeisky, *zt"l*.

sisters of *bachurim* in the yeshivah, explaining that it wasn't just an act of kindness, it was an integral part of his job. 'When a *bachur* has a sister who needs a *shidduch* it disturbs his learning, and his learning is my business. Therefore his sister's *shidduch* is also my business.' "

Reb Mendel once told a student first starting *shidduchim*: "The *Ibn Ezra* points out that Avraham made Eliezer swear concerning his search for a *shidduch* for Yitzchak with the expression, *the G-d of the heaven and the earth* (*Bereishis* 24:3). He explains that the pairing of young men and women is done in Heaven, and this is a *sod* (one of the hidden teachings of the Torah).

"Why is it a *sod* that matches are made in Heaven? Isn't everything in this world arranged in Heaven? The *Gemara* (*Sotah* 2a) says that forty days before a baby is formed, a Heavenly voice calls out, 'The daughter of so-and-so is destined for so-and-so.' Why does the Heavenly voice have to call out so early in the child's existence? Why can't Hashem just make the match when the time comes? The reason is that Hashem literally matches the souls of the two people before the child is formed. Later, when they grow up, all Hashem does is match their corporal forms here on earth. This is the secret the *Ibn Ezra* was referring to: It is a great miracle for Hashem to arrange circumstances so that two *naarishe yunge mentschen* (silly young people) will find favor in each other's eyes and want to get married.

"I was once at a *sheva berachos* in Shanghai which Rabbi Yechezkel Levenstein, the *mashgiach* of the Mirrer Yeshivah, also attended. He quoted the *Gemara*

At his daughter's wedding:
(L-R) Esther Hutner (Née Kaplan), R' Shaul Hutner, Reb Mendel, R' Chaim Benoliel, R' Dovid Lopian

which says that *shidduchim* are made in heaven and noted that the *Gemara* cites proof from the *Torah, Neviim* and *Kesuvim* (*Moed Katan* 18b). 'What novel concept is the *Gemara* teaching us?' he asked. 'Isn't *everything* that transpires on earth preordained in Heaven?' He answered that everything is, indeed, controlled by

Hashem, but Hashem generally runs the world in a concealed manner. When it comes to making *shidduchim*, however, His hand is clearly revealed. Therefore, a person should never despair if he encounters difficulties in the area of *shidduchim*, because it's all clearly in the hands of Hashem."

Someone once asked Reb Mendel what he felt was the right age for marriage. His answer: "A person first has to learn to live with himself before he can think about living with another person."

A student who had started dating once asked Reb Mendel whether, according to *halachah*, when he entered a building with a girl he should pass through the door first or should allow the girl to precede him. Reb Mendel retorted, "She's trying to decide if she should put her life in your hands and this is the only thing on your mind?"

Reb Mendel then explained: "Marriage looks different from the man's point of view than from the woman's. A man has a life outside his home, either in *kollel* or in business, while usually a woman's life is centered around the home. Therefore a boy must show respect to a girl who is thinking of putting her life in his hands, and honor her accordingly."[4]

⅗ ⅗ ⅗

Reb Mendel stressed the importance of natural affection between husband and wife. On the other hand, he also burst some romantic notions his students may have had about marriage. "What is a *kallah*?" he once asked his class in Chicago. Not waiting for a response, he answered his own question: "Look at your mother — your *kallah* is someone just like your mother."

⅗ ⅗ ⅗

While American philosophy treats the world as nothing but fun and games, Reb Mendel presented life to us as a series of responsibilities and obligations. "A person thinks about a nice wedding and doesn't think about the fact that afterwards he'll have to bear a yoke like his parents did. He prefers thinking about fun things, and nothing else.

---

4. See *Minchas Shlomo* 91:23.

"In America, first a child plays with toys and gets all sorts of sweets. When he's older, his interest turns to bicycles and cars. He thinks that when he gets married he'll play house with a family and buy a house and car and everything will be one big game. Of course that's all a big mistake — leisure destroys a person (*Kesubos* 59b). 'What is *good* for a man, to accept a yoke in one's youth' (*Eichah* 3:27). *Chazal* explain that this refers to a wife. Having a family isn't 'fun,' but if you can carry the yoke, you'll get millions in reward; and if you don't, you'll get a ton of *Gehinnom*."

s◆ s◆ s◆

Reb Mendel once drove a *bachur* from his home in Brooklyn to Philadelphia. About fifteen minutes after leaving his house, he suddenly turned around and started back towards home, telling the *bachur*, "Now you'll learn a big lesson about how to treat your wife." When he reached his house, he went inside briefly and came out with a thermos and a piece of cake his wife had prepared for him. "A woman's whole life is her husband," he explained, "and you have to show her that you appreciate whatever she does for you. Even when she bears children, she still only has her husband in mind. This is why Leah said upon the birth of Levi, 'Now my husband will accompany me' (*Bereishis* 29:34).

"The Creator teaches us in the Torah the reality about man and woman. To have a *chupah* underneath the heavens is a beautiful and fitting custom, because the marriage is also taking place in Heaven at the same time.

"To a woman, says the *Rambam*, her life has as much value as she feels she's worth to her husband. When her husband honors her, he shows that she is valuable to him. A wife is not a *chavrusa*, G-d forbid. It can cause a lot of trouble if you think in those terms — that sometimes you're right and sometimes she's right. No! Whatever a wife does is good and nice, and if you scold her and take that feeling of importance away from her, you've robbed her of her life."

s◆ s◆ s◆

A married *talmid* once questioned Reb Mendel's claim that everything a wife does is done for the sake of her husband, pointing out that his wife wore fancier clothing when she went out to a wedding than she would have at home. Reb Mendel began to chuckle and replied, "*Nu*, what I said is not like a piece of Torah, something you can ask questions on. It's only my personal view of the matter." But after reflecting for a moment, he continued, "Besides, how do you know that when your wife gets dressed up for a wedding she isn't doing it for your benefit? Maybe she only wants everyone to see what a pretty wife you have?

"The *Gemara* says that to a husband, a wife is like his own physical self (*ishto k'gufo*), but what is a husband to a wife? To her, he is her *neshamah* (soul)."

Reb Mendel once elaborated on this point, saying that a wife's whole connection to spirituality is through her husband. Reb Mendel's Rebbetzin is a pious and learned woman. When driving

together, they would often pass the time with the Rebbetzin saying the first half of a verse of *Tehillim* from memory and Reb Mendel completing the verse; they both knew the whole Book of *Tehillim* by heart. Yet Reb Mendel once told this author that in spite of her spirituality, if they did not go on a trip together during *Yom Tov*, she would not enjoy that *Yom Tov*, because a wife's enjoyment of *Yom Tov* is dependent on spending time with her husband.

Reb Mendel & his Rebbetzin

᠂᠂᠂᠂᠂᠂

One of the words the Torah uses for women is *nashim*. Rav Samson Raphael Hirsch explains (*Bereishis* 32:33) that this word derives from the word *nasheh*, "creditor." One Friday, Reb Mendel remarked to his son in connection with the work his wife was doing to prepare for Shabbos, "In the next world the women will tear pieces out of us. We'll have to give them spiritual reward in exchange for all the strenuous physical work they did in the house, and we won't have enough to repay them for all their labors."

Reb Mendel once said, "Even if you can't actually lend a hand, as long as you're at home, your wife still feels that you're a big help. It makes her feel secure, and she is able to take care of things better." (On another occasion, however, he remarked, "When a husband stays at home too much, he becomes a yoke on his wife, and when he leaves, she feels relieved.")

§➤ §➤ §➤

When Reb Mendel drove from Philadelphia to Brooklyn, he would stop a short distance from New York City to call and tell the Rebbetzin that he would be home soon. He explained to a student that since his wife enjoyed having him at home, he wanted to give her some peace of mind a little earlier. "When I tell her that I'll be home soon, she feels as if I'm already home and starts to feel better."

REB MENDEL'S PREMARITAL COUNSELING often consisted of one short parable: "Two birds were once sitting on a tree, and one

Advice for Living

of them said to the other, 'I can blow down this whole tree.' The bird who was listening flew away and a third bird who had overheard the conversation flew over and asked the braggart, 'How could you say you can blow down the tree — you know you can't!' The first bird answered, 'I was talking to my wife.' "

Reb Mendel then explained: "Although in general it's good to be humble, with your wife it's wrong. A wife has to think that her husband is capable of doing anything and everything. When Rachel was barren, she came to Jacob and demanded that he provide her with a child. Jacob told her, 'Am I in the place of G-d?' (*Bereishis* 30:1-2). This shows that Rachel thought that her husband possessed the powers of Hashem Himself!

"If a husband tells his wife that there's something he can't do, she thinks that he really can do it and that he just doesn't want to. If he does actually convince her that he is truly incapable of doing something, then he has destroyed part of himself in her eyes."

He once related that while trying to secure a visa to escape from Russia he often returned home frustrated after a long day of futile efforts. The Rebbetzin would look at him quizzically as if to ask, "Why didn't you get the visa?" He would say to himself, "What kind of question is that? It's not so simple and I'm not such a capable person, that's why I couldn't get the visa."

"It wasn't until many years later that I came to realize that she couldn't believe it was beyond my powers to procure a visa. That is how Hashem made a wife; every woman thinks her husband is capable of doing anything he wants to."

REB MENDEL WAS AWARE of his obligations to his family, but he did not allow himself to be consumed by them. One Friday he

A Sense of Balance

ended *shiur* later than usual. At the conclusion he pointed at one student and said, "I stayed late because I saw that *bachur* was determined to be fully involved in the *shiur* today, so just for him I stayed a bit later. What about my family and my other obligations? Don't think family is everything. When a person is married he begins to think that everything revolves around his family. At a certain age a new bike seems like everything in life, then later it's a car, then it's a wife, then family. No! *Hakol hevel* — it's all nothing (*Koheles* 12:13). The only thing that's true is the fear of Hashem."

At the same time, he knew that Torah study does not absolve a person from genuine family obligations. He excused himself from giving a *shiur* one day because he felt obligated to attend a *sheva berachos* for his granddaughter being given by the *chasan's* aunt. He explained that the aunt was a widow, and she might be hurt if the *kallah's* "distinguished" grandfather failed to attend. Reb Mendel observed, "I like to think I'm free of all other responsibilities, but I'm not. I hope to be back tomorrow night to make up for the lost *shiur*."

CHAPTER TEN

The Torah Way in Business

EB MENDEL loved the famous letter written by the *Rambam* to his student, Shmuel ibn Tibbon, when the latter was then

The Responsibility of a Doctor working on a translation of *The Guide for the Perplexed* from Arabic to Hebrew. In the letter, the *Rambam* warns his student that he will have little benefit from journeying from France to Egypt to see him since he has no time whatsoever to speak with him. The *Rambam* then proceeds to describe his typical day, which begins early in the morning in the Sultan's court and ends after nightfall with the *Rambam* still writing prescriptions for the many patients who have come to see him while lying flat on his back from fatigue and without the energy even to speak.

For Reb Mendel, the *Rambam* epitomized a doctor's dedication to his patients. Reb Mendel not only shared this letter with us, he encouraged one of his students to translate it and have it published in an English-language journal. Reb Mendel praised Dr. Julian Ungar, an internationally renowned neurosurgeon who used to voluntarily visit sick students in the dormitory, for the same type of dedication to healing:

"The pleasure that Doctor Ungar has from helping others is unbelievable. I have a nephew who went to the University of Virginia to study physics. After the craze died down for the particular topic he was studying, he found himself stuck there with his family. After a few years, he developed headaches and began shaking. The doctors diagnosed that he had Parkinson's disease. I wanted to visit him because someone who sits idle for a long time quickly becomes depressed.

"Doctor Ungar insisted on accompanying me on the visit. One plan was for us to meet in Washington D.C. and drive to Virginia from there. But then we found out that it takes three hours to get to Washington and another few hours to that part of Virginia, so we ruled that out. Next, Doctor Ungar suggested that we charter a plane to an airport close to the university, but the nearest airport turned out to be sixty-five miles away.

"Do you hear the ideas this doctor came up with? Such a *mentsch*. He wanted to charter a plane at his own expense! It didn't matter that he would miss a whole day of work or what it would cost. That he should do this seemed self-evident to him. And all I do is learn with him for fifteen minutes a few times a week. If you realize that the *Rambam* was many times greater in his concern for the sick, you will have some idea of the greatness of the *Rambam*."

S➤ S➤ S➤

On another occasion, Reb Mendel contrasted the *Rambam's* attitude with that commonly found in the medical profession today. "I go to a doctor who claims he can cure everything with nutrition. He has a staff of around forty nurses and secretaries working under him. My first visit cost me $200.00, and after giving me a very quick examination, he was ready to run out. I wanted to ask a question, but he told me, 'I don't answer any questions.'

" 'But, Doctor,' I said, 'I am a rabbi and rabbis always put aside our regular duties to answer questions.'

"He answered, '*We're* here to make money.' He said this without embarrassment or shame.

"It used to be that a doctor was embarrassed to take money, and you had to slip it into his hand when he was finished treating you. His only thought was to make people healthy; that he had to make a living was a separate matter, something tacitly understood. But that someone should be a doctor just for the money — who would ever have thought of such a thing?

"Now, Mr. Back, who has a car-repair shop in Philadelphia, is an example of what people used to be like. His first priority is to get your car running one hundred percent, just as if it were his own. He puts all his efforts into fixing it completely — the money is a separate thing. Of course, he has to eat, but for him that's something entirely separate.

"Baranovich was an old-time town. When I needed my shoes fixed, I would bring them to 'Avremele the *schuster*.' Not only would he fix the soles and heels, he would also patch the tops and sides of the shoe. One time I started to tell him where they needed mending, but he hushed me, saying, 'You don't have to explain to me where to fix your shoes. I always give the shoes I work on a thorough checking to make sure that everything that needs to be done is taken care of.'

"Some years later in Shanghai, I went to a shoe-repair shop frequented by the more stylish people in Shanghai. I showed the man something on one of the shoes, and he circled it with chalk and told me to come back in a few days. When I came back, I tried on the shoes and found that only the shoe he had chalked was fixed, but the other one still had a hole in it! When I complained that he had only fixed one shoe, he said, 'I only fix what you show me; what you don't show me I don't fix!' Do you see the difference between him and Avremele the *schuster*?"

♔ ♔ ♔

"My mother," he said, "was a remarkable person. Her whole week was spent going around town collecting for poor and needy families. In those days, you didn't buy a suit. First you went to a store and purchased material, which you then took to a tailor to have made into a suit. But my mother wouldn't purchase material off the roll, she would buy remnants from a roll, and from that the suit was made. Once I noticed a nice remnant in the store, a reddish brown, and I asked my mother to buy it, but she wouldn't. Instead, she bought material which was more expensive and not as nice from a certain *chassid*, who had a wife and a sick daughter to support.

"She didn't buy milk from the regular milkman, who made deliveries to people's houses early in the morning, but from a widow who had a child to support. This widow didn't bring the milk until the afternoon because she lived on the other side of town. Even though people drink milk mainly in the morning, our family went without milk for breakfast. Nowadays, they would call her crazy, but that's the difference between then and now."

Reb Mendel followed in his mother's footsteps. Before making a purchase, he tried to determine which store needed the business more. There was one grocer in Flatbush who had only a few items in stock, and consequently attracted very few customers. Reb Mendel made a point of buying from him even though his products were more expensive and usually had been on his shelves a long time. He once remarked to his son as they passed the grocery store, "Do you see how he stands there in the doorway waiting forlornly for a customer? Who knows if we won't look that way in the next world? The pious *Yidden* will be full of *mitzvos,* and others will just stand and look with sadness and envy."

ONE DAY THE *GEMARA* WE WERE LEARNING propelled Reb Mendel into a long discussion of changes in the way people

Uses and Misuses of Money
approach money since the days of the *Gemara.* "Imagine the following scenario: Someone wants to support a fellow Jew, but he knows he won't accept a gift. So what does he do? He goes out of his way to buy things from him. Let's say he walks into a hat store and asks how much a hat costs. The hatter says, 'Two dollars.' The buyer protests, 'Two dollars for such a nice hat — you should get five dollars for it!' But the hatter just wants people to enjoy wearing his hats, and refuses to take more than a small profit. Even though the buyer continues to insist that he take more, the seller only wants what's fair. That's how business was conducted in the days of the *Gemara.*

"Business then wasn't like it is today. Now we have banks to safeguard people's money, but then people wanted to use their money to help others. The reason people today are so interested in grabbing as much money as they can is that they think of their possessions as an extension of themselves. That's why people are reluctant to lend out their cars. They feel that their car is part of their soul."[1]

❧ ❧ ❧

"After I had been in Chicago for a while, a man I knew from Europe dropped by one day to see me. In the course of the conversation he asked me, 'Have you made any friends here?' I looked at him — what kind of expression is this, 'making friends'? How do you 'make friends'? That's such an American expression. In America you make friends, like the politicians do: 'I'll do this for you, and you do this for me.' That is what friendship means in America.

"When I first came to this country, I asked my brother, *alav hashalom*, who had been in Chicago since the late twenties, 'How does a person "make it," as you say, in America?' He answered, 'Whatever was considered deceitful in Europe, you'll succeed by doing in America!'

"In America the main thing in life is success, but how do you become a 'success'? By looking in the Torah and doing the exact opposite. The Torah says not to show off, so show off. The Torah says to be honest, so don't be honest. America is the Empire of the Dollar. Other than the dollar, nothing else matters, even though it's not written in the Constitution."

REB MENDEL was contemptuous of modern advertising. "Advertising has turned America into a mindless country," he

On Advertising

would say. "In Europe if there was a demand for something, then they made it; here they make the thing and then create the demand. They convince you to buy everything new and then to throw it away after you use it one time. Most people have their houses full of things they don't need — no wonder we are destroying all our natural resources down to the core of the earth.

---

1. Reb Mendel himself did not share this attitude. Once his car sideswiped one of the cement walls leading up to the Verrazano Bridge, but he just continued on his way. Apparently, another few scratches on his car did not matter to him, and the wall was still intact. At the other side of the bridge, a policeman who had seen the mishap pulled him over. "You know you just had an accident, Rabbi?" the officer barked. To Reb Mendel there was all the difference in the world between injury to a human being and a dent in a car. He smiled at the officer, put his hand on the man's shoulder, and said, "You're making a mistake, officer. *I* didn't have an accident. My *car* had an accident."

"Today, there are no appeals to the intelligence; everything is for the eyes — like styles and advertising. They take Coke and make it appear as distinguished as Scotch. Today a car is like a dress — every year you have to get a new one. It should be like a pair of rubbers. Of course, you need the body because the engine has to be covered. But that's not the essential part. A person's head is made for the brain. Hashem made it to look nice as well. You can put a hat on it, a face is attached to it, etc. But that's not the main thing.

"People are impressed by a beautiful car, but they don't consider how ugly they have to make themselves, with hard and sometimes dishonest work, in order to acquire it. Whenever I see a new car, I'm not the least bit impressed. I immediately visualize how it will look ten years from now when it's lying wheels-up in the junkyard."

⋅ *⋅* *⋅*

"An auto dealer sells a car for $7,999, not $8,000. I'm sick of this. Who do they think they're fooling? They think people are stupid, and they make us look so stupid. But they know that if the first number someone sees is a seven that's what makes the biggest impression.

"The Madison Avenue ads wield more influence than anything else. If a bill had been introduced in the '50s or early '60s to require people to buy only small cars, there would have been bigger protests than if America had declared war. But then the advertisers made small cars all the rage. You see how ads cause the public to grab all those foolish products like crazy. We must learn a lesson from this. If people swallow up foolishness with so much enthusiasm, then certainly we must pursue our Torah — every word of which is pure truth — with the same excitement and vigor."

ONE DAY REB MENDEL began our study of *Chochmah U'Mussar* with this introduction: "Clean out your ears of every-

On Jobs thing you've heard until now. Don't be foolish; don't miss out! Where else will you get another 'old Rebs' from the previous generation to teach you such things? If you pass up this chance now, you'll surely regret it later." With that he launched into a tirade about the concept of "jobs."

"In this country everyone has to have a job. When you meet somebody, the first thing you ask him is, 'And what do you do?' If someone doesn't have a job, he's viewed as if he has no life.

"Rava didn't have a job, and *Rashi* didn't have a job. Reb Elchonon held the position of *rosh yeshivah* but to him that was nothing like what people consider a job today. I told his son more than forty years ago that if Eliyahu HaNavi were to come and tell Reb Elchonon that his yeshivah could go on without him, he would immediately pack up and leave. He was there solely for the sake of spreading Torah.

"People in this country are just as happy to be a doctor or an electric-chair operator — whichever pays better. Everything is money. Being a judge is not something one does because he cannot tolerate injustice and criminality, but a 'job.' The policeman doesn't think of himself as protecting society from criminals, but as doing a 'job.'

"There are no 'jobs' in the Torah. Did Moshe have a 'job'? If someone is fit to do something, let him do it, and if he isn't fit, then forget it. When Moshe saw one Jew hitting another, his pure motivation compelled him to get involved, not like some of today's activists who would commit crimes if they could get away with it."

For the Sake of Others

"TO BE A PIOUS JEW does not mean you have to wear long *payos* and make yourself look religious. If you work for the good of others, and you don't take everything for yourself, that's called working for the sake of Heaven."

ᔐ ᔐ ᔐ

Reb Mendel once heard of a merchant who gave sizable donations of merchandise to worthy causes. He wasn't impressed. He explained that this merchant was just giving charity with the public's money, since his customers paid high prices for his products. It would be better for him, Rebbe said, to be charitable to the general public by charging them lower prices.

" 'The world is built with kindness' (*Tehillim* 89:3) and the real function of work is to help people. *Chazal* say that anyone who doesn't work is not a part of society (*Kiddushin* 40b). Every job, every product, should be done as a kindness to help others —

that's the nature of the creation and the essence of the human being. Just as the main part of a person is his heart, the organ which works without stop over an entire lifetime to serve the body, so too the main part of life is helping others.

"Do you think the lady who cooks in the yeshivah kitchen works for money? Such a thought is an insult to her. She prepares our meals with the exact same devotion with which the *roshei yeshivah* prepare their *shiurim*. I remember that once, when the yeshivah in Chicago was short of funds, they told the cook she couldn't give more than one portion to a boy. She just couldn't hold food back from the boys, so she quit her job."

On Independence

"THE *GEMARA* (*Berachos* 16b) relates that someone wanted to eulogize a slave by saying he was 'a good man who subsisted from the work of his hands,' but an objection was raised: 'If such praises are to be said for slaves, what praises will be left for better people?' From this you see that the praise, 'a good man who subsisted from the work of his hands,' includes everything, just like the words in *Shemoneh Esrei — the Powerful, the Great and the Mighty* — include all of Hashem's praises.

"The ability to work at a job was also given as a kindness from Hashem, to let us feel self-made and self-supporting. As *Chazal* teach, 'A person would rather have one measure of his own possessions than nine measures of something he receives from someone else' (*Bava Metzia* 38a). Hashem made the world so that if someone works, he'll succeed; and if he doesn't, he won't. This applies in the spiritual realm as well as in the material one. My Rebbe said that the reason communism failed was because it sought to uproot man's basic nature: the desire to live from his own efforts. When society was rearranged so that people had nothing of their own, and had to rely entirely on the government for all their needs, it took away their whole taste for life.

"We find this point in the Torah's laws concerning grafted trees. As long as a branch is nourished by what it received from the old tree, the laws of *orlah* don't apply to it, but once it starts to live on its own then they do. How do we determine this? The *Yerushalmi* says that if the leaves of the new tree point away from the ground, then we know it's living off the old tree's nutrition because it's ashamed to look the trunk in the face, since it's receiving a gift, and the nature of someone who receives a gift is to be ashamed. If, however, the leaves look downward, then we know it's on its own (*Mishnah Orlah* 1:5).

"The Torah says, *He who hates gifts shall live* (*Mishlei* 15:27), but the whole orientation of our society is to get something for nothing. Hashem created the world in order to bestow kindness on others. By giving to others we can make ourselves similar to Hashem. Even though our job is to give charity, a person should do everything in his power not to accept it. The goal of a person should be to bear a yoke and to stand on his own two feet; anyone who lives off others is missing something in himself. We find in the *Yerushalmi* that someone who had accepted charity was incapable of learning certain aspects of *Kabbalah*."[2]

⋗ ⋗ ⋗

Reb Mendel would try not to let anyone serve him in any way, not even by holding a door open for him or helping him put on his coat. One day he came into *shiur* and saw some boys still standing around talking. One of the boys saw Reb Mendel's look of disappointment, and told the others to be quiet, but Reb Mendel said, "No, don't," and himself motioned for the boys to sit down.

The *Gemara* (*Yoma* 83b) relates that once Reb Yehudah and Reb Yosi were walking on a road together when Reb Yehudah was suddenly seized by hunger to the point that he was in danger of dying. He saw a shepherd and forced him to give him his food. Reb Yosi then exclaimed to Reb Yehudah, "You forced someone to give you his food?!" As they approached the city, Reb Yosi suddenly collapsed from hunger. When the residents of the city saw him, they all ran out and surrounded him with pots of food. After Reb Yosi revived, Reb Yehudah told him, "I extorted from the shepherd, but you extorted from an entire city." From this *Gemara*, Reb Mendel concluded that if someone puts himself in a situation that requires him to accept help from others, it is as if he forced the other person to give against his will.

---

2. This discussion is in no way intended to diminish the importance of *kollel* in our times. The Chofetz Chaim rules (*Biur Halachah* 231:3) that the importance of working for a living notwithstanding, the needs in our current circumstances override other considerations and therefore *kollel* study is an honorable and worthwhile pursuit.

CHAPTER ELEVEN

The Jew in Today's Society

EB MENDEL once explained to us the fundamental philosophical differences between **Yaakov and Eisav — Two Separate Worlds** Yaakov and Eisav. "Someone once asked why the body, after it did so much good in its life, is buried and left to decay, while only the soul is rewarded after death. The question is based on a misconception. As the *Daas Tevunos* explains, Hashem does not withhold reward from any creature (*Pesachim* 118a), and it's precisely for this reason that the body will eventually be resurrected.

"Not only doesn't Eisav believe in resurrection of the dead, he also doesn't believe in the eternity of the soul. When Hashem created animals, He said, *Let the earth bring forth living creatures (nefesh chayah)* (*Bereishis* 1:24). The word *nefesh* also means 'soul,' because the animal soul comes from the same source as its earthly body, and when the body of an animal dies, its soul dies with it. Eisav thinks it's the same way with people."

S➤ S➤ S➤

Reb Mendel taught that a Jew's spiritual core is the root and essence of his being. "The *Mishnah* (*Sanhedrin* 90a) says, 'All Israel have a share in the World to Come, as it says (*Yeshayahu* 60:21): *They shall inherit the land forever; they are the branch of My planting.*' The soul of a Jew is planted in the World to Come; that is his true world and what he lives for. The world we live in is not our own, it's only a place where we can strive to accumulate Torah and good deeds.

"When a Jew returns to the Torah, he is only returning to his roots, and if he goes away from Torah he is going away from his roots. The *Kuzari* says a Jew might behave like a gentile and a gentile might behave like a Jew, but the gentile is still a gentile and the Jew is still a Jew."

Reb Mendel was once walking with a student near the yeshivah when 'Yankele the pauper' saw him from across the street. "Rabbi Kaplan! Rabbi Kaplan!" cried Yankele, waving his arms frantically. "How are you, Rabbi?"

Reb Mendel acknowledged Yankele's concern, and Yankele called out with a big smile, "Have a nice day!" Reb Mendel told the student, "You see how despite his poverty Yankele is still so concerned and friendly. The interest he takes in others is more genuine than that of many distinguished politicians."

☙ ☙ ☙

"Small people do big things and big people do small things. Reb Yeruchem Levovitz used to say that Yisro had to see the waters of the sea being split before he blessed Hashem, whereas a Jew makes a blessing on a simple glass of water. The wicked want to do only the "big" *mitzvos*, but the truth is that helping your next-door neighbor is no less important than helping people overseas in the Peace Corps. If you're really interested in helping people, you don't have to go to Africa. Someone could keep busy twenty-four hours a day just helping the residents of one apartment building."

☙ ☙ ☙

"Eisav is the classic case of someone who showed his father proper honor. Yet the Sages say that when he said, *Let the days of my father's death draw near* (*Bereishis* 27:41), he intended to kill his own father. An Eisav can be nice and friendly as long as things go according to his liking, but as soon as you rub him the wrong way he turns into a murderer. A Jew, however, always retains his good qualities, even under difficult circumstances. They may be concealed at times, but they stay embedded deep, deep inside.

"To Eisav, appearance is everything. The Sages compare Eisav to a pig that shows off its split hooves to make everyone think it's kosher while concealing its true nature. They can do the most hideous things and then try to make them seem perfectly legal. The Communists always claim that the country they're attacking did some terrible wrong that justifies — and even requires — them to destroy it. Why don't they just skip the rationalizations? But the truth is that the essence of Eisav's morality is to make things look proper. Even Hitler, may his name be erased, did that. First he had to write a book to give his bestiality a look of respectability."

"PHARAOH MADE THE NILE RIVER HIS GOD, and yet the Torah says that he stood over his river, meaning that his god was

Who Is Serving Whom?

enslaved to him. Concerning Avraham, however, the Torah tells us, *Hashem stood over Avraham* (*Bereishis* 17:22). Avraham bore the yoke of Heaven upon himself. Eisav does what he wants and thinks that even his gods exist only to help him to do what he wants. (Similarly, some Jews talk about 'my doctor,' 'my lawyer' and 'my rabbi,' as if their rabbi worked for them in the same way the doctor and the lawyer do. Instead of being someone to listen to, to accept guidance from, the rabbi is just there to serve their needs.)

"In today's world there's no concept of religion at all. The whole business with the Pilgrims, turkey and Santa Claus has nothing to do with religion — its only purpose is to drum up business. The store windows place a *menorah* together with a tree, and whichever group spends the most money, *harei zeh meshubach* (Behold, this one is praiseworthy)."

"IN ENGLISH THERE'S A SAYING, 'I'll tell you the truth.' Does that mean that until now he wasn't telling the truth? To Eisav

On the Media

falsehood is just as good as truth. I once knew a newspaperman who told me he would just as well write lies as the truth, as long as he could make them sound good. You can't assume everything they put in the papers is true. These fancy news magazines dress up the news so that everything is beautifully arranged, but they don't know the truth from a lie."

After hundreds of followers of the Reverend Jim Jones committed suicide, Reb Mendel linked this act of collective insanity to the effects of television.

"Those who killed themselves are products of television. When a child watches television, he loses his mind and his concept of self. If he sees a family show, he thinks he's part of that family. If people give their minds over to television, it's no wonder they give them over to a cult leader like that. The whole country is being destroyed by television. A person sits in front of it and vegetates. He can't stop himself from watching, like an addict can't live without drugs.

"We are not allowed to drink milk from a gentile or bread baked by a gentile. So why do we imagine that we can let them fill our heads with radio and television? How can Jews take that garbage into their homes? It's like having a sewer spewing forth all over a two-thousand-dollar carpet. It would be better to empty filth onto your carpet than to put a television there. When someone brings a television into his home, he brings a thousand demons in with it. You wouldn't suspect a *frum* Jew of being capable of murder. But if he watches murders day in and day out on television, it starts to seem normal to him. And then, even wearing *Rabbeinu Tam's tefillin* won't help."

Insensitivity to the Misfortunes of Others

"HOW CAN SOMEONE READ THE NEWSPAPERS? If the heartbreaking news they printed each day really bothered him, he wouldn't be able to read it. And if it doesn't, then reading it only serves to make him more hard-hearted to other people's suffering."

"A *bachur* once returned to the Mirrer Yeshivah after getting out of the Polish army. Reb Yeruchem embraced him warmly, but when another *bachur* followed suit, Reb Yeruchem asked him, "Now you embrace him. But did you miss even one night's sleep worrying about him?"

ک‍ ک‍ ک‍

Reb Mendel was once asked what makes someone a great general. "Not minding throwing away more soldiers in battle," he answered. During the Vietnam war, he once commented to the class, "When three Jewish soldiers were killed in battle, Ben-Gurion went out and cried in front of the troops. In Vietnam, however, where hundreds of American boys are dying every day, the leaders of the country are able to eat, drink and get a good night's sleep as usual."

"ONCE, I WAS ON MY WAY TO A WEDDING, and someone told me, 'Have a good time.' I couldn't understand him. You don't

Bringing Joy to Others
go to a wedding to have a good time. You go to give joy to the *chasan* and *kallah*. Today, however, people dance at a *chasunah* so they'll look nice in the pictures. Once the chicken is finished, they see no reason to stay. No one has patience to wait for the *sheva berachos*."

Reb Mendel once attended a wedding where one of the guests was a prominent Jewish personality. During the wedding, he noticed that the crowd gathered around the personality rather than the *chasan*. "Do they realize that there's a *wedding* going on?" he asked in wonder.

Reb Mendel with talmidim on Purim

"In earlier times, there was a bond of love among everyone at a *simchah*. This helps us understand the story of Kamtza and Bar Kamtza (*Gittin* 55b). Why did the host throw out Bar Kamtza? Why did it matter so much if his enemy was also at the party? In those days the feeling of unity and love was such that having someone there who wasn't your dear friend totally destroyed the *simchah*. It was as though a stranger was pushing his way into the family pictures.[1]

"Once I read about the expensive wedding of the daughter of a wealthy bar owner in Chicago. The groom didn't show up, and the bride hid herself in a room and cried all night. But the guests and family ate and danced through the night. The bride's father said they should enjoy themselves because the groom was going to pay for it anyway. For us, a *chasunah* is somewhere between the Chicago wedding and those in the time of the *Gemara*."

On Secular Education

"A MAN ONCE TOLD me his diamond ring had cost him $8,000. He obviously felt that one small expensive stone was worth dozens of larger inferior ones. Well, the Alter of Kelm said that all of Aristotle's philosophy wasn't worth even one line of Rabbeinu Yonah, and Rabbeinu Yonah knew that all his wisdom didn't equal one line of *Gemara*.

"Even the smallest Torah work contains more ethical wisdom than a whole secular library. To get a full understanding of even one word of *Tehillim*, you would have to master whole books, and the same applies to certain other Torah works as well."

§➤ §➤ §➤

"The yeshivah is open eighty percent of the time and we have an old run-down building, while the secular schools are used only twenty percent of the time, and they have beautiful buildings. Hashem gives them all the money, because He wants us to be *moser nefesh* for the truth."

§➤ §➤ §➤

"If it were up to me, I wouldn't let *bnei Torah* start 'school' until they're twenty years old. When they're young, they should

---

1. A *talmid* of Reb Mendel, Yochanan Tomar, recalls that he was standing in the back of the hall when family pictures were being taken. Reb Mendel called to him, "Come over here so you'll be in the pictures with us."

learn only Torah. Young people are innocent, and the Torah they learn is of unparalleled quality. It's like in business — you have to make the investment right at the beginning, as early as possible."

Reb Mendel removed his son from secular studies at a very young age. While the other children were studying English in the afternoon, his son learned in the *beis midrash* or just ran around there. Someone challenged Reb Mendel and suggested that it would be better for his son to do something constructive and disciplined rather than just run around by himself. Reb Mendel asked the Satmar Rebbe for his opinion and the Rebbe supported him on the basis of the *Maharsha* (to *Berachos* 28b) who says that it is good for a child to run around the feet of *talmidei chachamim* where he can pick up *midos tovos* at times when he is unable to learn Torah.

Eventually the matter came to the notice of the Board of Education, and two truant officers came to Reb Mendel's home to investigate. He explained to them in a courteous but resolute tone that his traditions did not allow him to do otherwise. The officers were so impressed that they did not bother him again.

S♠ S♠ S♠

Reb Mendel once asked Reb Shraga Moshe Kalmanowitz, *rosh yeshivah* of the Mirrer Yeshivah in New York, why it was necessary for the yeshivah to start English studies at such an early age. He considered such studies a waste of the intellect. Reb Kalmanowitz told him that parents would not send their children to a yeshivah without English studies. Reb Mendel insisted, however, that there should at least be an option for parents who didn't desire secular studies for their children.

Reb Mendel told us, "I have pity on you. How can you be absorbed in Torah if you have to sit and listen to English studies three hours a day?" When he saw how crestfallen his remark had left us, he added, "Let me give you a piece of good advice. While you're in English class, at least think of how much you want to learn Torah. If you do that, there won't be such a gap between your morning and evening learning."

DESPITE ALL THE DISPARAGING REMARKS he made about secular studies, Rebbe made a point of telling us that Reb

From the Torah's Perspective Elchonon allowed his son to learn Polish when he was sixteen. The point was that a Jew first has to learn to view the world through the lens of the Torah.

Reb Mendel was actually very well versed in worldly matters and felt that a good command of language was important to convey Torah ideas in a precise and vivid way. Often he would ask the class, "How do they say this in English?" After slowly spelling or pronouncing the word in question, he would ask, "What does it mean?" He didn't just want the dictionary definition but a feeling of how a word is used.

But for all his stress on being articulate in speech, the importance he placed on knowing the terminology of the *Gemara* was a hundred times greater. "The expressions hold the subject," he would say. "All the spirit and details of a law are encased in the way *Chazal* chose to express it."

s➤ s➤ s➤

Reb Mendel kept himself abreast of current affairs. Walking past a grocery store with a student, he might say, "Let's see what's doing in our *kleine medinele* (little country)," and bend over to read the headlines on the newspapers.

Avrohom Dov Owsianka was traveling with Rebbe in the Catskill mountains when Rebbe stopped at a store to buy a copy of *The Sunday New York Times.* He took only the front section and told the clerk he could keep the rest. Avrohom Dov asked Reb Mendel what the proper attitude is toward reading newspapers, but Rebbe appeared reluctant to answer. Later, Rebbe had to make a stop and told Avrohom Dov that he could read the paper until he returned. "Read what's doing in our country. It'll widen your scope and help you become concerned with the needs of more people."

Avrohom Dov then asked, "Should I look only at what's doing in our country?"

Rebbe answered, "To 'take on' the whole world is too difficult. Better concentrate on the concerns that are closest to you."

Rebbe was also familiar with the natural sciences and would frequently marvel at Hashem's wonders. Some boys once noticed a book on nuclear physics in one of the rooms in which he stayed during the week. Over the following weeks, they noted the progress of the bookmark. Another time a *bachur* left in the *shiur*-room a book on the theory of relativity he had borrowed for a report. During the lunch break, Rebbe was seen reading it. It was only when he realized he was being watched that he stopped.

A student in Chicago once noticed Reb Mendel carrying two books, one a *sefer* and the other a book on the chemistry of wine-making. The student asked Rebbe what the books were, and Rebbe replied, "This book is a *Meiri*, and the other one is not a *Meiri*." He did not want his knowledge of science to be known for fear that this would cause others to exaggerate the value of such knowledge, which was, in his opinion, the maidservant of Torah, but only if kept in perspective and confined to its proper time and place.[2]

---

2. Reb Mendel also meant this quite literally. A student happened to be in Reb Mendel's home when his young son returned home from school and placed his schoolbooks on the table. Reb Mendel immediately removed them from the table, chiding the boy, "How many times do I have to tell you: English books go on the floor — *sefarim* go on the table!" He then placed the books in a neat pile on the floor next to the wall.

CHAPTER TWELVE

Between Man and His Creator

Accepting the Yoke of Heaven

"In accepting the Torah, the Jewish people took upon themselves a greater responsibility than a surgeon has in the operating room. David HaMelech said that the proper way to serve Hashem is to *rejoice with trembling* (*Tehillim* 2:11). An astronaut sitting in his spacecraft enjoys his job and takes pride in it. At the same time, he knows how great his responsibility is and how careful he has to be about each move he makes, since even the smallest action can have tremendous consequences. Hashem made us like that astronaut. Even our smallest actions have enormous ramifications.

"Every Jew is capable of making himself into a holy of holies. What does it mean to be a 'holy of holies'? *Rashi* says it means nothing other than to fear Hashem and to accept the yoke of His kingship (*Rashi* to *Shir HaShirim* 1:1). In the morning prayers we say, 'And all (the angels) open their mouths ... in song and hymn — and bless, praise, glorify ... and accept the Kingship.' Singing Hashem's praises is of value only if it leads to accepting His Kingship.

"Don't think that saying *Shema* is anything like singing *The Star-Spangled Banner*. Accepting the yoke of Heaven means being willing to give up our lives. In Japan, until recently, it was expected that if someone failed to properly fulfill the mission the emperor ordered him to do, he would kill himself. They weren't lunatics; they lived solely to serve the emperor and if they failed in their duties there was no point in continuing to live.

"The yoke of kingship we bear is no less weighty, and there are times when we are also obligated to give up our lives. But for the most part our yoke is made up of ordinary day-to-day responsibilities. For Torah students, this means not looking at your watch to see if it's time for lunch and not chatting with your friends in the middle of learning. All this is part of the yoke for which we have to give of ourselves."

S➤ S➤ S➤

Reb Mendel used to express wonder at how Reb Chaim Ozer Grodzenski always behaved the same way in both public and private. Even in the privacy of his home, he was always dressed in a frock coat and hat. Once Reb Mendel mentioned his amazement to an old friend from Europe. The man had served as a liaison between the Jewish community of Vilna and government leaders, and in that capacity had often visited Reb Chaim Ozer's home. He told Reb Mendel, "Reb Chaim Ozer constantly had the first *halachah* of the *Shulchan Aruch* — 'I have placed Hashem before me always' — in mind. He actually sensed that Hashem was always in front of him."

When Reb Mendel told the class his friend's response, he added, "This man spent his days in the business world and still had a sensitivity to spiritual matters which I didn't possess. One of his ancestors once volunteered to be burned at the stake in order to save the Jewish population of his city from a blood libel. Can you see the greatness that resides in the descendant of such a *kadosh* (a holy person who gives up his life to sanctify Hashem's Name)?"

Converts

REB MENDEL WAS OVERWHELMED by the greatness of converts to Judaism, who voluntarily accepted upon themselves the yoke of Heaven. Concerning one convert who frequented the yeshivah, he used to say, "Whenever I see him, I feel like running over to him and asking, 'HOW DID

YOU DO IT!' He made it from being a gentile to being a Jew, while I can't even get from the bottom of one page of the *Gemara* to the top of the next!"

REB MENDEL TOLD US how the Jewish nation of old lived in a world of uncompromising truth: "The *Gemara* (*Bava Kama*

In the Times of the Gemara

117a) relates that Rabbi Yochanan was once sitting on cushions in the yeshivah while the students sat on the floor before him. Rav Kahana began to ask him questions which he could not answer. With each question another cushion was taken away from Rabbi Yochanan until he was left sitting on the floor. Since Rav Kahana was greater in Torah than Rabbi Yochanan, they gave him his due honor. In those days they lived on cash, not credit, and if a bigger scholar came, he took over and became the *rosh yeshivah*."

Rabbi Chanina explained the death of his son Shivchas at a young age as punishment for cutting down a fig tree before its time (*Bava Kama* 91b).

"Really," said Rebbe, "he did not have enough merits to live, but in Heaven they would not take his life had it not been for the tree. In a similar vein, the Chofetz Chaim explains with a parable why theft causes someone to be judged more harshly than other sins: Someone once opened a store with money he borrowed from many different people. At first he did well, but then things turned against him and his business deteriorated steadily. Eventually his creditors came to collect their money, but he didn't have anything to give them. The creditors knew that if they didn't grab the inventory he had in the store, they might lose their whole investment. But they also hoped that business would pick up and they would recoup all their money.

"Finally an aggressive creditor came along and began to grab merchandise in payment of his debt. When the other creditors saw what was going on, they naturally followed suit and soon the store was out of business.

"Similarly, even though someone might have a lot of sins, these sins have pity on his soul and give him a chance to repent. But since theft is an act of such brazenness, its accusing angel is also brazen — measure for measure — and demands immediate retribution. Here too, Rabbi Chanina's son cut down a tree, and so the Satan was allowed to cut him down.

"This parable is hard for us to understand, since it's far removed from our world. Nowadays if someone goes under in business, he files for bankruptcy and tells all his creditors, 'Tough luck.' Next week he opens up again under a new name! In Europe, if a father went bankrupt it was the greatest embarrassment for his children and family. He was in debt for his whole life and there was even a special derogatory name for children whose father had gone bankrupt."

⋟⋞ ⋟⋞ ⋟⋞

"The *Gemara* (*Berachos* 39a) tells the story of a young scholar whose teacher gave him permission to eat in his presence. When the student said a blessing in his rebbe's presence, his rebbe told him that he should have asked which blessing to say before he ate. That *talmid* died within a year. Why? Because in those times their whole being was devoted to fulfilling the Torah. Everyone's life was like a business with no credit. If you couldn't pay for it, you had to return it. Maybe this will help us understand the severity of the punishment of the twenty-four-thousand students of Rabbi Akiva who did not honor one another sufficiently. Since they were so great, so much more was demanded from them."

"SOME PEOPLE'S VIRTUES are still in a latent state like a flower bud before it opens. Hashem tests them in order to actualize their

Tidbits on Spirituality potential, and when they pass the test they are like a beautiful flower in full bloom."

⋟⋞ ⋟⋞ ⋟⋞

Rebbe saw a former student carrying a baby and commented that just as a parent has pleasure from his baby's every action, so Hashem has pleasure from even the smallest growth in spirituality.

⋟⋞ ⋟⋞ ⋟⋞

A student once asked Reb Mendel how to prevail in the battle against the evil inclination. Answered Reb Mendel, "There is no surefire recipe. You have to be like a bird trapped in a room trying to escape. First it flies to one window. If that doesn't work, it flies to another one. The important thing is to keep trying until you find a way out."

⋟⋞ ⋟⋞ ⋟⋞

The Sages say that a person should always view himself as half virtuous and half guilty, so that just one more *mitzvah* or one more *aveirah* will tip the scales of judgment (*Kiddushin* 40b). Reb Mendel explained their statement with a *mashal*: "The Sages mean that every *mitzvah* or *aveirah* is like a drop of color added to a can of white paint. The individual drops do not remain as distinct entities but rather merge with the whole can and change its color. The same thing is true in the spiritual world. The Sages use an expression, 'The words entered him like a snake's venom' (*Bereishis Rabbah* 55:18), meaning that the message penetrated inside him and spread throughout his body. Good and evil acts also have the ability to affect a person's entire body. One must always recognize that whatever he does at any time will change his color."

ᔓᔓ ᔓᔓ ᔓᔓ

"A sin is like a piece of chewing gum stuck on a wooden floor. It bothers people as they walk by and just hangs around gathering more and more dirt. Only with a lot of scrubbing can you get it out."

ᔓᔓ ᔓᔓ ᔓᔓ

"Fighting the *yetzer hara* is like playing tennis; you knock it away and it comes right back at you. You can't let yourself be distracted for a moment. But if you keep on playing, in the end you'll win."

"HASHEM GAVE EACH ANIMAL its own particular means of survival. A squirrel, for example, has the ability to spring suddenly from a sitting position. But we humans can't do that. Our survival depends on using our intellect. Hashem gave us vast intellect, but the only way to perfect it is through Torah.

Using Your Head

"The *Chovos HaLevavos* writes that a person's first teacher is his native intellect, and then he graduates and moves up a level to his next teacher, the Torah. But in our times, our intellects have become enslaved by our passions, as in the German saying: 'My desires create my thoughts.' It should be the other way around. Only if we free our intellect from the domination of our desires can it be a good rebbe."

ᔓᔓ ᔓᔓ ᔓᔓ

Reb Mendel taught us to see how many considerations must underlie any action. Once during *shiur*, a *bachur's* notes fell out of his *Gemara* onto the floor. The *bachur* moved quickly to pick up his notes, causing a loud grating noise which disturbed the entire class. Reb Mendel asked him, "Do you think your *sheimos* are so important that you can disturb the whole *shiur*?"

Later the same day, another boy also dropped his notes. Remembering the earlier incident, he simply ignored the notes which had fallen off his desk. Reb Mendel rebuked him, "What, you don't think the Torah is important enough to pick it up off the floor?"

s➤ s➤ s➤

Reb Mendel once commented about bright people who often seem oblivious to the needs of others, "Regarding their own needs they're as clever as foxes, but when it comes to the concerns of others, they're as foolish as cats."

How then can someone determine if his actions are pure and correct? The *Mishnah* (*Avos* 2:1) says, "What is the proper path a man should choose for himself? Whatever is pleasant for him and pleasant for other people as well." Reb Mendel explained the *Mishnah* as follows: "If you're in doubt as to whether what you're doing is proper, ask a friend if he approves of your actions. A friend who isn't swayed by what is prejudicing you can often see things in a clearer perspective."

Torah Is Great, for it Leads to Action

"IT'S A NICE CUSTOM TO LEARN LATE AT NIGHT, but not if it will make it hard for you to get up to *daven* in the morning. The *Yerushalmi* (*Berachos* 1:2) says that if someone learns Torah but does not put it into practice, it would have been better if he had never come into the world. This isn't a curse, but a simple fact. A fetus is taught the whole Torah before it is born, and the only reason it comes here at all is to act on what it has learned. Therefore if it does not act on what it has learned, it would have been better not to have come into the world at all and to have remained with all the souls up in Heaven."

"REB ELCHONON WAS CAREFUL to observe every *halachah* to the letter. Over the course of time, the Baranovich Yeshivah accu-

A Gadol —
Living Halachah

mulated many debts. Just to provide its students with the barest necessities, Reb Elchonon was forced to go to America for more than a year to raise money for the yeshivah. Despite returning to Baranovich late at night after an arduous trip, he was at the butcher shop by six o'clock the next morning. The surprised butcher asked him why he rushed over so soon after returning. Reb Elchonon answered that since, thank G-d, he had succeeded in raising money in America, the first thing he wanted to do was to pay off his debts. Before attending to the many other pressing matters that had accumulated in his absence, he went around to all the shopkeepers in town paying the yeshivah's bills."

§► §► §►

"At the outbreak of World War II in Europe there were hardly any private telephones. Just to make a simple telephone call you had to go to the post office. The Baranovich Yeshivah was then located in a small village many miles from Vilna with no post office. To make a call you had to first take a bus to the nearest town and then a train to Vilna. The Communists didn't let yeshivah boys use the buses so we had to make the slow trip by horse and buggy. Boys went through this trouble just to say a few words to their families. Once the baker gave us his driver and horse and buggy on the condition that only three people would ride in it at a time. So Reb Elchonon sat in the front, while I sat in the back with another student.

"On the way, we passed a young *bachur* who was walking on the road, and the driver stopped to pick him up. The *bachur* explained that the baker's wife had been touched by the sad look on his face and had told him to walk ahead on the road in the hope of hitching a ride in her husband's wagon.

"As we continued on our way, Reb Elchonon grew restless and began muttering to himself, 'I don't know how we can do this — how is it allowed?' We overheard him and explained to him that the baker's wife had told the *bachur* he could get a ride with us, but he brushed this aside, saying, 'It's not her wagon to give us permission.'

"One of us said, 'Yes, but if the owner had seen the boy on the road himself, he would certainly have picked him up.' To this, Reb Elchonon replied that we cannot presume another's mind. When the boy saw that Reb Elchonon didn't think he was allowed to ride with us, he jumped off the wagon and walked the rest of the way to town.

"Reb Elchonon then told us a story about the Chofetz Chaim. Once he was heard moaning, 'What's going to be with me in Heaven because of the *sefarim* I sold to people that contained misprints? Do you think this is a petty case? No! It's a matter of FIRE!" Even though the Chofetz Chaim hired people to check his *sefarim* for mistakes, he was still scared that there would be complaints in Heaven that he hadn't checked them himself. It didn't matter that his intention in writing his works was to serve the public; because he took money for them, he was afraid.

"Incidentally, after the boy jumped off, Reb Elchonon began to worry for the boy's safety, since the local peasants might throw stones at him. The happy outcome was that we just missed our train and had to wait another few hours for the next one, during which time the boy arrived. Reb Elchonon was very relieved to see that he was safe. Then we all traveled together to Vilna."

ז־ ז־ ז־

Reb Mendel used to relate the following story with awe and enthusiasm. Just after the War, the Satmar Rebbe visited Chicago and stayed at the home of a wealthy man. Later, the Rebbe made a *shidduch* for his host's daughter, but the marriage ended in divorce. The next time the Satmar Rebbe had reason to come to Chicago, he was afraid that his former host would feel uncomfortable if he were to stay with him again. On the other hand, he knew it would cause the man embarrassment if he stayed anywhere else. In the end, he decided not to go to Chicago at all, even though he had an important reason to be there. This shows how careful the Satmar Rebbe was in observing the *halachah* that a traveler should not change his place of lodging (*Arachin* 16b).

"YOU CAN'T FEEL THE SPECIAL QUALITY of a *sefer* by holding it in your hands. You have to study it first. *Tefillin,* however, are a gift from Hashem, and con-

The Power of Tefillin

vey a special power by just having the words rest on your hands and head. Wearing them gives us the ability to see into the World to Come. If you wonder how this can be, consider that your eyes, which are nothing more than balls of gel, can see to the end of the horizon. It should be no wonder, then, that *tefillin* can let you see in the World to Come."

REB MENDEL USED TO SAY with great awe, "*Tehillim* — it's a wonder a human being actually wrote them!

The Power of Tehillim

"When you say *Tehillim*, your heart has to melt and break. At the beginning of World War II, Rav Zalman Sorotzkin of Lutsk managed to get across a border to safety together with his wife, while the Brisker Rav had to leave his wife behind. When the Brisker Rav's son asked him why the Lutsker Rav had been able to sneak his wife out with him while he couldn't, the Brisker Rav answered, 'What the Lutsker Rav can accomplish with his *Tehillim*, I can't do with my Torah.' "

"WHENEVER REB ELCHONON HAD GUESTS in his house, he made a point of learning Torah with them, saying that part of the

On Hachnasas Orchim

mitzvah of taking in guests is to learn with them."

A *bachur* who was spending Shabbos at a yeshivah in Brooklyn asked Reb Mendel whether he should accept an invitation to someone's home for a Shabbos meal or eat in the yeshivah where he would be able to return to his learning sooner. Reb Mendel answered that it is part of the *mitzvah* of *hachnasas orchim* to be a guest and enable other people to fulfill the *mitzvah*.

"THERE IS A CUSTOM not to remove anything from the house of a mourner. Once, in Chicago, I paid a condolence call to the family of a rabbi with whom I had been very close. There I saw a

On Comforting Mourners

sefer I had been unable to locate for a long time. Since the children were not very religious and were unlikely to use the *sefarim* anyway, I asked the son if I could have the *sefer*. The son said nothing but gave me a funny look.

"It was at that moment that I understood the reason for the custom not to take anything from a house of mourning. When you visit a mourner, you have to go for no reason other than to offer comfort and consolation. If you have any other motive, you cannot fulfill the *mitzvah* properly and the mourner feels it. The son sensed that I had something other than his feelings on my mind."

REB MENDEL TAUGHT US that each *Yom Tov* is capable of leaving a lasting effect for the entire year to come. Someone once asked Rebbe during Pesach, "How is your **Yom Tov** Pesach?" He answered, "I won't be able to tell you that until next year. All I can tell you now is how last Pesach was."

Yet the spiritual benefits of a *Yom Tov* were not something that one acquired automatically. At the end of one *Yom Tov*, Reb Mendel remarked to a visitor from another yeshivah, "Well, *Yom Tov* is nearly over already. It's sad that it's ending."

The visitor replied, "Our *rosh yeshivah* taught us to say that we've added a *Yom Tov* to our account."

Reb Mendel quipped back, "If you really did, then so much the better, but how can you be sure?"

Knowing that the influence of a *Yom Tov* lingers over the course of a whole year, we must be especially careful to guard its sanctity.

Reb Mendel once told us, "When I was in the wine business, an I.R.S. agent once came to my house on Succos and I offered him some very good food. He told me, 'You know, I like your holidays. There's a holiday for blintzes, a holiday for kreplach and a holiday for latkes.' That was his idea of a *Yom Tov*.

"Today people think that one *Yom Tov* is for trips, another one for concerts and so on. Chanukah has become a jolly time, especially since it coincides with the Santa Claus business. For this reason, if it were up to me I would place it instead between Rosh Hashanah and Yom Kippur. *Chochmah U'Mussar* compares the *mitzvah* of lighting the *menorah* on Chanukah to tying a ribbon around your finger as a reminder of something important. The purpose of Chanukah is to remind us of Hashem's kindness and greatness. But merely performing the external actions is like tying a ribbon without any idea of what it was intended to remind you of."

"JUST LIKE WATER CLEANS FLOORS, so too the waters of a *mikveh* clean a person's soul from impurities that have become

On Purity
attached to it. The holy works say that one is elevated (*misaleh*) by going in a *mikveh*. Really this means that he becomes nullified (as in the Mishnaic expression *oleh b'echad u'meah* — nullified by being diluted in a hundred parts). If you nullify your body through immersing yourself in the *mikveh*, you become pure.

"There are other forms of immersion as well. The *Rambam* (*Mikvaos* 11:12) says that someone who immerses himself in the wisdom of Torah also becomes pure.

"Learning on Friday afternoon is a greater preparation for Shabbos than shaving and showering. Torah is a *misnagdishe mikveh*. If you also want to clean yourself you can go to the *mikveh*, but if you contaminate your body by running after physical pleasures, the *mikveh* won't do anything for you. You'll leave it exactly the way you came in.

"There is still another form of immersion. The interior of a person is also compared to water, as Shlomo HaMelech says, *Deep waters are in the heart of man, and an understanding person will draw them out* (*Mishlei* 20:5). Each person has to draw out what's inside himself. Rabbeinu Yonah writes that this is the meaning of Hillel's saying, 'If I'm here, everything is here.' All we have to do is bring out our true inner selves; once we do this, nothing else is lacking. In order to bring out our true essence, we have to first nullify the superficialities of our physical personalities.

"A person is supposed to tell his body, 'Shut up, body!' and then his *neshamah* will come out."[1]

WHEN REB MENDEL would see a one-year-old baby he would comment: "*Chazal* say that Shaul HaMelech at thirty was like a

Purity of Innocence
one-year-old in innocence (*Yoma* 22b). Look at a baby's face. That look does not remain for long. By the time a baby is two, it already doesn't have the same innocence as a one-year-old." Reb Mendel was told that a biography was written about a natural healer who was able

---

1. Some commentators interpret this concept as the meaning of R' Shimon ben Gamliel's statement in *Avos* 1:17.

to look into a person's eyes and see his ailments as well as his personality. When asked who had the most interesting eyes he ever

saw, the healer, a non-Jew, answered, "The Grand Rabbi of Satmar. The Rabbi's family asked me to see him in order that I prescribe a diet for him, so I looked into his eyes. I have never seen such pure eyes in my entire life." Reb Mendel corrected, "Not 'pure' eyes; in the Rebbe of Satmar he saw the eyes of a child."

Reb Mendel with a great-grandson

The Jewish People — Strong Even After a Crash

"IN THE NEWSPAPERS we see so many pictures of auto accidents that you'd think nobody ever reaches their destination. But the truth is that most of the time cars don't crash. The same is true of the Jewish people: the Torah lists their faults, but most of the time our people haven't had 'accidents.'

"If I wanted to buy a new car, I wouldn't care so much how it looks in the showroom; I'd want to see what happens to it after a crash. If it still looks like a car, then it's for me. Before Yitzchak blessed Yaakov, he first wanted to know how his children would look — not when they were being righteous, but how they would hold out after a crash.

"The *Midrash* says that Yitzchak had a vision of someone named Yosi from Shisha, a turncoat who defected to the Romans at the time of the destruction of the Second Temple. When the Romans came to destroy the *Beis HaMikdash*, they were afraid to enter. Instead they asked for a Jewish volunteer to first defile the Holy Temple and promised that he could keep whatever vessel he brought out. Yosi of Shisha betrayed his people — he entered the *Beis HaMikdash* and took out the *Menorah*.

"The Romans objected, 'It is not seemly for a commoner to use such a vessel. Go again, and this time whatever you take you may keep.'

"This time, however, Yosi refused to return. So the Romans offered to give him all the taxes of the city for three years if he went back. Still he refused, saying, 'It's enough that I have angered my G-d once; should I anger Him a second time?'

"This reply infuriated the Romans and they tortured Yosi to death. As he was dying, he cried out, 'Woe to me that I have angered my Creator!'

"When Yitzchak saw that this was how even the traitors among the Jews would act, he knew he could give Yaakov his blessings."

CHAPTER THIRTEEN

Emunah

"THERE'S NOTHING IN CREATION that *has* to be the way it is. My Rebbe told me that even the fact that objects take up space is only because the Creator made the world to be like that. He could just as easily have made a world in which objects don't occupy space, just as the *Aron* did not take up any space in the Holy of Holies. My nephew the physicist tells me that in physics they talk about an object that can be here and not here — two opposites at the same time. That is like what I've said."

It Ain't Necessarily So

"ALTHOUGH OUR ACTIONS may emulate the traits of Hashem, our actions do not really possess His true traits. Just as Hashem is infinite, so too are His traits, and we can never come to comprehend their essence. This is like a motorized doll that a person can make. Even if he makes it sense objects so that it doesn't bump into them, will that doll ever be able to understand why the human being made it? So too, even though we can have mercy on something, it's impossible to understand His attribute of mercy."

Beyond Comprehension

"THE *GEMARA* SAYS Acheir (Elisha ben Avuyah) did not repent because he heard a Divine voice proclaim, 'Everyone may repent,

Teshuvah — Coming Back Home

with the exception of Acheir.' The *Shelah* writes that this was a mistake on his part; he should have ignored the Divine message and repented anyway.

"I once gave my young son a good spanking and he ran away from the house. Before long, however, he returned home, since there was nowhere else in the world for him to go. So too, nothing in the world is true except Hashem and His Torah — so eventually you have to come back to Him.

"I was on a subway in New York and I saw a man literally kick a woman friend out the doors of the train. The woman was crying bitterly, and she jumped back onto the train through a different door and grabbed his leg. The man was trying to kick her off but she continued to cling to his leg. She had no existence beyond him, and eventually he had no choice but to accept her back."

"Listen to a parable that someone fifty years older than you is trying to teach you, and maybe in fifty years you'll also come to think the same way."

S➤ S➤ S➤

SOMEONE ONCE ASKED R' MENDEL where he was a teacher. He replied that he taught at the Philadelphia Yeshivah. The person

There's Only One Boss

said, "Oh, you work for Rabbi Kamenetzky?"

"No," Reb Mendel answered, "we both work for the same Boss."

Once Reb Mendel pulled into a service station to fill up his gas tank and for no apparent reason the young attendant told him to turn the car around and go to another pump. Rebbe asked him why, and the attendant replied, "The boss says so."

Pointing up to heaven, Reb Mendel said, "There is only one Boss," and drove away.

WHEN REB MENDEL was preparing to leave Chicago and move to New York, there were no available teaching positions there, so

Placing Ourselves in Hashem's Hands

he decided to reestablish his wine business in New York. After a long search he found a winemaker who was going out of business, and bought several enormous wooden vats for hundreds of dollars. He and his family then spent nearly a week dismantling and transporting the vats to the basement of an apartment building where he had received permission to store the wood. Reb Mendel then returned to Chicago to continue saying his *shiur* until the end of the term. On his next visit to New York, some months later, Reb Mendel went to check on the vats and discovered to his surprise that they had disappeared.

In the courtyard of the building, he found a large wooden hut constructed from what was unmistakably the thick wooden slats of his wine vats. His children were outraged by the theft, but Reb Mendel gestured with his hand as if to say, "Forget it," and returned home without a word of complaint, despite the fact that he was now unable to resume his wine business and had no other means of supporting his family.

Thirty years later, he reflected on that episode. "I have to thank Hashem for what happened to my vats. Who knows, if it weren't for that, I might have wound up as a winemaker and not continued teaching Torah."

୨୨ ୨୨ ୨୨

Just before his daughter's *chupah*, which was scheduled to take place in the Bronx, Reb Mendel made one last run to Brooklyn to pick up guests. On the way, he encountered a massive traffic jam which added nearly an hour and a half to his trip. When he finally reached the wedding hall, his son noticed how relaxed he looked, and asked him how he had been able to remain so calm while he was stalled in traffic, knowing that he was delaying the wedding. Reb Mendel made a motion as if he were unscrewing an imaginary radiator cap on the side of his waist and replied, "I opened the valve and let out the steam."

His son explained later, "The safety valve was his *bitachon*. He would always say, 'I am Yours and my aspirations are in Your hands.[1] We are all in Your hands — and they are good hands.' "

୨୨ ୨୨ ୨୨

---

1. From the supplications accompanying the Priestly Blessings of the Festivals.

No matter what difficulties he encountered in life, his unwavering faith enabled him to remain calm and to transmit joy to those around him. He remained by himself in Chicago one winter after his family had moved to New York. When he joined them for Pesach, he taught them a song he had composed based on the verse (*Yirmiyahu* 6:16), *So said Hashem, 'Stand on the roads and see and ask which is the good road, and go on it and find tranquillity for your soul.'* Years later, the boys in his *shiur* would come to his home on Purim and ask him to sing that song. Usually he told them, "This song is for older men, not young people."

During the period he was separated from his family, Reb Mendel used to compose melodies for verses from *Tanach* relating to *bitachon*. On the long drive between Chicago and New York, he often sang these melodies.

LATE ONE NIGHT the Rebbetzin was sitting in a chair holding an infant grandchild when the telephone rang. As she carried the

Hashem Guards His Loved Ones

baby across the room to answer the call, a large chunk of the ceiling came crashing down onto the exact place she had just left! She lifted the receiver to hear Reb Mendel asking anxiously if everything was all right. Astonished, she told him about the miracle that had saved her life that very moment and asked him how he knew he should call just then. Reb Mendel replied that he had fallen asleep and had dreamt that a lion was about to leap out of the ceiling. He awoke from his nightmare and rushed to the telephone to make sure everyone was safe at home.

§► §► §►

Once, a gentile family moved in down the street from the Kaplan home in Bensonhurst. The neighbors were all frightened of them, as they had a reputation for being violent people. Shortly after moving in, they began harassing the Kaplan family and caused hundreds of dollars worth of damage to the Kaplan's home. One gentile neighbor who was on friendly terms with the Rebbetzin informed her who had caused the trouble and asked what she planned to do. The Rebbetzin replied, "I won't do anything," and then added, pointing upwards, "He'll take care of them." The neighbor repeated to the other family what Mrs. Kaplan had said.

Some months later, the mother in the family started screaming at the Rebbetzin, "Witch! Witch!" Only later did the Rebbetzin learn that from the time that the family had started to harass the Kaplans they had been plagued with nothing but tragedy. The girl who had knocked out their windows was killed in an automobile accident, her older brother lost an eye in a fight, another brother was sent to prison and the father became very sick from the whole ordeal. The family soon moved away and was never heard from again.

Beyond the Laws of Nature

VARIOUS LEGENDS CIRCULATED AMONG STUDENTS at the yeshivah of Reb Mendel's extraordinary abilities. Often his cryptic remarks left all those who knew him filled with wonder.

After *davening* one Sunday morning, Reb Mendel raced over to Mr. Shalom Esrig and told him that his *tefillin* were not kosher. Mr. Esrig was dumbfounded since his *tefillin* had just been checked by a *sofer*. But he took Reb Mendel's advice and had them checked by another *sofer*. The second *sofer* found an error that had been overlooked in the earlier examination.

S➤ S➤ S➤

For a period of time, Reb Mendel was limited to a diet that consisted mainly of avocados and lemons. His grandson Yechiel Mordechai wondered how someone could eat such unappetizing foods. Seeing his grandson's expression, Reb Mendel coaxed him into trying the mixture.

"I hate avocados!" replied the grandson.

"Try it anyway," said Reb Mendel. "If Hashem made something, you shouldn't say you hate it. Perhaps you could say you dislike something, but not that you hate it." After much effort, Reb Mendel finally succeeded in convincing his grandson to try the combination, and after tasting some, the grandson admitted that it was not as bad as he had expected. Reb Mendel commented, "Yes, it's a sophisticated flavor, and in time you'll get to like it." Then he added, "There will come a time that you'll be in a yeshivah far away, and you won't have anything to eat. Then you'll eat avocado and lemon." At the time, Yechiel Mordechai gave little thought to his grandfather's cryptic remark.

Reb Mendel with Yechiel Mordechai
at Camp Ohr Shraga

Five years later Yechiel Mordechai was in a yeshivah run by the Lakewood Kollel in Melbourne, Australia. Late one night, he went to the kitchen to look for something to eat. The refrigerator and all the cupboards were bare.

As he headed up the stairs to his room, Yechiel Mordechai heard a knock on the door below. Wondering who it could be so late at night, he went down and opened the door to find a member of the community who wanted to give the bachurim some fruits he had left over from a party he had made that evening. Yechiel Mordechai opened the box and found that it contained nothing but avocados. Disappointed, he put it in the refrigerator and went back upstairs.

Five minutes later there was another knock on the door. This time it was a rebbe from the yeshivah who said his children had picked the lemon tree in their backyard that day and wanted to give some to the boys in yeshivah. Yechiel Mordechai had a vague recollection that the two fruits made a good combination, so he sat down and had the late-night snack for which he had been looking.

Only after he finished enjoying the avocados with lemon did he remember his grandfather's mysterious remark five years earlier.

S๖ S๖ S๖

Three years after Reb Mendel passed away, a former student decided to leave full-time yeshivah study temporarily in order to complete a Torah project he had undertaken. Shortly after starting the project, Reb Mendel appeared to him in a dream and told him, "You *must* spend more time learning Torah."

"Rebbe, please tell me what they're saying about me in Heaven," he pleaded.

At this Reb Mendel simply smiled and said, "These questions you're not allowed to ask." The dream ended and he woke up. The next day he related this dream to Reb Mendel's son and discussed what he should do. In the end, he decided to continue working on the project, but also to learn for several more hours each day.

A few days later, he was in the passenger seat of a car turning left at a busy intersection when an oncoming car crashed into the car he was in. Although the front end of the car was crushed like an accordion, he miraculously suffered only a few fractured bones. Had the collision occurred a mere fraction of a second later, the point of impact would have been just where he was sitting!

Reflecting on this experience, he was grateful for Reb Mendel's warning to increase his merits through Torah study, but wondered whether the accident might have been completely averted had he taken the advice more seriously and returned to full-time learning. As David HaMelech says of a *tzaddik* (*Tehillim* 34:21), *He protects all his bones, not even one of them was broken.*

On Eretz Yisrael and the Beis HaMikdash

"YERUSHALAYIM WAS CALLED 'the joy of all the earth' (*Tehillim* 48:3). To what can this be compared? Imagine a city in which sick or crippled people went to sleep at night and woke up perfectly strong and healthy. Wouldn't masses flock to this city? A sin is a lot worse than being sick or deformed. And what did *bnei Yisrael* do? They came to *Yerushalayim*, brought a sacrifice in the Temple, spent the night there and the following day would return home beautifully cleansed of sin."

S๖ S๖ S๖

'When the Jews first entered *Eretz Yisrael*, a lottery was held to distribute the land, and the parcel each person received in that lottery was exactly the plot of land that was meant for him. Each piece of land in *Eretz Yisrael* was custom tailored to the spiritual level and nature of the person for whom it was designated. Reuven couldn't live on Chaim's land or vice versa.

"The *Kuzari* explains why we say that the *Shechinah* rests in Jerusalem even though Hashem's glory fills the entire world. While it's true that every part of the human body is alive, only the face shows emotion, and *Eretz Yisrael* is the 'face' of the world.

Reb Chaim Wysokar, zt"l

"If someone is holy, then he can be buried in *Eretz Yisrael*, but if he isn't, the *Yerushalmi* says that the land complains, 'Why do you defile me?' Yet today they make a business out of burying people there.

"The *Chazon Ish* rarely went up to Jerusalem — perhaps because he was embarrassed to go. Now people go to *Eretz Yisrael* for a vacation like they go to Florida. Reb Chaim Wysokar[2] once visited *Eretz Yisrael* and went to the *Kosel HaMaaravi*. When he was about to return to America, he was asked why he didn't go back to the *Kosel* one last time. He answered, 'I don't want to lose the feeling I had the first time I saw it.'

"If you go to the *Kosel* with a flashlight, you can look down and see how many layers of stone there are embedded in the ground. Why did the foundation have to be so deep? Because the *Beis HaMikdash* isn't a building in the normal sense of the word.

---

2. One of the outstanding scholars in the Mirrer Yeshivah in Europe who later was head of Yeshivah Beis HaTalmud in Brooklyn. He was a *mussar* giant whom Reb Mendel greatly respected, saying of him, *"Bai em is noch a rainer vinkel* — He still has a pure corner," referring to his unrelenting honesty and adherence to the teachings of *mussar*.

Whenever we try to make it into one, it gets taken away from us. It is deeply rooted into the ground to show how deeply rooted it is in the hearts of our people.

"Shlomo HaMelech said, *I see slaves riding on horses, and officers walking on the ground* (*Koheles* 10:7). *Chazal* tell us that this passage refers to the time when Nevuchadnetzar would come and destroy the *Beis HaMikdash*. They say that when he destroyed it, he was riding a horse and the angel Gavriel came and led him into the Holy of Holies: Nevuchadnetzar was the slave riding on the horse, and Gavriel was the officer leading him. How could our good friend Gavriel do such a thing? Because it was no longer the *Beis HaMikdash*. At that time it was only a building. The *Beis HaMikdash* isn't a building — it's the heart of the Jewish people.

"When *Chazal* said that the city of Betar was destroyed because of a chicken and a rooster (*Gittin* 35b), the chicken was only the spark. The people's sins had grown so great that it needed just one spark to start a conflagration."

THE DAY FOLLOWING the death of Reb Elchonon's grandson, Reb Elchonon Meir Wasserman, Rebbe came to *shiur* looking unusually haggard. Rebbe had shared the

On Suffering

family's burden throughout the young man's illness, as if he were a member of Rebbe's own family. That day Rebbe ended the *shiur* earlier than usual and made a few remarks about the sad occasion:

". . . He passed away yesterday, and his whole family — including his uncle, Rabbi Simcha Wasserman, as well as his mother and sister — accompanied his remains to *Eretz Yisrael*. They didn't go for the sake of making a big funeral, as you might think. They went simply because they couldn't bring themselves to leave him. He was like a magnet; he had a soul that was out of this world, and they couldn't bring themselves to part from him. He sparkled with the qualities of Reb Elchonon — so many of them. I have to go now as I'm tired, but first I'll relate to you a thought from the *Daas Tevunos*, which will be good for me to hear as well.

"Hashem didn't create people to make trouble for them, Heaven forbid. He created people to give them enjoyment and goodness. Had Adam HaRishon done what he was supposed to do, Hashem's ultimate plan would have been fulfilled at the very beginning. But Adam didn't do what he should have, and for the next six thousand years we have the task of sterilizing ourselves. After his sin, what could have been accomplished in one day now has to take six thousand years. It's just like at a large convention, there are many meetings going on in different rooms but they're all interconnected and directed towards a common goal. So too the Creator arranges everything that happens in the world towards one goal, the goal that Adam could have accomplished by himself. Everything in the world is part of one long process. There are no new accounts being opened, and Hashem has His reasons for everything He does."

S➤ S➤ S➤

On another occasion, Rebbe discussed with us Iyov's complaint that people seem to undergo a lot of undeserved suffering. The *Ramban*, he said, answers that much of the inexplicable suffering in the world enables people to correct the damage caused by their sins in previous lives.

"In Czarist Russia they used to take Jewish children away from their homes to serve in the army for many years. At the time many people wondered why these children were made to suffer so. Many never married after their service was over and they had great difficulty reintegrating themselves into the community.

"The Chofetz Chaim explained to Reb Elchonon that in the time of Gideon, during the period of the Judges, many Jews served idols. In order to give them a chance of winning a place in the World to Come, Hashem sent them back to earth in another incarnation and gave them the opportunity to prove their devotion to Judaism under trying conditions such as those in the Czar's army. From this we see that sometimes Hashem can carry someone's sin on account, so to speak, for thousands of years until He arranges a way for the sins to be rectified."

ONE PESACH, a student visited Reb Mendel in his home. After serving his visitor some nuts and homemade wine, Reb Mendel

Redemption in the Midst of Exile

asked, "Pesach is a time of redemption. How can we feel redemption if our brethren are suffering so much in *Eretz Yisrael* and other places around the world?"

In answer, he referred to the description of Hashem in the second blessing of *Shemoneh Esrei*: *The King Who causes death and restores life and makes salvation flourish.* "Why did the Sages who composed this prayer see fit to include a blessing about the fact that Hashem causes death? The answer is that death is necessary to prepare the body for the 'restoring of life,' which will come at the time of the resurrection of the dead. Thus we bless Hashem even for causing death.

"In comparison to the resurrection and eternal life, the period of death is totally negligible, as David HaMelech says (*Tehillim* 126:1), *When Hashem will return the captivity of Zion, we will be like dreamers.* The *Rishonim* say that this means our joy in the salvation will be so great that all the persecutions we've suffered in the centuries of exile will seem like no more than a dream. While someone is dreaming, he thinks his dream is actually happening. But after he wakes up, he sees that it was all nothing. So too the redemption will be so great that the exile we're in now will seem like it was all a dream."

❧ ❧ ❧

Reb Mendel's deep faith in Hashem did not lessen his acute sensitivity to the suffering of others. During the recitation of the story of the Ten Martyrs on Yom Kippur, he would become so overwrought with emotion at times that he had to leave the *beis midrash* to continue his *davening* outside. Yet he would sometimes say, "When we hear the story of the Ten Martyrs we cry, but the *Midrash* relates that for the martyrs themselves it was like a parade, a cause for great celebration."

"Everything in creation has an outer facet and an inner facet, including people and even the Torah. With all its good and evil, the world seems to be getting more mixed up and chaotic. Yet *Daas Tevunos* explains that all this is part of Hashem's direct plan leading to the end of days, when He will reveal how He has guided all the events of history. To give an analogy, we know that scientists studying the ocean discovered a current of warm water flowing in its own path in the midst of the ocean's turmoil!"

❧ ❧ ❧

"*Daas Tevunos* gives us a way of understanding the death of the Ten Martyrs. All the suffering in the world has to happen in order to complete Hashem's plan for the fulfillment of creation. The *Gemara* (*Bava Metzia* 85a) relates that the suffering of R' Yehudah HaNasi was the result of an incident in which he failed to show compassion for a calf that had escaped from a butcher. His suffering was destined to come about, but it needed an action to bring it on. I feel the same way about the great destruction [the Holocaust]; all that suffering had to happen to fulfill Hashem's ultimate plan of creation."

Although the *Daas Tevunos* discusses this deep and complex subject at great length, Rebbe merely wished to tell us that the only way to fathom the dimension of the destruction is to have faith in the ways of Hashem, ways which limited mortals cannot fathom.

The Jews who spent World War II in Shanghai had little idea what was going on in Europe, until suddenly one day the news came that all their families had been killed, and everyone was in a state of shock. Reb Mendel recalled that what brought him back to his senses was the thought that "nowhere in the Torah does it say that I have to understand what the Creator does."

s➤ s➤ s➤

Reb Mendel held in awe anyone who had survived the concentration camps with his faith intact. Whenever he met such people, he would ask them how they had accomplished such a feat.

A STUDENT IN THE *SHIUR* was named Streicher, but Reb Mendel always called him "Estreicher." He told the class that he

On the Holocaust

mispronounced his name deliberately: "It hurts me to call him Streicher, the name of one of the most horrible of the S.S. murderers. It pains me too much to call him by that name ..."

Reb Mendel felt so much anguish in connection with the Holocaust that he rarely talked about it. One day, twenty minutes before the end of *shiur*, a *bachur* brought up the topic. When Reb Mendel opened his mouth to answer him, his voice broke on the first word. He tried several times to speak, but could not get out even one word. Finally, he stood up and left the room for the remainder of the period. He was unable to return to continue the *shiur*.

The first time Reb Mendel had to teach the tractate *Bava Kama* in Chicago, he would occasionally shed a tear during *shiur*. The students did not understand what was bothering him. Finally one boy mustered his courage and asked what Rebbe found so depressing about that particular *masechta*. Reb Mendel answered that learning the *masechta* reminded him of the rebbe from whom he had learned it as a child. At the beginning of the war, when this teacher was taken away to a concentration camp, he fought with the Nazis to allow him to take his *Gemara Bava Kama* along.

$$S \triangleright \ S \triangleright \ S \triangleright$$

Every year on Purim, Reb Elchonon used to retell the famous story of the exorcism of a *dybbuk*, in which he had been personally involved. One year, however, he stopped telling the story. Reb Mendel explained that Reb Elchonon realized the extent to which Hashem was concealing His presence in the world during the period leading up to World War II. He considered it inappropriate to bring up a story that so clearly demonstrated Hashem's direct role in the world at such a time.

"One of the *kinos* we say on Tishah B'Av contrasts the glory of the Jews on their Exodus from Egypt with the degradation they suffered when they were banished from Jerusalem. One great thinker explained that the Exodus showed that there is an Omnipotent Power Who controls the world, and the exile from Jerusalem showed the role of that Power just as clearly. So did the destruction in Europe. After the redemption we will see that everything Hashem does, even when He metes out justice, is done with total righteousness. But meanwhile, we're like small children ...

"In the Mirrer Yeshivah in Europe I studied with the author of the *Yonas Aylem*, an older *bachur* who was considered to be the best student of all the yeshivos in Europe. The *mashgiach* asked him to learn with me for one term, and the next term he chose to learn with me on his own, and that made me feel great. He was killed by the Germans in the war.

"The prophet says that everything the gentiles took away from us will be restored. *Chazal* say that this promise refers to the martyrdom of Rabbi Akiva and his colleagues. *Chazal* are referring to *everything* — even the Torah that was lost will be returned at the time of the redemption.

"During the war a Jew was less safe in the street than an animal. Did you ever see how a bug, when he comes out of his hole, runs around nervously until he finds another hole and then hides in it as quickly as possible? The Jews in Europe had even less security than that. When I walk in Boro Park, I feel good because I see all the restoration that has occurred. And just like Hashem has restored this much, the day will come when He will restore everything else the Jewish people had, physically as well as spiritually."

CHAPTER FOURTEEN

The World of Mussar

THE GOAL OF *MUSSAR*, Reb Mendel taught, is not to make people into saints, but into human beings. "You don't have **A Mentsch** to be a *tzaddik*," he would say, "you have to be a *mentsch*. The *Rambam* says this explicitly at the end of *Hilchos Shmittah V'Yovel*: ' ... not only the tribe of Levi, but any human being ... who desires to know Hashem and go on the straight path as Hashem intended when He created him...'

"In my teachers I saw only *mentschlichkeit*, not *tzidkus*. If you can see someone's piety visibly gushing from him, that's proof that he hasn't yet become a truly straight and righteous person. It's possible to be a *tzaddik* and still not be a *mentsch*."

Reb Mendel once said of someone he knew that he had "lost control of his steering wheel." For him this was the opposite of a *mentsch*, whose distinguishing characteristic is his mastery over himself, over his baser nature and his weaknesses.

৯ ৯ ৯

"The *Midrash* relates that the Greeks indicted Rabbi Yosi Ben Yoezer for observing the Torah and *mitzvos* and sentenced him to death. When they took him out to be executed, his nephew — who was an apostate — followed behind on a horse (in those days riding a horse was a mark of distinction, like a limousine today), and said to Rabbi Yosi, 'Look at the difference between us. You are being led to your death for keeping the Torah, while I, who am unobservant, live a life of honor and pleasure.'

"Replied his uncle, 'If a life of pleasure like yours is the way Hashem rewards those who rebel against Him, how much more will He reward those who heed His will?'

"But Hashem has no greater servant than you, and look where you are headed,' the nephew retorted.

"Rabbi Yosi answered, 'If this is the way He punishes someone who follows His will, how much more so will He punish those who rebel against Him.'

"These words penetrated the nephew's soul like a snake's venom, and he immediately inflicted on himself all four forms of death which *beis din* could have imposed. Just one incisive comment was enough to make him repent totally!

"We see what a *mentsch* the nephew was from the way he changed his life from one truthful statement. Reb Itzele Peterburger once met Reb Yosef Yoizl Horowitz, who was in business at the time, and asked him why he didn't return to learning Torah. Reb Yosef Yoizel replied, 'What will I live with?' Reb Itzele answered immediately, 'What will you die with?' This question made such an impression on Reb Yosef Yoizl that he returned to learning and eventually became the Alter of Novardhok."

৯ ৯ ৯

While Reb Mendel used the term *mentsch* to describe a person who was genuinely capable of growing and changing himself, he generally used the term *tzaddik* to refer to someone whose piety was only superficial. "Today we don't know what a true *tzaddik* is," he once said. "What we see nowadays isn't piety, it's just style." He was particularly wary of *bachurim* who excelled at acts of piety. He told us about a former Communist who repented of his earlier ways and came to learn at the Mirrer Yeshivah in Europe. At first this *bachur* would fast frequently, *daven* excessively long, and engage in other forms of extreme behavior. As time went on, however, his self-imposed acts of piety began to decrease. When another student told Reb Yeruchem Levovitz about these changes, Reb Yeruchem replied, "The worse he gets (i.e., the less he makes a show of his piety), the better he gets."

Reb Mendel's point was that jumping to higher levels before mastering basic *mentschlichkeit* can only lead to failure.

"SOME PEOPLE GO AROUND COLLECTING MONEY with the attitude, 'You have to give me money because I'm the cream of

True Piety, False Piety

the world and you're nothing. The only way you'll ever have any merit is by giving me your money.' They feel that they're doing you a favor by taking your money.

"*Nu*, this attitude is also a kindness from Hashem. Normally it's hard for a Jew to ask others for money, but these people enjoy it as if it's a sport, a form of hunting, and that's a kindness from Hashem.

"When someone gives you *tzedakah* money, you shouldn't say, '*Tizku l'mitzvos*' but rather, 'Thank you,' to show that you appreciate the fact that he gave you something."

S❧ S❧ S❧

A wealthy man with whom Reb Mendel had been close in Chicago once asked his advice about how much of his money he should bequeath to his children in his will and how much he should give to charity. Reb Mendel told him to leave the greater part to his children. Since the children were not religious, Reb Mendel felt that leaving too much to charity would arouse their antagonism towards Judaism. On the other hand, if the man left most of his money to them, it might cause them to look more favorably on his religious beliefs and possibly to even start observing Shabbos as a result.

S❧ S❧ S❧

Reb Mendel encouraged everyone to act in a fashion that was cognizant of his own needs as well as those of others. He once asked a student riding in his car why he wasn't sharing the box of cookies he was eating with the other students in the car. The embarrassed boy promptly gave the box to the others and told them to finish it. But Reb Mendel was still not satisfied. "You don't have to give the whole thing away. Keep some for yourself," he told the boy.

SOMEONE ONCE ASKED REB MENDEL why it is greater to be a *mentsch* than a *"tzaddik."* He explained as follows: "A *tzaddik*

Mentsch or Tzaddik

takes on stringencies that aren't commensurate with his true spiritual state, sort of like wearing fancy jewelry. Jewelry doesn't change the essence of the wearer; it always remains external. True, some of the people who do these things are true *tzaddikim*, but very often it's just jewelry that they throw on to make themselves look better. You can put a *gartel* around a desk too, but the desk will still be a desk.

"I've seen people *davening vasikin* at the *Kosel* in exactly the same way I see ordinary people *davening* in Brooklyn. Don't think that just because you go to *Eretz Yisrael* and stand by the *Kosel* — which is the holy of holies — that you'll automatically become a holy of holies yourself. It doesn't work that way.

"The problem with doing an external action that's not right for you is that you might start to think that you've actually attained a higher level. First you should internalize that higher level, and only then will the external actions take on meaning. Hundreds of years ago, the scholars of Italy did not wear beards. They believed that beards were fitting only for those on the spiritual level of their contemporaries in *Eretz Yisrael*."

"THERE'S AN OLD QUESTION: why does Rosh Hashanah come before Yom Kippur, when really the opposite would seem

How to Repent

to make more sense? Shouldn't we first repent our sins and then be judged? However, there is a danger in dwelling on our sins, even when we're repenting for them. If we think about our sins too much, we might come to think about how much fun they were and try to imagine ways to have even more fun next year! So we have to feel the fear of judgment first and then we can start to think about our sins.

"That is why the Torah sandwiches the sin of the Golden Calf in the middle of the description of the building of the Tabernacle. If you just start off learning about the Golden Calf, you might get too interested in it. (You might wonder what was so attractive about the Golden Calf, but you should realize that in earlier times idolatry had as much seductive power as cigarettes and business do today.) Therefore the Torah goes back to the account of the Tabernacle immediately after the story of the Golden Calf.

"The main thing about Yom Kippur is not to bang your chest, but to look for ways to improve yourself. Nowadays people enjoy saying a long *viduy* on Yom Kippur. Reb Chaim Ozer Grodzenski and Reb Elchonon were brothers-in-law, and one year Reb Elchonon asked Reb Chaim Ozer how his Yom Kippur fast had gone. Reb Chaim Ozer answered that the fast was bearable but confessing his sins was too hard for him.[1] That's how the *al cheits* are supposed to be — more painful than the fast.

"That's how we should feel, but most of us feel as much pain when we say our confession as we do when we blow the *shofar*. Ideally we shouldn't be able to get the words out of our mouths and we should be falling on the floor and hiding our faces in shame. When Nathan the prophet rebuked David HaMelech, David merely said, 'I have sinned to Hashem.' He just couldn't say any more."

Serving Hashem on Your Level

CHAZAL SAY that when good things happen to us in this world we recite the blessing, "Who is good and does good," while on bad events the blessing is, "Blessed is the True Judge." In the World to Come, however, we will say, "Who is good and does good," regarding any event which transpires, since it will be evident that all is for the good. Reb Mendel asked: If we believe that everything is for the good, why don't we recite the blessing, "Who is good and does good," in this world as well?

He also asked a question about the text of *Bircas HaMazon*. "Instead of thanking Hashem only for the food we have just eaten, we bless Him for nourishing the entire world: '...Who nourishes

---

1. "*Der taanis iz noch oistzuhalten, aber de al cheits zenen nit durchtzutragen.*"

the world, in His goodness, with grace, kindness and mercy.' If so, why is it necessary to eat in order to say the Grace After Meals? Even if someone has only seen other people eating, he should still be able to say these blessings."

Yet another question: "The *Gemara* (*Kiddushin* 31b) relates that one of the Sages would stand up whenever his mother entered the room and say, 'I am standing because the *Shechinah* is here.' Why did he stand only for *his* mother? He should have stood up for other mothers as well!"

To answer all these questions, Reb Mendel told the following story: "After World War II, I attended a conference on the suffering of the Jews during the war. The first speaker was Pierre Von Kassin, one of the righteous gentiles of the world, who had written about the plight of the Jews during the war. The second speaker was Reuven Dofni, an Israeli who parachuted into Europe during the war to fight with the partisans. He also spoke about what Jews went through during the war, but his words left an unimaginably more powerful impact on the audience than those of the first speaker. Von Kassin spoke about things he had only heard from others, while Dofni spoke from his own firsthand experiences, and the effect was entirely different.

"What we are required to do in life is based not on what we know but rather on what we feel, what we live through. The truth is that we should be required to stand up for all mothers, but if we did that, it would only be because we have an abstract knowledge of the holiness that accompanies them, and that knowledge is not enough to make a person truly sense the *Shechinah..* In whom do we actually *feel* Hashem's Presence? In our own mothers!

"Similarly, we should say, '...Who nourishes the world, in His goodness, with grace, kindness and mercy,' whenever we see anyone eat, even if we don't touch a morsel ourselves, but that would also be purely intellectual. It's only when we ourselves satisfy our hunger that we can bless Hashem for nourishing the world in His mercy and really mean it.

"Also, the blessing '...Who is good and does good' should be said on the bad in this world as well, but again that would be based only on our knowledge that Hashem does only good. It's only in the World to Come that we'll be able to truly feel in the depths of our hearts that even the bad is for the good. In this world, the most we can perceive is that He is the true judge."[2]

s➤ s➤ s➤

Reb Mendel once dictated a *kvitel* to a man who would bring it to the *Kosel*. In it he asked for health for himself and his family, *nachas* and a year of learning. He told the man, "You are probably wondering why I didn't place my request for learning at the top of the list. My true desires are in the order I told them to you, and before the *Kosel* only the truth is acceptable."

REB MENDEL ONCE POINTED OUT to the class, "*Tosafos* says here, '*b'ezras Hashem*,' but not once in the entire *Chochmah*

To Serve Hashem in Truth

U'Mussar by the Alter of Kelm does he write *baruch Hashem* or *b'ezras Hashem*. The only reason we can throw these phrases around is that we are not so honest. The Alter of Kelm wrote with total honesty, and he realized that he wasn't like the *baalai Tosafos*, who were on such a lofty level that they could truly write and feel *baruch Hashem* and *b'ezras Hashem*.

"The Alter of Kelm was extremely careful never to do anything above his true spiritual level. For example, he wouldn't say the traditional *Ushpizin* on Succos to invite the Patriarchs and other *tzaddikim* into his *succah*. He said that if they actually came to his *succah*, he would feel so unworthy to be in their presence that he would have to leave. He also would not kiss a *sefer Torah* because he said he didn't feel he loved the Torah enough, and perhaps the Torah wouldn't want him to kiss it. Maybe it would say, 'Don't kiss me, I don't need your kisses. If you want to show that you love me, you should go and make a better effort to fulfill what's written in me.' Everyone in the Kelm Yeshivah knew not to stand up when the Alter entered the room. Once, a new student stood up for him, and the Alter immediately went to a *mussar* room and spent an hour learning *mussar*. From this you see what a clean soul he had."

---

2. Heard by Rabbi Chaim Zelig Fasman at Reb Mendel's house on Purim.

"AT THE SCHOOL OF THE ALTER OF KELM they taught one thing: The first law in the *Shulchan Aruch* is not to be a fool. Today

The Golden Rule of Mussar

bachurim run to weddings as if they're going to do the biggest *mitzvah* in the world, but how do they know? How can they be so sure they're going to add to their friend's joy, and not just to have a good time and get together with their friends? The *mussar* schools taught self-scrutiny, which means not fooling yourself and thinking you're going to a wedding purely for Hashem's sake when you're really going just to have a good time.

"Reb Yeruchem once told us that even when the Alter of Kelm was very sick and weak, his *mussar* talks still lasted three or four hours at a time. When he finished speaking, he was so exhausted that his doctors ordered him to rest for at least fifteen minutes and sometimes for half an hour. Initially he would do as they said and lie down, but after five minutes he would jump up from his bed and start yelling at himself, '*Atzlus*! (Laziness!)'

"Reb Yeruchem used to say, 'What the Alter considered laziness would seem to anyone else nothing short of superhuman dedication, while what I consider dedication still has plenty of laziness in it. The Alter was always worried he was being lazy. But we are really lazy and just imagine that we're being cautious.' Reb Yeruchem himself was always careful about his health and took precautions against exerting himself unduly, but he always suspected that his real motive was laziness."

Reb Mendel was always careful not to make himself look holier than he actually was. After delivering a *mussar* talk to several students, he told a boy who wanted to discuss one point at length, "They're serving lunch in the dining room and if we keep talking you'll miss your lunch." As the boy was walking away, Reb Mendel called him back with a sheepish smile and admitted that his concern wasn't entirely altruistic: "Really, I'm also hungry, and I wanted to eat, too."

One day Reb Mendel began the *shiur*, "My Rebbe ..." Suddenly he stopped, and then began to make fun of himself for sounding boastful, "Ha! My Rebbe, my Rebbe. Ha! ..." He was trying to dismiss any conceit he might have felt for thinking that he was worthy to be a student of such a great person.

"Most of us are convinced that we'll go straight to *Gan Eden*, yet even Rabban Yochanan Ben Zakai was uncertain where he would be led after his death (*Berachos* 28b). Once I met a rabbi from an non-observant congregation who told me that he had mercy on his congregants because he didn't think they would get into *Olam Haba*. Really, he should have been concerned about whether he would make it there himself."

A *baal teshuvah* once asked Reb Mendel why he referred to the *yetzer hara* as the *baal davar* (literally: litigant). Reb Mendel responded with the following two stories: "The *mashgiach* in Reb Elchonon's yeshivah, Reb Yisrael Yaakov, was a genuine *tzaddik*. The Chofetz Chaim used to tell people who came to him for blessings, 'Why are you coming to me? You should go to Reb Yisrael Yaakov for a blessing.' Reb Yisrael Yaakov used to go alone late at night to visit his mother and people would ask him, 'How can you go out so late by yourself? Doesn't the *Gemara* say that it's dangerous to go alone at night?' He answered them, 'I don't walk alone.' "

At this point Reb Mendel stopped to ask, "What do you think he was about to say? What would someone who fit your concept of a *tzaddik* say? 'Hashem is always with me,' right? But what did he actually say? 'The *baal davar* is always with me.' He was a great man who knew just where he was holding.

"The second story is about a pious elderly Jew who lived a long time ago. He decided that he could no longer bear the impurity of the Diaspora; he had to move to *Eretz Yisrael*. So he packed his bags and set out on the long and difficult journey. Upon his arrival, he kissed the ground with love and then jubilantly went to the *Kosel* to thank Hashem for allowing him to succeed in his quest. When he came to the *Kosel,* he saw the *yetzer hara* standing there next to him.

"The *tzaddik* was shocked— he couldn't believe his eyes. 'What are you doing here?' he asked. 'I thought I left you behind at home.'

"The *yetzer hara* began to laugh and then said, 'You fool! Who do you think brought you here!' "

Reb Mendel was once asked why he did not go to live in *Eretz*

Yisrael. Reb Mendel replied, "If I could leave the *yetzer hara* behind, I would go. The problem is that wherever I go he comes along!"

§⁕ §⁕ §⁕

When an activist in a certain communal matter was carried away by his own zealousness, Reb Mendel remarked, "A person goes to do a *mitzvah* and he isn't aware that the *baal davar* has jumped onto his wagon and is riding along with him. We can see this from the verse (*Vayikra* 19:17), *You shall surely rebuke your friend and not bear a sin for him.* Even when someone performs the *mitzvah* of giving rebuke, he still has to be on his guard against being overzealous and coming to sin."

Reb Mendel illustrated the pervasiveness of the *baal davar* with the following story: "The Kotzker *chassidim* tell about a great *tzaddik* who was about to pass away from this world. His friends and followers gathered around his deathbed, and in the last few seconds of his life someone asked him, 'Do you have a *yetzer hara* now also?'

" 'Certainly,' the *tzaddik* replied.

" 'What kind of *yetzer hara* could you have at a time like this?' the friend asked in astonishment.

"The *tzaddik* replied, 'The *yetzer hara* is telling me to scream a long, loud *Shema Yisrael* so that people will say my soul left the world with the *Shema* on my lips.' "

REB MENDEL ONCE COMMENTED, "Did you ever notice that it is yeshivah students in particular who are constantly reproaching themselves for wasting time from Torah study? Listen to what a great man, Reb Yeruchem Levovitz, had to say: 'In the areas where you think you're failing, that's where you are really good. However, it's where you think you are good, and certainly where you think you are perfect, that you are lacking.' The *yetzer hara* tries to not even let you think about your true weaknesses so that your eyes will stay completely closed, and you'll never be able to improve yourself.

Strategies of the Yetzer Hara

"Reb Elchonon used to say in the name of the Chofetz Chaim, 'Since the *mitzvah* of Torah study is greater than all the other *mitzvos,* the *yetzer hara* will let a Jew do all the other *mitzvos* in the world in order to prevent him from learning Torah.' "

Reb Mendel was an idealist, but practical. He understood very well that necessity could not be ignored, but he wanted us never to forget that there was an ideal and we should strive for it. So it was with his attitude toward the need for women to work outside the home. He knew that the self-sacrifice of such women made it possible for their husbands to learn and develop into *talmidei chachamim,* and that these devoted wives and mothers were pillars of Torah life. But he would not let us forget that it would be better if Jewish women could occupy their traditional throne as queens of their households.

He would say, "And what's the *yetzer hara's* main objective with women? Not to be a *tzenua*! *Tznius* is more than just wearing proper clothing — that's basic *halachah.* People define *tznius* to their own liking — like a chicken that everyone can stuff with whatever he likes. The real meaning of *tznius* for a woman is to avoid the public arena and maintain segregation of the sexes. *All the honor of the king's daughter is within (Tehillim* 45:14). Since this is the most important attribute for a woman to possess, the *yetzer hara* will allow a woman to run around and do all the acts of kindness in the world, as long as she does not stay home. The Alter of Kelm's daughter lived on the floor above the yeshivah's *beis midrash* and used the same steps that the *bachurim* used to get to the *beis midrash,* but the *bachurim* said that they didn't remember ever seeing her. That's not just piety, that's genuine *tznius."*

"REB ELCHONON USED TO SAY that when a child gets bored in his crib and bangs his head, it's due to the *yetzer hara.* From this we see what an enemy the *yetzer hara* is. The *yetzer hara* will make a yeshivah *bachur* feel moody and depressed, even

The Yetzer Hara — a Physical Enemy as Well as a Spiritual One

when everything is going well and he really should be happy, because his goal is to hurt people. In spiritual matters this can mean making someone depressed so that he can't learn well, which is the *yetzer hara's* greatest objective. But when he can't do that, as with a baby, he causes the person physical pain, which is also an accomplishment for him."

REB MENDEL ONCE NOTICED a boy toying with his wristwatch during *shiur* and asked him, "Why are you looking at your watch?

It's the Small Things that Distract

Don't worry, it's working fine. It's a wonder how someone can be sidetracked by such foolishness. The Satan tried and tried to prevent Avraham and Yitzchak from going to the *Akeidah*. First, he appeared to Avraham as an old man and said, 'Old man, have you lost your mind? You were given a son when you were one hundred years old and now you're going to slaughter him!' Avraham replied, 'That is my intention.' The Satan countered, 'Tomorrow people will try you as a murderer!' Again Avraham paid no attention to him.

Then he appeared to Yitzchak as a young man and said, 'You are the only son of your poor old mother. Are you going to let yourself be killed?' Yitzchak also answered, 'That is my intention.' The Satan then tried many different tactics to divert Yitzchak, even creating a river and threatening to drown him. But nothing worked. What question did the Satan ask that finally managed to move Yitzchak a little? 'What will happen to all the pretty things your mother made for you?' That had an effect on Yitzchak; sometimes it's the little things that touch a person's heart."

CHAPTER FIFTEEN

The Fruits of Mussar

Don't Give Spiritually — Give Materially

FTER A LONG ROAD TRIP, Reb Mendel stopped in an unfamiliar city. He managed to locate a *shul* and waited there for the morning *minyan* to start. Tired as he was from the long journey, it took all his strength to *daven* with concentration. After *davening*, he was approached by a member of the *minyan* who said, "Excuse me, but I noticed that you remained seated during the prayer of *VaYevareich David.* Isn't it customary to stand at that point?"

Reb Mendel replied, "If you're really interested in my welfare, why don't you first ask me if I have a place to eat breakfast?"

The point Reb Mendel was attempting to convey is from his favorite *mussar* work, *Chochmah U'Mussar*, by the Alter of Kelm. The Alter points out that the Torah is replete with numerous injunctions to concern ourselves with the physical well-being of our fellow Jew, and only one *mitzvah* to concern ourselves with his spiritual well-being, demonstrating that our primary responsibility is to enhance our fellow's physical well-being. People, however, frequently appear to be more solicitous of the spiritual well-being than the physical well-being of others. This is so, the Alter explains, because being concerned with another's spiritual state costs nothing. Thus, it is really the low value placed on spiritual matters which leads people to give priority to their neighbor's spiritual condition. The correct approach is that only after one has proven his concern for another's material well-being should he worry about the other's spiritual well-being (vol.II p. 242).

The Alter of Kelm's point was nicely illustrated by the following incident involving Reb Mendel.

He told a *bachur* who was responsible for waking up the other boys for *Shacharis*, "Your job has two contradictory elements. On the one hand, you're doing everyone a great kindness by waking them up so that they can get to *davening* on time. This aspect is referred to in the *sefarim* as *tzurah* (true essence). At the same time, you are required to do an act that is just the opposite of kindness, i.e., depriving them of sleep against their will. This is called the *chomer* (purely physical) aspect of the action. Since the physical side in a person is usually stronger than the spiritual side, most people usually gravitate to the *chomer* of their actions rather than the *tzurah*.

"That is why, says *Chochmah U'Mussar*, doctors often are cruel people. On the surface you would imagine them to be the kindest of people since they spend their whole day helping others. Yet, even though the *tzurah* of their work is to help people, the *chomer* of what they do, the external action, frequently involves inflicting pain on their patients, whether by cutting into them surgically or charging them high fees."

Reb Mendel advised that boy to make a special effort to do acts of kindness for others so his physical actions would also be consistent with the kindness he was, in fact, doing by awakening others. Reb Mendel used to say, "I don't like the people who wake everyone up for *davening*. If you want to do someone a favor, bring him breakfast in bed. Only if you would be willing to do that do you have the right to wake him up for *Shacharis*."

S➤ S➤ S➤

Torah law says that if there is a need to violate Shabbos in order to save a life, it is better for an adult to do so rather than a child. Reb Mendel explained that children see only the physical aspects of actions. Thus the child will only be aware of the physical act of desecrating Shabbos. An adult, however, is aware of the essence of the action, which is the *mitzvah* of saving a human life. Thus the desecration of Shabbos will not have a negative effect on the adult, as it might on the child.

In this connection, Reb Mendel told us a story he had heard from Rabbi Moshe Soloveitchik. Reb Moshe's son became so ill on Friday night that a doctor had to be summoned. The boy's grandfather, Reb Chaim Brisker, was present and asked the doctor if he wanted the kerosene lamp brighter or moved closer. The doctor nodded to indicate that it would indeed help his examination of the patient. When Reb Chaim told his son to move the lamp, Reb Moshe looked questioningly at his father, who snapped at him, "*Am haaretz*! Why are you afraid of a *mitzvah*! You aren't worthy of this *mitzvah*!" Reb Chaim then moved the lamp closer to his sick grandson.

Reb Mendel explained that Reb Chaim called his son an *am haaretz* (the worst insult in the Brisker lexicon) since Torah scholars are always expected to look at the underlying purpose of their actions, the inner essence. Reb Moshe should have recognized that moving the lamp closer would have been a *mitzvah* rather than a desecration of Shabbos. The *Rambam* defines an *am haaretz* as someone who is aware only of what his senses perceive rather than of the underlying reality. Thus the term *am haaretz* does not refer to someone ignorant of Torah, as is commonly thought, but rather to a simple person whose perceptions are all limited to earthly matters. Man's goal is to make himself more spiritual by subduing the earthly side of his nature.[1]

ONE HOT SUMMER DAY, soon after Reb Mendel moved to New York, he had occasion to drive to the Lower East Side with his

**Gratitude —
To What Extent**

daughter. He did not have change for the parking meter, and asked his daughter to wait in the car until he returned. After a few minutes, however, she found the hot car unbearable and went to stand in the shade of a nearby building. There she was cornered by a missionary who proceeded to harass her. She was desperate

---

1. When Reb Mendel told us this story, he praised Rabbi Moshe Soloveitchik for his willingness to relate this story in public in spite of the embarrassment it must have caused him.

to break away but felt duty bound to stay near the car. Suddenly there appeared out of nowhere a vagrant bundled up in two coats and three hats in spite of the stifling heat. He stared at the empty parking meter for a short while and then, for no apparent reason, put a dime in the meter and walked away. Free at last from her guard post, Reb Mendel's daughter immediately fled from the missionary and ran to join her father to whom she excitedly related the whole incident.

After listening to her story, Reb Mendel insisted on searching the entire neighborhood to find the beggar in order to repay him for his kindness. His search, however, proved futile.

Reb Mendel did not say another word about the incident. The following week, however, he walked into the house, his face beaming with happiness. "Finally I found him," he told his daughter excitedly, "and I gave him a few dollars!"

ᔆᗷ ᔆᗷ ᔆᗷ

Reb Mendel befriended a young *baal teshuvah*, who worked at the yeshivah in Philadelphia, and fretted constantly about the young man's frail constitution. Once Reb Mendel found him working on a ladder and insisted on standing there for an hour holding the ladder steady until the job was finished.

That Pesach, a woman in Philadelphia — Mrs. Weiss — invited the young man to stay in her home for the entire holiday. When Reb Mendel heard about the Weiss' hospitality, he was so appreciative that he gave Mrs. Weiss, who collected antique coins, two antique silver dollars he had once received as the *Kohen* for a *Pidyon HaBen*. To this day, Mrs. Weiss still cannot understand why Reb Mendel was so grateful for an act of hospitality from which he did not personally benefit.

ᔆᗷ ᔆᗷ ᔆᗷ

When Reb Mendel first arrived in Chicago, his older brother Reb Hertzl Kaplan was already saying a *shiur* in the yeshivah. Not only did Reb Hertzl persuade the yeshivah to hire Reb Mendel, he also volunteered to move to a less

Reb Mendel & Reb Hertzl

advanced *shiur* to allow his younger brother to take over the one he himself had been saying.

When Reb Hertzl became critically ill in 1948, Reb Mendel offered to Hashem the remaining years of his life to keep his brother alive. He felt that his debt to his brother overrode even his obligations to his own family since his brother had saved all of their lives by sending the money they needed to escape from Europe.

Shortly before Reb Mendel passed away, he mentioned to his youngest daughter that when Reb Hertzl had been ill later in life, he had given Reb Hertzl five years of his own life. (Reb Mendel lived to 72, Reb Hertzl to 77.) He then related the following story, illustrating the ability to give away one's merits on behalf of another:

The Chofetz Chaim once sent two young Torah scholars to convince the storekeepers in a certain village to close their shops on Shabbos. The two scholars fulfilled their mission and returned to the Chofetz Chaim's home. As they entered, they saw a man crying to the Chofetz Chaim that his wife was deathly ill. The Chofetz Chaim turned to the two scholars and asked them if they were willing to donate the reward they earned for their efforts for Shabbos observance and give it over to the sick woman. The men agreed and the woman miraculously recovered.

Reb Mendel always displayed great appreciation to his rebbe, Reb Elchonon Wasserman. He kept in constant communication with Reb Elchonon's children and grandchildren and tried to help then in any way possible. When Reb Elchonon's grandson Elchonon Meir contracted a life-threatening disease, Reb Mendel did everything in his power to save his life.

While the author was studying in the Mirrer Yeshivah in Brooklyn, Reb Mendel approached him one Shabbos afternoon and said that he had arranged for Elchonon Meir's wife and mother to come to the *beis midrash* to pray together with his own Rebbetzin. He told them to come well past midnight when no one would be in the *beis midrash,* to stand in front of the *Aron,* before the Torah scrolls, and beseech Hashem to save the young man's life. He asked the author to stop anyone from interfering with them. That night, it was very moving to see the three women, wrapped in shawls, enter the dark, empty *beis midrash,* in the dim light of the *ner tamid,* and cry and pray to Hashem.

After Reb Mendel's passing, Rabbi Dan Segal, formerly the *mashgiach* of the Mirrer Yeshivah in Brooklyn, related that when Elchonon Meir was sick, Reb Mendel had asked him to explain the procedure for giving away some of one's years for the benefit of another. To Reb Mendel it was obvious that his debt to Reb Elchonon required him to offer years of his own life to save his grandson. Reb Mendel also approached colleagues who had studied under Reb Elchonon in Baranovich with the request that they do the same.

ᔿ ᔿ ᔿ

Elchonon Meir Wasserman, zt"l

Reb Mendel taught that when one does a favor for someone else, he should not have any thought of receiving anything in return, not even a "thank you." He would tell us the story of how the *kollel* in Baranovich was founded. Originally the young married scholars in Baranovich learned individually in scattered locations throughout the town. Reb Elchonon decided that it would be better to have them all in one place, and raised money to start a *kollel* and pay them salaries. Nonetheless, Reb Elchonon never expected the slightest show of appreciation from the *kollel* students, to the extent that he did not even expect them to greet him with a *"Gut Shabbos."*

Despite everything Reb Mendel did for his students, he would never accept any show of appreciation from them. Even to a "thank you," he would respond curtly, *"Far vas a dank?!"* ("What do you mean, thank you?") He felt that he was simply doing his job, for which no one owed him anything.

RABBI BEREL WEIN relates the following story from Reb Mendel's days in Chicago:

Saving People from Embarrassment

"The boys were dissatisfied with the yeshivah cook because the food rarely varied. After being served egg salad and red jello for lunch thirteen days in a row, a group of *bachurim* sent a sarcastic letter of complaint to the yeshivah's administration: ". . .Perhaps there could be a little variety. How about yellow jello and red egg salad?" The administration responded and the menu was varied slightly. But the cook was totally destroyed. She was so upset that she couldn't greet anyone or serve food to the *bachurim* for months.

"One day in *shiur*, Reb Mendel interrupted our regular learning to talk about the importance of not embarrassing others. He quoted the *Gemara* (*Berachos* 43b) that says that it's better to jump into a fiery furnace than to embarrass someone in public. None of the students realized how this *Gemara* applied to them until Reb Mendel concluded, 'It would be better to eat nothing but jello and egg salad for a whole lifetime than to embarrass someone publicly.' Suddenly, we realized that he was talking to us. . ."

ﺱ ﺱ ﺱ

We were once discussing the requirement to extend Shabbos into the week by delaying *havdalah*, when Reb Mendel related an

experience that showed his great sensitivity towards other people's feelings. "One of my neighbors in Chicago went away one Shabbos, and towards the end of the day his wife came over and asked if she could hear me make *havdalah*. In those days, few people waited even an hour after nightfall and this woman appeared at my door barely half an hour after sunset. When I asked her if it wasn't a little early for *havdalah*, she told me that her husband made *havdalah* at this time every week. Although it was still Shabbos for me, I thought to myself, 'Her husband is also *frum* and if I tell her it's still Shabbos for me, I'll be suggesting to her that there is something wrong with what her husband does.' I remembered this *Gemara* that we were discussing and made *havdalah* for her without a candle."

✎ ✎ ✎

Reb Mendel always made a point of being friendly with all the workers in the yeshivah. In appreciation of Reb Mendel's friend-ship, a non-religious Russian worker once brought some of his wife's home-baked bread and gave it to a *bachur* with instructions to serve it to Reb Mendel at lunch. Innocently, the *bachur* did just that. It was not until Reb Mendel had taken a few bites of the bread and remarked on how good it tasted that the *bachur* told him its source. Instinctively Reb Mendel started to cough the bread up. Then, just as suddenly, he sensed how foolish the *bachur* was feel-ing. He regained his composure, and with a wave of his hand dismissed the matter, telling the *bachur*, "Don't worry, it's noth-ing."

One Shabbos morning while davening at the Mirrer Yeshivah in Brooklyn, a sick old man sat next to Reb Mendel. In the middle of *davening*, he began to vomit on the floor. While everyone else immediately moved away from the sick man, Reb Mendel didn't move from his seat the entire *davening* and chatted amiably and quite naturally to the man whenever it was permissible for him to talk. He acted as if nothing at all had happened, in order not to cause the man any embarrassment.

One day in *shiur* a student fell asleep and began to snore. His neighbor gave him a gentle nudge to wake him up, but Reb Mendel stopped him: "Let him sleep. It says in *halachah* that you're supposed to wake someone up to say *Shema*, but nowhere does it say you have to disturb him to listen to my *shiur*."

He then seized the opportunity to speak about the prohibition against disturbing people's sleep. The sleeping student must have sensed the change in Rebbe's voice because he began to emerge from his nap. Realizing that the sleeper would be very embarrassed if he were to awaken to find that everyone was looking at him and that Rebbe was talking about disturbing someone's sleep, Reb

Mendel stopped abruptly in the middle of a sentence and resumed his discussion of the *Gemara*: "...And with this the *Ramban's* question is answered and we can go further in the *Gemara*."

REB MENDEL TAUGHT: "We must treat another person's body as if it were a *sefer Torah*." Both have to be approached with the utmost care and consideration.

The Way to Appease

Once a boy fell asleep in *shiur*, and the boy sitting behind him began to gently kick his friend's dangling hand in order to wake him up. Reb Mendel saw this and told the boy who was kicking to bring water so the other boy could wash his hands (since a shoe had touched his hand and he was forbidden to learn). The boy stayed in his seat, refusing to go. Reb Mendel said, "If you won't go, I'll have to go myself," and began to get up from his seat. When the boy saw this, he quickly got up and went to bring the other boy some water.[2]

Reb Mendel often said that in today's society people use phrases like "Thank you" or "I'm sorry" with a total lack of sincerity. Once on a long trip with several students, Reb Mendel grew tired and stopped at a large service station to rest. He parked in a quiet corner and put his head down to rest. After fifteen minutes an attendant came over and said, "Excuse me, can I help you?" Reb Mendel answered, "Yes. Tell your boss that he has a place like a drugstore; everything is well organized and it's in perfect shape."

After the attendant left, a student asked what the attendant had wanted and Reb Mendel answered, "He asked me if he could help me, but what he really meant to tell me was, 'Get out of here!'"

§► §► §►

One Purim some boys hung a mocking caricature by the seat of one of the rebbes. Reb Mendel was very upset by this public embarrassment of a rebbe. He told the "artist" to appease the rebbe by buying a set of *sefarim* that cost around fifty dollars (a large amount at that time) and offering him an apology. "It has to cost money," Reb Mendel said. "Today, words are cheap. Only by giving away your own money can you demonstrate that you're truly sorry."

_____
2. Related by Shlomo Dick.

"ALTHOUGH THE DESIRE FOR HONOR is a terrible thing," Reb Mendel once said, "we are still required to give honor to others.

On Honor But when you're on the receiving end, you should take a laxative to wash it out. A person can easily become a spiritual cripple from receiving honor.

"A *baal gaavah* is a person who, whenever they start calling out someone's name for an *aliyah* to the Torah, immediately thinks they mean him."

ℰ✦ ℰ✦ ℰ✦

One day after *Shacharis* in yeshivah, an old man with a long white beard stood up in front of the *beis midrash* and delivered a tirade blasting the *rosh yeshivah* for not taking any role in what he called the "salvation of the Jewish people." That day in *shiur* Reb Mendel asked a student what he thought about the tirade. The student replied that the man was an idealist who was willing to make a fool of himself for what he felt was right.

Reb Mendel laughed and said, "When people are young their personalities are relatively simple, but when they grow older they become more complicated. Sometimes a person can get so tangled up that he himself doesn't even know what's really driving him to act the way he does. That old man is smarter than we are, but with this idea and that idea racing around in his head, he does stupid things.

"The biggest trial an older person has is the desire for honor. The *yetzer hara* reminds him of all the worthy things he's done in his life and tells him he deserves to be called for one of the honored Torah readings. This is why, if he doesn't get the honor, he is devastated. This trial is a lot harder for an older person to overcome than it is for a younger one."

For health reasons, Reb Mendel went swimming each week at a local pool. He usually went when only adults were present. On one occasion, when he was accompanied by his grandson, they noticed the pool full of young children. His grandson asked him what he was going to do, as it wasn't *kavodik* to swim together with little children. Rebbe laughed, "What do you think I am? I'm *basar v'dam*, too!" and with that he jumped into the water together with the children.

Nonetheless, Reb Mendel was aware that in some situations, one must not only accept honor but actively pursue it:

"The *mashgiach* of the Baranovich Yeshivah, Reb Yisrael Yaakov, was the humblest of men. Once, when the *bachurim* tried to pick him up on a chair during a *simchah*, he refused by sitting on the floor. He would spare no effort to gladden a *chasan* and *kallah*, and would totally demean himself with his antics.

"Once he was invited to speak at the dedication of a new yeshivah building. The deputy mayor of the city, who was also the president of a secular Zionist school, was also present. The deputy mayor spoke first, and when he finished, they called upon Reb Yisrael Yaakov. The *mashgiach*, who considered the arrangement of the speakers an affront to the Torah, acted very insulted that he had not been asked to speak first, and refused to speak at all. A big commotion ensued and the organizers all came and apologized to him. But Reb Yisrael Yaakov continued to voice his resentment loudly enough for everyone to hear: 'At the very least there should have been some kind of separation. First they should have called on a flour miller from the marketplace, and then have had me speak!'

"Finally he allowed himself to be placated and agreed to speak. He gave a powerful address which far outshone the first speaker and afterwards took command of the whole ceremony. He made an appeal for the yeshivah and even played the fiddle to entertain the audience. It required a great effort on his part to overcome his normal modesty and act so brazenly, but he did it for Hashem's honor, to demonstrate the superiority of Torah scholars over the nonreligious."[3]

ה‎ ה‎ ה‎

Reb Mendel always fled from all kinds of honor and fanfare. One former student who was involved in organizing youth activities tried a number of times to get him to speak, always without success. Once, however, a *rosh yeshivah* who had been scheduled to speak at a large Torah assembly bowed out just as the announcements were about to be printed. The young man frantically called Reb Mendel to ask what to do since it would be impossible to arrange for a comparable speaker on such short notice. Under the

---

3. In a similar vein, Reb Mendel once related that the Chofetz Chaim sometimes made a point of jumping off a wagon while it was still in motion in order to show his nimbleness. He would remark, "People shouldn't say that yeshivah men are sluggards."

circumstances, Reb Mendel unhesitatingly agreed to speak. (This was one of the only times he spoke at a public assembly.)

Similarly, Reb Mendel always declined the honor of officiating at the weddings of his students. Once, however, when he heard that another notable, who had been scheduled to officiate, had withdrawn at the last minute, Reb Mendel sent the *chasan* a message that he would be willing to do the honors.

Accepting the Truth

"SOME COMMENTATORS SAY THAT THE SIN of Nadav and Avihu[4] was drinking wine before they entered the *Mishkan*. Immediately following the story of their deaths, the Torah forbids a *Kohen* from bringing an offering after drinking wine. Hashem later told this law directly to Aharon as a reward for his unquestioning acceptance of the Divine judgment on his two sons.

"Perhaps we can understand this as follows. Normally, parents are prejudiced in favor of their children and try to minimize their shortcomings. Aharon, however, remained totally silent and accepted the fact that his sons had sinned greatly and deserved the punishment they received. This was the merit that earned him the great honor of having this command issued as a direct prophecy to him."

Reb Mendel was also capable of owning up to the truth even in situations when it hurt, embarrassed or offended him. In his years in Chicago, he rented a basement from a "pious" Jew to use for his wine-making operation. This basement was cold and damp and an unbearable place to work. Once the lights went out and Reb Mendel called up to the landlord, "Please put on the lights. It's dark down here!"

The landlord answered him from upstairs, "We Jews don't say that something's dark, we say it's not light." Reb Mendel remained silent at the time, but later he confessed to his son, "At first, I thought of telling him, 'Here I am stuck in your pitch-black basement and you're telling me how to *talk*?' But then I realized that he was right, for the *Gemara* at the beginning of *Pesachim* spends two pages discussing that point."[5]

---

4. Aharon's two sons whose lives were taken by Hashem when they brought an unauthorized incense offering.
5. The first *Mishnah* in Tractate *Pesachim* euphemistically describes night as "the light." The *Gemara* then digresses for several pages on the importance of speaking in a refined manner.

CHAPTER SIXTEEN

Education for a Holy Nation

"AT MOUNT SINAI, Moshe explained all the detailed laws of *tefillin*. And the truth is that all of them can be derived from the written Torah, but we don't see them there; we don't feel them with our senses.

Seeing the Torah

"The Chofetz Chaim could feel a verse in the Torah as if it were a tangible object. To someone on such a high spiritual level, there is no difference between the physical objects in front of him and a verse in the Torah.

"A person can only see what he's capable of conceiving, and that depends totally on who he is. The degree to which a person is totally wrapped up in the material world determines how he'll learn *mussar*. A full stomach gives you a different outlook on life.

"When I was a child in *cheder*, an old Chassidic Jew once explained to me the difference between the *Gemara* and the *Zohar*. In the *Gemara* it always says, 'Ta shema — come and hear,' while the *Zohar* says 'Ta chazi — come and see.' When the Torah was given on Mount Sinai everyone 'saw' the thunder, even though normally you can't see sounds. So too the phrase 'Ta chazi' implies that you can see the concept.

"The reality is that whenever someone does a *mitzvah*, he changes the world around him. We find in the *Gemara* (*Berachos* 17a) the blessing, 'May you see your world in your lifetime,' meaning may you see all the spiritual perfection created by your *mitzvos*. The opposite is true with *aveiros*: when someone does an *aveirah*, he creates impurity, destruction, and a destroying angel, which becomes attached to that person until the day he dies and then accompanies him into the next world. *Chazal* say that if Joseph had sinned with Potiphar's wife, that sin would have created a reality — a spiritual monster — which would have clung to him in the World to Come. The Torah teaches us to do good and stay away from evil, but the *Zohar* 'reveals' more than the revealed Torah does. From the *Gemara* you can only 'hear' the concepts; in the *Zohar* you can 'see' them.

"Being a *mekubal* doesn't just mean learning and knowing *Kabbalah*. It means being an entirely different type of person, a spiritual person. I once heard from a *mekubal* that anyone who still has a taste for meat won't understand that sphere of study."

A student asked Reb Mendel if he could study *Yosher Divrei Emes,* and received the reply, "That work is only for *hecherer mentschen* (elevated people) since it discusses Kabbalistic concepts." Then he added, "If someone can refrain from eating one of the tastier foods they serve at lunch, then he can read the *sefer.*"

REB MENDEL EXPLAINED TO US how difficult it is to eat correctly. "The easiest thing to do is to learn; *davening* is harder than learning and hardest of all is eating. If

On Asceticism

someone is truly great, he'll be able to give his eating as much sanctity as his Torah study.

"When you eat, 'flies' (i.e., the attachment to the material side of food that disturbs your spiritual balance) attach themselves to you. The *Zohar* (Section III, 191b) says that the purpose of *Bircas HaMazon* is to dislodge the 'flies' that stick to your soul while you're eating."

One evening after a fast, as Reb Mendel watched the *bachurim* hurry to the dining room to break their fast, he remarked, "You can lose everything you've accomplished during a whole day of fasting by the way you run to eat afterwards. The Alter of Kelm used to say that the meals we eat on Succos consume the Yom Kippur fast."

৯▶ ৯▶ ৯▶

Rabbi Aharon Sonnenshein, however, recalls that Reb Mendel never spoke about abstinence except in small doses. More commonly he would tell students to "enjoy *zich* (enjoy yourselves)." In general he encouraged us to be happy, and to take pleasure in the fine things Hashem gives the world. This advice, however, was always tempered by a reservation: " 'Enjoying *zich*' is fine, but if you make it into an obsession then it's no longer 'enjoying *zich*.' "

Sometimes he would slip this topic into his *shiur* indirectly. For example, as he repeated a quote from the *Maharsha* during *shiur*, he said, "Each one of the ten times I've said this *Maharsha* I've enjoyed it, but not as much as you enjoy soda. Reb Elchonon used to measure his tea — sometimes he'd take a half cup and sometimes a quarter of a cup. (In those days, tea was like soda is today.)"

Reb Leizer Horedzeisky, zt"l

Seeing the looks on our faces, he added, "From your expressions I see you don't understand why he bothered to measure it. Surely you remember the *Mishnah* (*Avos* 6:4), 'Water in measure you should drink.' But nowadays *bachurim* carry large bottles of soda in their arms like a *sefer Torah* and put it in the refrigerator as if it were an *Aron Kodesh*. Their attachment to soda comes entirely from the power of advertising, that's all it is.

"At first, they didn't allow a soda machine in Yeshivah Beis HaTalmud — the very thought was considered a disgrace! When they were still in East New York, not even cooled water was available. Once a *bachur* arranged to have a water cooler installed at the back of the *beis midrash* and as soon as Reb Leizer Horedziesky[1] saw it, he picked the whole

---

1. One of the "old school." Originally from the Mirrer Yeshiva in Europe, he was later one of the *gedolim* in the Yeshivah Beis HaTalmud in New York.

machine up and carried it outside, saying, 'This is a *beis midrash,* not a park.'

"In America, people are used to learning in luxury, and you can't take it away from them. When we grew up in Europe, we weren't accustomed to the pleasures Americans take for granted. Some American boys learned at the yeshivah in Mir in my time. They stayed with a local family, and one day they asked for some cake. The lady of the house asked them what the occasion was. Europeans couldn't understand how anyone could eat cake in the middle of the week for no special occasion.

"We'll have to do *teshuvah* for all the pleasures we had in our younger years. The *Gemara* says that in order to merit the 'cream of Torah,' you first have to give back the milk you drank as a baby. This means you have to reject the pleasures you had in your earliest youth, just as you're ashamed now of the train set and baseball cards you have lying in the closet at home."

૬ ૬ ૬

"If you could keep yourself from drinking soda for a whole month, it would be as good as the biggest fast."

૬ ૬ ૬

"*Prishus* (abstinence) is to eat what you don't like, more than to not eat what you do like."

૬ ૬ ૬

"A good way to work on perfecting yourself is to let the food sit in front of you at lunch for a while before you eat it. Once, in Chicago, I noticed that a student of mine seemed weak. When I questioned him, he confessed that he'd been fasting a few times a week. I suggested to him that instead of fasting entirely, it would be better to let the food sit on the table in front of him for a while before eating. He later told me that he had tried to take my advice but hadn't succeeded. It's easier not to eat at all than to eat in a proper fashion."

૬ ૬ ૬

Regarding himself, Reb Mendel was an ascetic. Once a student brought him his lunch in the yeshivah dining room. When he realized that Reb Mendel's strict diet would not allow him to eat most of the food on the menu, the boy suggested various other foods that were available in the kitchen. The boy offered him cottage cheese and sour cream. Reb Mendel said, "I'll take the cheese, but

I don't need the sour cream." When the boy asked why he didn't want the sour cream, he answered, "It's better not to get too involved in these pleasures. The *sefarim* say that the pleasures of this world are like the skin of the snake (meaning that they give strength to the *yetzer hara*)."[2]

ᔐ ᔐ ᔐ

He never applied his own strictures to others, however. He always taught that serving Hashem requires an attitude of joy and happiness, and encouraged anyone who was unhappy or discouraged to enjoy some physical pleasure in order to lift his spirits. After speaking against excessive pleasures in *shiur*, he called one very serious *bachur* aside and told him, "Don't take what I said today too seriously. I didn't mean that you should put everything I said into practice. I just wanted to tell you the way things really are. Even though we're not on that level, it's still good to know about it, just as we like to know how the major league players are doing even though we are only spectators.

"*Chazal* say that a person should always ask himself, 'When will my actions reach the levels of Avraham, Yitzchak and Yaakov?' (*Tanna d'vei Eliyahu* 25). "We think it means like this," said Rebbe, holding both index fingers side by side, "but really it means like this," and he moved one finger a foot ahead of the other. "We can't dream of equaling their level. The most we can hope for is to touch the bottom of their feet."

One day, when Rebbe noticed that the *shiur* had continued on past the official ending time, he said, "I can't hold you here any longer. My Torah is just as important and enjoyable as eating, but your eating is also my Torah."

ᔐ ᔐ ᔐ

A Torah scholar who was always very serious once approached Reb Mendel and asked him, "Reb Mendel, why are you always smiling?" Reb Mendel was surprised at the question. "Why, that's our purpose in life!"

In practice, Rebbe never attempted to dissuade students from anything they needed for their basic physical comfort and peace of mind. A student who enjoyed classical music once asked Rebbe's opinion about it and was told, "It's no weakness. On the contrary,

---

2. Related by Avraham Dov Owsianka.

it shows that you have a certain delicacy of feeling."

Senior students in the yeshivah were assigned to small *chaburos* in which the students took turns presenting their original Torah thoughts to the group. In one such group, refreshments were served. Some students in the other group felt this custom was not in keeping with the proper spirit of the Torah. When a student from the "refreshment" group asked Rebbe's opinion, he smiled and said that he did not think it was a bad idea at all.

One summer at camp, within a short time of his arrival he found a farm nearby that sold fresh milk, a cleft in a mountain from which pure spring water flowed, and a patch of wild berries. At times during the summer he would return to camp with buckets and bottles filled with his newly discovered treasures for everyone to enjoy.

When he was swimming alone in the pool with the camp director, Rabbi Leumai Shalam, Reb Mendel commented, "The pleasure we now have from swimming in the pool is worth a million dollars. All the effort and money you've put into the camp is worth it just for this alone." Since the director was always under pressure and had to make frequent trips to the city to raise money and attend to other camp business, Rebbe wanted him to cherish the pleasure he had at that moment and to appreciate the gifts Hashem grants us in life.

REB MENDEL EXPLAINED the statement in *Bircas HaMazon* that "Hashem nourishes the entire world in His goodness, with grace,

Thought for Food

kindness and mercy" as follows: "Meat tastes good, and so do potatoes. But when you eat potatoes together with meat, they taste even better. In the same way a mother prepares a meal for her son, that's how Hashem prepares food for us.

"One of the great people of the previous generation said, 'If we said *Bircas HaMazon* properly, we would realize that food was created to give us the opportunity to bless Hashem for it.' "

୫ ୫ ୫

One year on Tu BeShvat, the new year for fruit trees, Reb Mendel told the class the following:

"If you really want to do the trees a favor and give them merits, then when you hold a fruit in your hand, take a careful look at it and think about how kind Hashem is to create such a fruit. That's the greatest merit the tree can have. When you recite the blessing in a rush and stuff the fruit into your mouth as quickly as possible, the tree barely has any merit at all.

"Did you know that food is entitled to the same respect as *sefarim*? In the time of the *Gemara*, people wouldn't leave food on the street; they would pick it up or put it to the side. You have to work on yourself to be aware that food comes from Hashem, and not from California or Florida. The fact that we don't see food growing makes it easier to forget that it's Hashem Who provides our food. The disrespect with which people treat food shows that they don't really believe it's from Hashem, which is why they can't make a proper blessing over it either.

"David HaMelech once treated clothing with disrespect, and because of this his clothes did not keep him warm in his later years. His clothes were telling him, 'I'm not yours to be scorned.' I've heard it said that our purpose in Creation is to respect and appreciate everything in it. If someone disdains objects, it leads him to look down on people as well. This in turn leads to *lashon hara* and eventually even to giving false testimony, which is a denial of Hashem himself.

"You have to see the Creator in the world, even though He doesn't show Himself. He's still everywhere to be seen. Your main challenge is to grow up and use your minds. You have to be a *lamdan* and a *baal machshavah* not only as far as learning is concerned but in all other aspects of your lives as well. Don't think you need a white beard to reach that level — you can do it now.

"I once heard a beautiful thought: when someone receives a gift, he should keep it rather than give it away. Certainly, then, one should never just take the food Hashem gives us and throw it away. The cook in yeshivah is more idealistic about her work than a doctor — you have no idea how much it hurts her when boys throw away their portions. That's what babies do: if they like a food they eat it, and if they don't they just throw it away. You have to grow up and put *everything* you learn into practice, not just those things that you enjoy, while discarding the rest.

"American boys want to take on only those aspects of *tzidkus* that appeal to them. But it's not so easy to be a *tzaddik*. One must give thought about how to go about doing even a "simple" *mitzvah*. The Brisker Rav was extremely strict concerning the *mitzvah* of visiting the sick. He felt that even though it's very important to visit someone who isn't well, you can't just go whenever you want to. First, you have to think about whether the visit will be too great a strain on the patient, and whether he'll want you to see him in his present condition. Many times, people only think of one aspect of an issue, but the Brisker Rav was a *baal machshavah*. He kept all angles of the situation in mind."

ONE DAY IN THE MIDDLE OF *SHIUR* Rebbe asked for a particular *sefer*. Two students handed him two separate copies, one new

Holy Books and Holy People

and one used. Reb Mendel took the used one, saying, "I like learning from an old *sefer* since it's been learned from more and has more holiness in it. You'll get more Divine inspiration by learning from it. But learning a *blatt Gemara* has more holiness than the *Gemara* itself. Similarly, the body of a Torah scholar acquires as much holiness as an old *sefer*."

REB MENDEL SAID, "Reb Yisrael Yaakov said that the Heavenly signs that inform a person of his spiritual level (see

Extrasensory Perceptions

Orach Chaim 615:2) do not exist in our times. My teachers told me that today we shouldn't concern ourselves with the meaning of dreams. But the Brisker Rav did because, as he said, his father had a *Shulchan Aruch* on thoughts. For some people, dreams still have meaning.

"There is another form of extrasensory perception that's not as mystical as *Ruach HaKodesh* or dreams — the capacity to feel fear though the cause of that fear is far away. Rabbi Ephraim Epstein, the brother of the *Levush Mordechai*, told me that at the time of the Hebron Massacre of 1929, he woke up in the middle of the night and sat trembling in fear at the edge of his bed without any idea what was wrong. The next morning he learned that his son, who was learning in Hebron at the time, had been killed in the pogrom. 'This,' he said, 'is what the *Gemara* (*Bava Basra 16b*) meant in relating that the friends of Iyov knew when to come visit him because something was wrong with their tree.' We see from this how strongly one person can be connected with another."

REB MENDEL WENT TO GREAT LENGTHS to fulfill the Torah's command, *You shall be holy* (*Vayikra* 19:2). He was once with a stu-

Sensitivity to Holiness

dent in a public building and on his way out noticed a group of women entering the building coming towards him. Rather than leave through the front door as he had planned to, he turned around and left the building through a back door and circled around the building to avoid passing the women.

Any immodest discussion made him physically nauseous. A student once asked his advice on how to approach a group of non-religious teenagers who were far more interested in their social lives than in Torah. The question elicited a sickly look from Reb Mendel. Eventually he suggested that the student learn *Gemara* with them, and hopefully the Torah's light would lead the boys to higher aspirations. The student followed this advice, and within a short time, these teenagers developed a love of learning and their personalities underwent a complete transformation.

Once when Reb Mendel was teaching us the *Gemara* about someone who rents a cow for the purpose of sinning, an uncomfortable look came across his face. He said sadly, "Well, there are sick people in the world. *Chazal* delved into all types of mud for our benefit, to teach us Torah."

A student observed that Reb Mendel always kept a solitary left-hand glove in the front of his car so as not to touch the hand of female toll collectors. He donned the glove before reaching the booth so as not to embarrass the woman. If the collector was a man, Reb Mendel would remove it.

ﺱ ﺱ ﺱ

Once he brought his car in for repairs at a garage owned by a Jew he knew. Not finding the owner in his office, he went to the shop area, where a group of gentile workers were engaged in conversation. Noticing an indecent picture on the wall, Reb Mendel immediately stalked over and ripped the picture down, totally ignoring the presence of the workers. One of the mechanics gave a nervous laugh and said to his companion, "I see the Rabbi doesn't like this kind of picture."

In relating this story, Reb Mendel's son commented that Reb Mendel was not acting out of ordinary *frumkeit*; rather, he saw the picture as a spiritual menace to the workers themselves, as well as to society at large. He recalled that after the deterioration of the neighborhood in Chicago in which Reb Mendel lived, he rented a garage for his winery from the pastor of a local church. Reb Mendel used to advise the pastor not to preach lofty religious ideas to his congregants, but just to stress the importance of acting decently, and avoiding liquor and other vices.

⌘ ⌘ ⌘

Reb Mendel's sensitivity to holiness did not deter him from acting when he felt it necessary. He was shopping in a grocery store when he saw an improperly dressed woman haggling with the storekeeper to give her a pack of cigarettes, even though she did not have the full amount it cost. Reb Mendel gave the *bachur* accompanying him the nickel she lacked and told him in a sorrowful voice to give it to the owner, commenting, "*Es is a rachmanus oif a mentsch* — It's a pity when a human being comes to such a state (to have to demean herself to haggle over a pack of cigarettes)."

CHAPTER SEVENTEEN

To Serve the Public

"**R**ABBI YAAKOV OF LISA, the author of *Nesivos HaMishpat*, was widely acclaimed as the leader of his generation.

Merits for Mitzvos
While he labored tirelessly all his life on behalf of the entire Jewish people, his great achievements were matched by his humility. Towards the end of his life, after all the *sefarim* he had written, he decided to publish a *siddur*. He was afraid that errors might have crept into his Torah, and he would lack the merit to be admitted into *Olam Haba*. Therefore, he wrote the *Siddur Derech Chaim* as an act of kindness for the Jewish people to help him merit a place in the World to Come.

"In order to do big *mitzvos*, one must have great merits. A person can't just wake up one day and say 'Now I'm ready,' and expect to perform a big *mitzvah*. One needs enough merit (either ancestral merits or the merits of having done many *mitzvos* previously) to be able to accomplish great things.

"The *Beis Yosef* (Rabbi Yosef Karo) is a case in point of great merit leading to Divine assistance in performing great *mitzvos*. Did you know that there were many scholars who were greater than the *Beis Yosef*? Yet he merited to write the *Shulchan Aruch*, and they did not. Rabbi Yonasan Eibeshutz (*Urim VeTumim* 48b) said that the *Beis Yosef* couldn't figure out all the intricate Talmudic calculations of the authorities who preceded him. But the *Beis Yosef* was given special Divine assistance to write only the correct *halachah*."

REB MENDEL TOOK A VERY LOW-KEY APPROACH to *kiruv rechokim*. "Before you start trying to make someone *frum*, first make him into a *mentsch*," he told us.

On Kiruv Rechokim

The Mirrer Yeshivah in Brooklyn had an outreach program through which non-religious Russian boys came to the yeshivah one morning each week to learn with designated study partners in the *beis midrash*. One day, after Reb Mendel *davened Shacharis* in the yeshivah, he went to the yeshivah dining room with one of the students. When he noticed the boisterous Russian boys eating breakfast, he asked what they were doing there and was told that the boys came for breakfast and then went to learn with their study partners in the *beis midrash*. He commented that just having the boys eat together with *bnei Torah* was worth as much as all the learning they did afterwards.

჻ ჻ ჻

Reb Mendel often went out of his way to befriend non-religious Jews, without making any overt effort to bring them closer to Torah and *mitzvos*.

Once he flew to Switzerland. In the airport, he saw three young hippies, who he suspected were Jewish. He went over to them, greeted them warmly and, after exchanging pleasantries, told the scruffiest-looking member of the group that he had the face of an angel. Reb Mendel then said that he was an old man who needed someone to drive him around in Switzerland, and asked whether they'd be interested. (Typically, he convinced the recipients of his kindness that they were doing him the favor.) They readily agreed, but pointed out that they needed a place to stay. "Oh, that's no problem at all," he replied, and went to a pay phone to call his host, an old friend of his.

After exchanging warm greetings, Reb Mendel said, "Listen, Reb Chaim, I need to ask you a favor. I have three distinguished guests accompanying me. Can they stay over with me at your house?"

His host answered that, much to his dismay, he had no room for another three guests. But Reb Mendel brushed his objections aside on the grounds that these guests could sleep on the floor in his room.

Throughout his stay in Switzerland, Reb Mendel was escorted by these three "distinguished guests" wherever he went. Before he parted from his young traveling companions, he told them to look him up when they returned to America.

Some time later, a former student of Reb Mendel's was approached one day in the *beis midrash* of the Lakewood Yeshivah by three hippies. "Is your name _____?" they asked.

"Yes," replied the *bachur*, a bit nervously.

"We have something to give you from the Rebbe."

The *bachur* could not imagine what in the world was going on. "What Rebbe?" he asked incredulously.

"You know, Rabbi Kaplan!" they answered, holding out a bag of cassette tapes. "He asked us to give you this." The hippies explained that upon their return to the United States they had visited Rebbe in Philadelphia. When they were leaving, he asked them to stop in Lakewood on their way to New York to deliver tapes he had borrowed from this *bachur*. The *bachur* realized that the tapes were a pretext to get his "distinguished guests" to visit Lakewood and hopefully arouse in them an interest in Torah study. He quickly seized the opportunity and gave the young people a guided tour of the yeshivah.

Even Children

REB MENDEL'S OUTREACH extended even to children. A non-religious secretary in the yeshivah once brought her nine-year-old son with her to work. When Reb Mendel saw the little boy playing in the hall, he called him over, pointed to a *Chumash* and asked, "Do you know what this is?"

"Sure," the boy answered, "it's a Bible."

"No," answered Reb Mendel, "this is a *Chumash*." He then pulled up two chairs and sat with the boy for an hour, teaching him *Chumash* on a level the child could understand and appreciate. Later that day someone asked Reb Mendel why he had devoted so much of his time to a nine-year-old boy. Answered Reb Mendel, "I hope that I've planted a seed that will grow years from now."

REB MENDEL ONCE ASKED A STUDENT (now a successful Torah educator) to get involved in reaching out to a certain

The Delayed Reaction

Russian boy from a non-religious family. The student put a lot of effort into learning with the boy, and then even more effort into persuading the local yeshivah to accept him as a student. But when it came time for the boy to register at the yeshivah, his parents were uncooperative to the point of rudeness. The principal of the school later berated Reb Mendel's student for causing him so much trouble. It took all the student's diplomatic skills to placate the principal.

After a week of classes, another parent informed the boy's mother that she was expected to participate in a car pool. The mother replied that she was too busy and that the other mothers would have to bear the burden of shuttling her son back and forth. Needless to say, this upset the other parents, who complained to the principal. He again vented his frustration on Reb Mendel's student and blamed him for causing all these problems.

By this time, the student had reached the point of exasperation. He went to see Reb Mendel just as he was about to retire for the night. 'How much do I have to do for this child?" he called out angrily.

Reb Mendel snapped back, "Hashem tolerates him, so you'll have to tolerate him too!" and slammed the door to his room behind him. The next time he saw his student, however, he went over to him and told him in a gentler tone, "We have to try to do what we can — no more. We don't know how successful our actions will be; we just have to plant seeds. It could be that in ten years you'll see fruits."

The student accepted Reb Mendel's admonition and continued his efforts with the boy and his family. A short time afterwards, however, the family moved away suddenly and lost all contact with the student.

Ten years later, the student noticed a bearded young man enter the *beis midrash* of his *kollel*. Looking at the name embroidered on the visitor's *tallis* bag, he could not believe that this was the very same boy he had helped many years before. The boy told him that both he and his parents had become completely religious.

ONE SUMMER, Reb Mendel stayed at a summer camp which worked with young people from non-religious backgrounds.

But Without Compromise

Sometimes he felt that the camp went too far in its attempts to provide the campers with a good time. "Why do you always have to provide them with 'fun'?" he asked the camp directors. "Why don't you get them to do something constructive, like picking blueberries, for a change?"

When Reb Mendel questioned the necessity of taking boys to a country fair, the camp director told him, "This is the only way to bring these children to Torah observance. If we don't give them this trip, we'll lose them."

Reb Mendel replied curtly, "So you'll lose them."

At the time, the camp director was shocked at Reb Mendel's reply. Later, however, he understood Reb Mendel's point: while telling the boys that Torah is supreme, the camp was conveying through its activities the message that having a good time is paramount. At the most, the camp would produce kids who give lip service to the importance of Torah while continuing to do whatever they want.

S❧ S❧ S❧

Once, Reb Mendel and his son were given a ride from the Catskills to New York City by a young non-religious college professor. In the course of the conversation the young man revealed that he intended to marry a gentile. This pained Reb Mendel to no end. Though the young man was doing him a big favor, Reb Mendel did not hesitate to express himself.

"In times of old," he began, "when the Jewish nation was a kingdom and we had self-rule, someone could *kill* you for what you are planning to do. It's better for a Jew to be dead than to be married to a gentile woman." From the back seat, Reb Mendel's son saw the driver's neck turn red and the hair on the back of his neck actually stand up from fear. These words obviously had a powerful effect on the man, and he promised to give the matter further consideration.

AS A CHILD, Reb Mendel memorized the Books of *Iyov*, *Mishlei* and *Tehillim* in their entirety. Throughout his life he minimized

On Education such accomplishments, on the grounds that they were common among many *cheder* children in those days.

"Once," he related, "my rebbe confiscated a boy's collection of candy wrappers and said that the only way he could get it back was to learn *Mishlei* by heart. By Friday, the boy had memorized half of it. From this we see that toughness is a most successful form of education."

Reb Mendel was a master of the delicate art of coaxing and pushing children in Torah study. Once he took his fourteen-year-old grandson with him on a long car trip. Noticing that his grandson was spending the whole time looking at the scenery, Reb Mendel said, "You enjoy looking out the window, but you won't want to do it the *entire* time, so maybe you can help me out with the *Gemara* I'm learning. Why don't you learn with me for ten minutes and then look out the window for twenty minutes?" The youth agreed, and they started learning together. At the end of the first ten minutes, Reb Mendel said, "Let's learn for just another few minutes. You won't regret it." As time went on, his grandson grew so involved in the *Gemara* that most of the trip was spent learning with his grandfather.

ꙮ ꙮ ꙮ

"Children in Pre-1A should be learning *Chumash* already! At that age children may not be mature enough to master the intricacies of *Gemara*, but they can memorize hundreds of facts — and that's a lot better than the 'half-*Shas* of foolishness' children usually have in their heads. They can learn tractate *Mikvaos* with tons of *halachos*, and it's not so dry.

"Children don't learn *Chumash* properly here because they study English in the afternoon and all the Torah is pushed out of them. In Europe, little kids learned Torah like they play with toys today. One game they used to play was to look at the interesting shapes on the pages in the *Gemara*: one page had only one or two lines of *Gemara*, on another page there was the shape of a building, another one had the shape of a hammer, and so on. They also used to dance on the steps of a building to the chant of a *Mishnah*.

"Children in Europe had an entirely different concept of fun. When I was a small child, I used to play with the son of the Baranovicher Rav, and we would climb up on the bookshelves that lined the walls of the Rav's house and memorize the names of all the *sefarim*. Then we tested each other to see if we could identify a particular *sefer* by its size and shape.

"In America, children play 'Johnny on the Pony' and 'Red Rover.' In Europe they played the same games, but they gave them names from *Chumash*: '*Sus V'rochvo*' ('*The horse and its rider*,' *Shemos* 15:1), or '*Sh'lach es Haanashim*' ('*Send out the men*,' *Bamidbar* 13:2). Even for little children, Torah was the reality; they grew up with Torah as their whole life.

"I just can't understand why people need to buy toys for children. They'll play with anything they find. If you put two children together, one of them gets down and the other one jumps on him, and they'll play 'horse.' It's that simple! What do they need with complicated toys, and specially made items? In Europe, kids were kids too, but parents would not allow their children to be stuffed with all types of foolishness."

REB MENDEL EXPRESSED HIS APPROVAL when he saw a *bachur* dressed in a tuxedo and top hat one Purim. "I like the way you've

Appreciation of Beauty

dressed up," he said. "It's attractive and dignified. I don't understand how anyone can make himself look ugly on Purim, but that's today's generation. It used to be that dolls looked nice and sweet. Today, however, they make ugly dolls, and everyone grabs them up."

ه ه ه

"Once I was driving across the Verrazano Bridge with a distinguished *rosh yeshivah* and I noticed him staring at the magnificent and imposing bridge with great intensity. I asked him what he saw in the bridge, and he replied, 'When you look at something great, it makes you great.' The same is true with certain Torah works that were written for great scholars, not ordinary people like us. You might wonder why we study them since we don't really understand them anyway. The fact is, however, that just by looking at the *sefer,* we also become greater."

Reb Mendel particularly admired the beauty of the original edition of *Chochmah U'Mussar,* a large volume with wide margins. He commented, "A book is nicer with a margin, which is why a *sefer Torah* has to have a lot of space at the top and bottom. But young people don't think so; they like things in miniature."

REB MENDEL LOVED CHILDREN and treated other people's children as if they were his own. Once he stopped in the middle

On Love and Discipline

of speaking to a student and ran to check on a crying baby. On his return, he explained, "You can't just let a baby cry!" Still, he understood that at times it is better to let a child cry. He once saw a small child walking around crying and did nothing. He showed the *bachur* with whom he was speaking that at times the child stopped crying in order to stomp through puddles that lay in his path. "You see," said Reb Mendel, laughing, "as soon as he steps in the puddle he forgets what he's crying about. A child's crying doesn't always express what he's feeling. Sometimes it's just a tool for him to get what he wants."

ه ه ه

Children loved Reb Mendel. The eight-year-old son of Reb Dovid Shmidt, a former student of Reb Mendel, often urged his father to take him to Reb Mendel's house on Shabbos, even though it was nearly an hour's walk away.

In general, he favored talking gently and with love to children. He once heard his son speaking sternly to one of his children and asked the son, "Is that the tone in which I spoke to you when you were a child?"

On the other hand, he did not forget that he who spares the rod spoils the child. Children are almost never spanked in America, he noted. "When the father gets angry he knows he's not allowed to spank the child in his anger, and after his anger subsides, he then forgets about spanking him. The Brisker Rav, however, used to call his children together at the end of the week and tell them calmly, 'Moshe, Monday night you did this and this, so you get one *patch*. Thursday you did this, so you get another *patch*. . .'"

A *KOLLEL* STUDENT at the Mirrer Yeshivah in Brooklyn, who was a mentor to many of the younger *bachurim* in the yeshivah, once

Positive Criticism

noticed a *bachur* beginning to spend excessively long periods of time in the *Shemoneh Esrei* prayer and taking on other extreme forms of piety. The man asked Reb Mendel if he should try to convince the boy to refrain from his extreme behavior.

Reb Mendel told him that before Reb Yeruchem Levovitz accepted the position of *mashgiach* of the Mirrer Yeshivah in Poland, he returned to Kelm for a period of time. When he was later asked what he had learned, Reb Yeruchem replied: "The first rule in being a *mashgiach* is not to make things worse. A *mashgiach* must first make certain that his actions won't undo any positive aspects of the existing situation."

Reb Mendel lived by this rule and was extremely careful before offering criticism or advice. He spent several summers at a camp which did outreach work with non-religious youth. Though his main contact with the campers was during *davening*, Reb Mendel nevertheless concerned himself with the campers' welfare.

One day after *Shacharis* he said to one of the counselors, "It seems to me that many of the boys have *pasul tefillin*. Have a look around, and if you see anyone whose *tefillin* look shoddy, suggest that they make a *berachah* on yours after *davening*. That's what we did in the Mirrer Yeshivah in Europe, where not all the *bachurim* could afford the best *tefillin*. While I'm here you can also bring me some pairs to look at."

At that point Reb Mendel happened to notice a boy wearing a pair of *tefillin* that appeared cheaply crafted, and he asked the boy if he might look at them. After looking at the *tefillin* for a while, Reb Mendel asked their owner, "What kind of car would you like — a

Cadillac or a Chevy? I'm sure you'd rather have a Cadillac. Well, these *tefillin* are like a Chevy."

Reb Mendel gave him the *tefillin* back. As the boy turned to put them away, Reb Mendel asked how much he had paid for them. Without turning around, the boy replied, "Two hundred dollars." Reb Mendel looked worried and said quietly to the counselor, "*Oy*, now he's offended. I can't believe he paid two hundred dollars — it's not true. I don't know why I said what I did, and I regret it. This can tarnish the whole camp." Then he walked over to the boy and said, "Excuse me, I'm sorry. If they cost two hundred dollars, then they must be a Cadillac."

For the rest of that summer, Rebbe was worried his remark might have caused a negative effect, and he frequently asked how "the boy with the *tefillin*" was.

Usually Reb Mendel was careful to cushion his constructive criticism with delicacy and tact. He once saw a boy in yeshivah whose *tefillin* were on loosely. Rebbe went up to him and engaged him in a conversation about the laws of *tefillin*. First they discussed different *Gemaras*, including the reasoning behind them, and then they looked up the appropriate decisions of the *Mishnah Berurah*. In the course of their "research," they encountered the *halachah* that specifies the proper place for *tefillin* to rest.

A former student of Reb Mendel's was a slightly absent-minded genius, and Reb Mendel was concerned that he wasn't paying enough attention to his wife. One day, he heard that his former student was in New York for a brief stay. After several calls, he found out that the man was learning in a *beis midrash* in Boro Park. Reb Mendel went there and sat down to learn.

Eventually the young man noticed Reb Mendel and they greeted each other warmly. Reb Mendel acted as if the meeting was a complete surprise, and asked his former student to step outside for a few minutes. As they were walking around, they passed a gift store. Reb Mendel stopped to look in the display window and pointed out to the young man how much women enjoy receiving presents from their husbands. Reb Mendel was pleased to note, as he parted from his former student, that the young man walked into the store to buy his wife a present.

CHAPTER EIGHTEEN

Life and Human Nature

"**R**EB EPHRAIM EPSTEIN, the brother of the *Levush Mordechai* and a *rav* in Chicago, was extremely quick in everything

On Youth he did, even at the age of eighty-two. Even at this advanced age, he continued to raise large sums of money for the Hebron Yeshivah in Jerusalem and he would learn Torah for hours at a time while standing. He used to say, 'What can we do? Old people don't have any strength and young people don't have any sense.' But the truth is it's better this way. The young can listen to their elders and have the benefit of both strength and wisdom.

"The impressions of youth last a lifetime. The *Gemaras* that you learn now will be a part of you for the next fifty years, but what you learn later in life lasts a much shorter time. We think that when we're young we don't have to watch out for our health, but the truth is just the opposite; in our youth

Reb Ephraim Epstein, zt"l

we have to be more careful than in our older years. The *amora* Shmuel said that his well-being as an adult was only due to the oil his mother rubbed on his skin as a child.

"The Sages say that a person isn't punished in Heaven for his sins until he reaches the age of twenty, but even so it's good to avoid sins before then. It's like a car going downhill; if you don't stop it at the beginning of its descent, it's much harder to stop later."

REB MENDEL TREATED ELDERLY PEOPLE with the utmost honor. Once he was talking with a student when an unlearned old

Respect for the Elderly

man walked into the room. Reb Mendel stopped in the middle of a sentence, excused himself and ran over to greet the man warmly.

In camp, an elderly Jew sometimes came to visit his relatives and stayed on the campgrounds. He used to sit down at the table while Reb Mendel was giving a class in *Chochmah U'Mussar*. Whenever he came, Rebbe would turn to him and give him a quick review of what had been said previously, even though the man usually fell asleep within the first few minutes. If the chapter was too difficult for the man to follow, Rebbe would stop the *shiur* and change to an easier chapter. Even though the man appeared to understand little of what was being said, Reb Mendel often looked towards him as if he wanted an affirmation to his interpretations of the text.

"*CHOCHMAH U'MUSSAR* (Chapter 10) stresses that one should not wait until his old age to bear the yoke of communal concerns.

Illusions of Old Age

Young people are flexible and can adapt themselves to the needs of others, while older people become set in their ways and find it more difficult to adjust.

"When people get old and begin to speak frequently about *Mashiach*, it's usually not because they have such a strong belief in *Mashiach*, but rather because they don't want to die.

"Young people look at an old person as someone who is going to die. Old people, however, try not to think about it — they go to Florida to have a good time. Part of a person thinks he will live forever (*Zohar*, *Naso* III 126). Even in old age, he doesn't think that he is approaching the end of his life. Rather, he tells himself, 'If I lived so long already, I certainly will live a lot longer.'

"Actually, this instinctive feeling of immortality has its roots in man's creation, since before Adam's sin, man was intended to live forever. Indeed, after *techiyas hameisim* the body will live eternally. It is only our present physical state that is destined to end, and ironically this is what people mistakenly imagine will endure forever."

"WHEN SOMEONE PASSES MIDDLE AGE, he has a tendency to spend time worrying about honor and how others view him. He

The Quest for Honor begins to improve his behavior so that they'll be able to write nice things on his gravestone. Rather than worry about how others view them, people should really be concerned about how they are viewed by Hashem, before Whom they will soon be judged.

"Everyone thinks he's the righteous of the righteous, especially as he grows older and begins to feel even more embarrassed about arriving in Heaven empty-handed. It's then that he's most likely to convince himself that he's great. Old people begin to speak with great piety. They tell themselves, 'People don't give me honor because they don't realize how great I am, but I know the truth.' All of this is just the work of the *yetzer hara*. In this respect, a young person is more honest; it's a lot harder to overcome the tendency to deceive yourself when you're older than when you're young.

"At a gathering of Torah scholars, a rav once remarked that a person becomes better in old age. Reb Leib Chasman, the *mashgiach* of the Hebron Yeshivah, was so agitated by this remark that he banged his cane loudly on the floor several times, and cried out, 'No! When you get older, you get worse! You get worse!' The truth is that the speaker was right — in some ways you do get better with old age. But with regard to the ability to view oneself honestly, Reb Leib Chasman was right."

๑ ๑ ๑

A *bachur* told Reb Mendel he had seen two old men with long white beards having a heated argument, which eventually ended in a fistfight. Reb Mendel asked the *bachur*, who was quite disturbed by the incident, "Why are you so bothered? Do you think that just because someone eats potatoes for seventy years, he becomes a mature old man? They're still the same children as when they were seven years old. If a person doesn't work on his *midos*, he won't mature automatically when he reaches old age."

THROUGHOUT HIS LIFE, Reb Mendel was extremely youthful in spirit and action. A businessman who *davened* at the Mirrer Yeshivah in Brooklyn arrived at the yeshivah early one Shabbos morning to find the front door locked. He noticed a frock coat lying on the lawn by the window of the coatroom, and saw someone trying to climb in through the window. Tapping the person on the back, he was shocked to see it was Reb Mendel. "What are you trying to do?" he asked. "Inside there's a six-foot drop from the window to the floor!"

Young at Heart — Old in Mind

"So what?" asked Reb Mendel, feigning insult. "You think I can't do it?!"

By the time Reb Mendel returned to his summer bungalow colony from Philadelphia late on Friday afternoon, the four-foot gate surrounding the swimming pool was often locked. But this did not deter him in the slightest. Although he was well into his sixties, he would simply back up several steps to get a running start and then vault over the fence.

For all his youthful vigor, Reb Mendel never lost sight of what awaits a person at the end of his days. Once he picked up a young hippie who was hitch-hiking. The boy asked him his age, which Reb Mendel told him. The hitchhiker then said, "You are forty years older than me." Reb Mendel replied, "I'm not forty years older; I'm forty years closer...," and pointed his finger upwards.

Reb Mendel once said, "I am aware of what's coming in the next world. Whenever I look at the world around me, I already see Hashem — in the handiwork of His creations — and I am comforted."

ɛ♣ ɛ♣ ɛ♣

Although Reb Mendel spoke about death, it never made his *talmidim* morbid. He succeeded in destroying their tendency to worship their bodies, by devaluing the physical side of life which contemporary society so emphasizes. He had a talent for breaking the false idols of American culture — without breaking *talmidim* in the process. He taught that a cemetery is just a parking lot for people, a place to leave the body when it gets used up.

Potential — A Gift of Fire

"THE SAGES TELL US that out of one thousand students who embark on the path of Torah study, only one emerges worthy of rendering halachic decisions (*Vayikra Rabbah* 2:1). Hashem endows some people with more natural gifts — such as superior intelligence and less of a propensity towards being distracted — than others. Albert Einstein had the potential to be a Torah giant bringing eternal life to the world; instead, he gave the world an atom bomb with which to destroy itself. Natural abilities are like a fire; if they're misdirected they become destructive.

"*Yichus* is also a gift of fire. Torah is the vessel that can safely handle the fire, but if someone doesn't have Torah, then all his inherited talents and energy become a fire that can consume him. If he doesn't use his fire for Torah, then it will be used for other things, or will ultimately consume the person himself..."

The Spiritual Power of Inheritance

A STUDENT ONCE TOLD REB MENDEL that he had consulted a young *mekubal* about a woman who suffered from a bad ulcer. The *mekubal* said that the woman would recover, and then added that her sickness came about because of her unyielding nature. Reb Mendel concurred with the *mekubal's* assessment of the woman's condition.

Someone asked him, "How is it possible that this young *mekubal*, who devotes most of his time to business, can know so much?" Reb Mendel answered, "He had a father who was also a *mekubal*, and just like Shlomo HaMelech became what he was because he was the son of David HaMelech, so he also became what he is because of his father."

ॐ ॐ ॐ

Reb Mendel told one diligent student who was discouraged by lack of success in his studies: "Anything you learn becomes part of your personality and an inheritance for your children. I once had a student who was a descendant of the *Chida*, and he always answered questions in the style of the *Chida*, even though he had never learned any of the *Chida's* works. In Chicago, I met a man who understood *lamdus* and could sit down with Torah scholars and present exceptionally good arguments. I used to wonder how this simple Jew, who had not learned that much Torah, was able to reason so deeply, until I learned that his father was an author of Torah works.

"Someone should not be discouraged if he toils in Torah and still doesn't become a *lamdan*, or if he sees that people many years younger than himself learn better than he does. It could well be that they inherited special talents from ancestors who were Torah scholars. In the same way, whatever efforts a person puts into learning, even if he doesn't succeed in making himself into a great Torah scholar, will nonetheless have the effect of helping his children and later descendants grow great in Torah.

"And what about weak people like myself who don't have the stamina to learn sixteen hours a day? What can we do to earn a share in the World to Come and to merit holy offspring and descendants? Imagine for a moment that through your efforts and your merits you can make yourself worthy of having a descendant who will be a prophet. That by itself would be enough to give you comfort and to make all the travails and suffering of a whole lifetime worthwhile. That is what Lemech meant when he said on the birth of Noach (*Bereishis* 5:29), *This one will bring us comfort from our work and our pain. Chazal* (*Yalkut Yehoshua* 2:9) say that Chuldah became a prophetess in the merit of her ancestress, Rachav, who excelled in doing kindness to others. Whenever I think about this saying of *Chazal*, it gives me strength and hope. Even if my own Torah is deficient and I'm lacking in innate qualities and strengths, I can still merit to have holy descendants just through the *z'chus* of doing kindness alone."

AFTER RAV PASSED AWAY, ten of his students gathered together and each one committed himself to adopting one of his

The Legacy of the Great

teacher's outstanding character traits. Reb Mendel asked, "Why was it only *after* Rav passed away that they decided to divide up his character traits — why didn't they resolve to emulate those traits during his lifetime as well? We see that just as in monetary matters, inheritance only takes place after the parent's death, so too in spiritual matters there is an inheritance that takes effect only after death. We find this also with the prophet Elisha when his teacher Eliyahu passed away (*Melachim* II 2:9)."

When the Satmar Rebbe, *zt"l*, passed away, Reb Mendel called his relatives and said, "*Kumt, mir gehen tzu der levayeh. Efshar vet men kenen eppes krigen* — Come, let's go to the funeral. Perhaps we will be able to inherit something from him by being there."

CHAPTER NINETEEN

On Peace and Unity

"IT IS SAID that every generation has thirty-six hidden *tzaddikim*. Reb Yisrael Salanter used to say that no such great men are found in our times. He reasoned that in our times there is so much to be done that no *tzaddik* could afford to remain hidden. The *Gemara* (*Succah* 45b), however, says explicitly that there will always be thirty-six *tzaddikim* in the world. So we must say that today the qualities of these thirty-six *tzaddikim* no longer reside in thirty-six individuals, but are spread out among the Jewish people. And the only time the Jewish people as a whole possess the qualities of complete *tzaddikim* is when there is unity among all Jews. Then, all the parts come together to form a complete whole. The Jewish people is referred to as *shoshanas Yaakov*, 'the rose of Jacob.' How are we like a flower? Just as many small petals are only beautiful when they are bound together to form the flower, so the Jewish people must be bound together.

"The *Midrash* (*Vayikra Rabbah* 26:2) says that the soldiers of King Shaul fell in battle because there was talebearing among them. But those of King Ahab were victorious in battle, even though they worshiped idols, because they did not slander one another. They felt so much love and unity that there was no tale-bearing among them. Through this, their good qualities became united. When the body of the Jewish people possesses all the qualities in their totality, no one could possibly harm them."

REB MENDEL USED TO SAY, "You have to live with someone else's good qualities, not with his weaknesses."

Seeing the Good in Every Person

A student asked Reb Mendel to point out his shortcomings. In response, Reb Mendel told him a story about Reb Yeruchem Levovitz. "A boy in the Mirrer Yeshivah asked his rebbe for a letter of recommendation to another yeshivah. The rebbe could think of no particular quality to extol and mentioned his problem to Reb Yeruchem. Reb Yeruchem got very upset with the rebbe. 'How is it possible that you don't see any good qualities in a boy?' he asked. 'I could speak for hours about the good qualities of every boy in this yeshivah!'

When he told this story, Reb Mendel added, "You learn from this story that you are supposed to study another person to see his strengths, not his weaknesses."

ᔋ ᔋ ᔋ

Another student asked Reb Mendel how one Torah leader could speak very sharply against another in public. Seeing that the boy was greatly bothered by the matter, Reb Mendel told him the following story from his Chicago days:

"A *rav* I was friendly with told me that a certain boy was a *mechalel Shabbos*. I knew the boy was good and I couldn't believe it, but I also knew that the *rav* was a great man who wouldn't lie. So I looked at each one separately. The *rav* was an honest person so if he said something it had to be true. The boy was also a very fine boy who would never be a *mechalel Shabbos*. So the *rav* remained kosher in my eyes, and so did the boy!"

ᔋ ᔋ ᔋ

The Sages say that it is greater to show someone a smile than to give milk to a thirsty person (*Kesubos* 111b). Reb Mendel explained that when we give a thirsty person milk, we do so out of pity. It is a much higher level to rejoice in your friend's good qualities and success. A smile shows you appreciate the other person's good qualities. Such rejoicing is more difficult than pity, and therefore a much greater *mitzvah*.

"Reb Yeruchem used to say, 'A person feels that he's deficient and needs improvement only in those areas in which he has already achieved some success. But the *yetzer hara* prevents him from seeing those areas in which he is completely lacking. Thus one can be great in nearly all areas, and still be totally lacking in one particular area.'

"Sometimes when we see a person of stature who is lacking in one area, we tend to think that we must be mistaken about his good qualities as well. But Reb Yeruchem shows us that this is wrong. It is possible to possess many merits and yet be completely lacking in one area."

Reb Mendel was a shrewd observer of people and often discovered positive qualities unnoticed by others. He was sitting in the Mirrer Yeshivah in Brooklyn with a student when the yeshivah's handyman entered the *beis midrash* to speak to the *rosh yeshivah*. Reb Mendel spent some time pointing out to the student many admirable aspects of the handyman's demeanor and conduct.

He always saw the positive side in every Jew. A student once told him about someone who had lost his faith during the Holocaust. Reb Mendel corrected him: "Don't say he's not a believer. He could very well be a bigger believer than any of us. I'm sure he feels that Hashem is his Father. His only mistake is that he thinks he can have grievances against Hashem, like a son who is angry at his father and wants to have nothing more to do with him."

Every person, he said, has special qualities shared by no one else. As an example, he noted that Reb Elchonon's approach to learning could not have been more different than that of Rabbi David Rappaport, and yet when the latter's work *Tzemach David* was published, Reb Elchonon immediately hired him and put him in charge of half the yeshivah. Reb Elchonon knew that neither approach was "inferior," and that both he and Reb David had something unique to give the *bachurim*.

"The *Midrash* (*Tanchuma, Pinchas*) tells us: 'Just as no two people have exactly the same facial features, so too no two people think exactly alike.' This analogy teaches us that just as it would be absurd for someone to complain that others don't look like him, he also shouldn't be upset or offended that others think differently than he does."

"HASHEM FINDS THE GOOD IN EVERY PERSON'S ACTION and stores it in His treasure house. The verse *If there is only one* **Hashem** *defending angel among a thousand* (*Iyov* 33:23) **Finds the** applies to each individual action as well: if **Good Amidst** nine hundred and ninety-nine parts of a given action are bad but a thousandth of it is **the Bad** pure — Hashem uses that merit to save the person (*Shabbos* 32a)."

Reb Mendel advised people to emulate Hashem in this respect. He taught us that whenever we have a complaint against someone, we should recall at the same time all his merits — just the opposite of the prevailing practice of buttressing any complaint with an exhaustive list of all the other failings of the object of the complaint.

"THE *YALKUT* SAYS THAT IN THE WORLD TO COME, Hashem will sit together with the *tzaddikim* at a feast. When the time **Praising the** comes for *Bircas HaMazon*, the cup will be **Qualities of a** given to David HaMelech, and those who are sitting in *Gehinnom* will answer *amen* to **Fellow Man** his blessing. When Hashem hears the *amen* of those in *Gehinnom*, He will take them out and allow them to enter *Gan Eden* and join the *tzaddikim* there, as the prophet says, פתחו שערים ויבא גוי צדיק שמר אמנים, *Open the gates and allow the righteous nation to come, they who keep the faith* (*Yeshayahu* 26:2) (*Yalkut Shimoni* 429).[1]

"This is amazing. Just for answering *amen* the wicked will be permitted to enter *Gan Eden*! Don't we answer *amen* all the time?

"Perhaps this problem can be resolved as follows. Answering *amen* is an affirmation of belief that the statement is true. Thus

---

1. Reb Mendel pointed out, "From here we see that *Gan Eden* is right next to *Gehinnom*, as the Sages said, 'There is only a hairsbreadth between *Gan Eden* and *Gehinnom*.' This does not mean, as commonly thought, that the lowest level of *Gan Eden* is a hairsbreadth above *Gehinnom*. Rather, corresponding to all the different levels of *Gan Eden*, from the lowest to the highest, there are parallel levels of *Gehinnom*, each a hairsbreadth away. No matter what heights a person may reach, he is always only a hairsbreadth away from *Gehinnom*."

when someone answers *amen* to a *tzaddik's* blessing, he shows that he agrees that the statement he has just heard is true. The wicked about whom the *Yalkut* is speaking are people who during their lifetimes didn't live like *tzaddikim,* but who nonetheless admitted that the way of life of *tzaddikim* is the proper one. They themselves didn't follow that path for numerous reasons — because of difficulties they may have had in life, or because they never had an opportunity to learn Torah, or simply out of personal weakness — but they still praised the way of *tzaddikim* as the proper way of life. That is why they say *amen*. It is for this feeling that they had while they were alive that they will be privileged to leave *Gehinnom* and enter *Gan Eden*."

At this point Reb Mendel paused, and then added, "I have always been worried about my judgment in the next world, and this thought gives me comfort. I am a *chassid* of all good Jews, no matter what group they belong to. I believe that they are all good and righteous people. Even though I personally may be unable to follow in their way, I can still say *amen* to all their good actions. This in itself is enough for a person to be admitted to *Gan Eden*. Indeed, *Chazal* tell us that one who answers *amen* in this world will merit to answer *amen* in the World to Come, as well.

"Recognizing and affirming the ways of *tzaddikim* is the foundation uniting the Jewish people. There is a natural tendency not to admit someone's good qualities or to downplay them. The failure to appreciate the good qualities of a fellow Jew is the source of all disunity."

"THE GIVING OF GIFTS is supposed to increase love and friendship among Jews. But we give *mishloach manos* on Purim today out

Avoiding Selfishness of a sense of obligation, not to bring out our feelings of love for our fellow Jew, which is what the *mitzvah* was originally intended to accomplish."

Reb Mendel urged us not to be self-centered, even in our learning. "Don't learn in order to become a *rosh yeshivah*." he would say. "Learn in order to be able to help someone else." In the same way, he frowned on two-seat sports cars as selfish because of their lack of passenger seats.

Every field of activity, he stressed, provides an opportunity either to bring people closer together or to distance them from one another. He used to quote Rabbi Leib Malin, *zt"l*: "Even when someone does a mundane act such as driving a car, he does not remain the same person. Either he improves himself by doing acts of kindness and utilizing opportunities to show respect for other drivers, or he reinforces his selfishness and other bad character traits."

Reb Yeruchem loathed waiting rooms, Reb Mendel used to tell us, because of the humiliation inflicted on all those forced to wait a long time prior to being admitted into the inner sanctum of some benefactor.

Reb Mendel would contrast this to the *Rambam.* In his letter to Shmuel ibn Tibbon, *Rambam* describes how, when he would return from his day at the sultan's palace, he would find a crowd of sick people waiting to be seen by him. He would dismount from his donkey, and immediately go to greet them: 'I would entreat and beg them to overlook their honor and indulge me a few moments. I then partook of some light food, which is the only meal I ate in twenty-four hours.'

Reb Mendel expressed annoyance with people who put large desks in their offices. "Do you know why a person likes to sit behind a big desk?" he asked. "Only in order to keep visitors far away from him!"

"David HaMelech didn't keep company with the '*sheine*' (successful) Jews. He surrounded himself with people who needed him, the broken and downtrodden."

ૐ ૐ ૐ

"My friend from Europe, Reb Shmuel Charkover, the author of the *Ner Shmuel,* had all the fine qualities you could imagine. He once stayed at our summer cottage for a week, and one evening he was seen sitting and taking Russian lessons from an old woman who had a nearby bungalow. In truth, he could read and speak Russian just as well as she could, but since she was a distinguished person who didn't have any children, honor or money, he let her have the satisfaction of teaching him Russian. He made believe he didn't even know one word!"

Reb Mendel used this same approach. It bothered him that a distinguished young doctor who learned with him in the yeshivah treated him as a rebbe. Therefore Reb Mendel made a point of asking him for medical advice in order to reciprocate the honor in

The farewell party for R' Shmuel Charkover (seated, fourth from right) in Shanghai

return. "Giving a person honor is very important," Reb Mendel said. "A person's honor is his soul, as David HaMelech said, *Awake, my honor!* (*Tehillim* 57:9), which really means 'Awake, my soul.' "

AT THE CONCLUSION OF *SHIUR* ONE DAY, Reb Mendel said, "Now we've concluded our discussion of this topic. In English
No End they say, 'The End' or 'That's it, it's all over.' In Yiddish, there's no such expression, since nothing really ends. The word *ge'endikt* means we're holding off for the moment, but the words still live on. Certain streets are marked as 'Dead End,' but among Jews there is no such thing as a 'Dead End,' because no situation is ever hopeless — no one is ever lost beyond hope."

CHAPTER TWENTY
Memories

Reb Mendel in Chicago

Rabbi Chaim Zelig Fasman,
student of Reb Mendel in Chicago,
presently *Rosh Kollel* in Los Angeles

I do not know of another rebbe in America who left as great an impact on his students as Reb Mendel. Even though he spoke mostly in Yiddish and the boys spoke only English, we still communicated very well with each other. The first year we learned Bava Kama up until the sixth chapter. It was then that I had my first taste of diligent Torah study.

His main concern was to make the boys think. He would ask us, "What do you think?" and when we told him, he would take the opposite position. After discussing the various angles to the Gemara, he would continue, "What does Rashi say?" and prod us to discover that Rashi had a completely different approach to the topic. His goal was to get us to come to everything ourselves.

ৰ ৰ ৰ

We once asked him why he didn't sell his wine in the taverns where his profits would be much greater. He answered, "We have to try to make the world a better place — not to make things worse."

ৰ ৰ ৰ

Reb Mendel had a student who was outstanding in every respect. He was the son of a doctor, and after high school, he entered college with the intention of becoming a doctor. Reb Mendel was extremely disturbed that such a fine student was leaving yeshivah. Even after the boy entered college, Rebbe drove there to talk to him. He was uncomfortable on a campus setting and asked me to join him.

He spent a long time speaking with the young man. Although the boy was respectful and appreciative of Rebbe's concern, he was not persuaded to return to yeshivah. As we walked to the car to return to the yeshivah, Reb Mendel told me, "This trip was not in vain. If it did not help him, it will at least help his grandchildren."

Those few words left a lifelong impression on me. Whenever I have encountered difficulties in my work in teaching and outreach, I always draw comfort and inspiration from Reb Mendel's far-sighted perspective.

Rabbi Moshe Gottesman,
student of Reb Mendel from Chicago,
Dean of Hebrew Academy of Nassau County,
and Director of Camp Sdei Chemed International

Forty years after I was a student in Reb Mendel's shiur, he is still a part of my family. He was like a father to me, and my children grew up thinking of Yom Tov as the time when they would get to see Reb Mendel. He let us become part of his family, part of his life.

I did not have a father figure in Chicago; Reb Mendel was the one I looked up to then and throughout my life. To this day, whenever I am about to do something, I ask myself, "What would Reb Mendel have done? How would he have answered this question?" The strong commitment his students have to Torah, to tzedakah and to chesed is not something he taught us, but something we absorbed from watching him.

He was the type of rebbe whom everyone felt touched by. He knew about each individual — whether or not he ate, whether he was happy or in pain. When we spoke with him, we felt that at that moment only we existed for him. He made us feel that the entire world was created for us. When we went through hard times, he lifted us out of despair. We didn't need a psychiatrist, we just spoke to him. And when we finished speaking to him, we felt like different people.

I changed my whole life because of him. When I was in yeshivah, I had a small business on the side and was quite successful at it. At one point, I was thinking of leaving yeshivah and going into business full time. Reb Mendel came over to me and explained that however successful I might be in business, it was more important to stay in Torah and Torah education. And if today I am a dean of three schools with a thousand students, I have Reb Mendel Kaplan to thank.

ᔍᕐ ᔍᕐ ᔍᕐ

In those days, everyone in Chicago ran to the movies on Motzaei Shabbos. Reb Mendel once told us in shiur, "The flashing lights of the marquee call out, 'Come in, come in.' You have to learn to look at those lights and say, 'I'm not coming in. I'm stronger than you.'" We tried, and eventually we stopped going.

He did not give grades on his report cards or tests; instead he wrote a short phrase for each boy. On one of my report cards he just wrote the verse, If she is as strong as a wall, we shall build on her a fortress of silver (Shir HaShirim 8:9).

ᔍᕐ ᔍᕐ ᔍᕐ

"Money is not to be counted," he told me. "Never tell anyone how much you make, how much you've done, because that's not important. If you do a chesed, that's good to remember. Tzedakah, mitzvos, they're good to count, but whatever money you make — forget about it."

I was one of the first boys to work at his winery. To boost profits, I suggested adding water to the wine (which was legal and a common practice). He told me, "Moshe, you have to be honest — not only to the people you deal with, but also to the grapes."

ᔍᕐ ᔍᕐ ᔍᕐ

Reb Mendel did not need words to communicate. His expressions, his eyes, spoke more than words. Boys who did not even speak Yiddish wanted very much to be in his shiur, just to be near him. Later, they slowly began to learn Yiddish.

A person needs a rebbe to guide him always, and someone like Reb Mendel is impossible to replace. All that remains now is to tell my grandchildren and students about Reb Mendel, and hope that they too will learn and grow from the life he led and taught us to lead.

Rabbi Yitzchok Perman,
Maggid Shiur, Philadelphia Yeshivah

From Reb Mendel, I began to understand what it means to be a gaon in gemilas chesed. He saw the needs of other people more clearly and knew better than ordinary people how to help them.

A meshulach came to the yeshivah and Reb Mendel gave him a donation. Later Reb Mendel became aware that this meshulach was a Torah scholar and a student of some of the great scholars of Eretz Yisrael. He wanted to give him a larger donation, but felt it would not be right to simply give him more money. Instead he went up to the meshulach and drew him into a conversation. After hearing from him stories about the Tchebiner Rav, the Steipler Gaon, and other gedolim, Reb Mendel told him, "Ah, these stories are worth ten dollars," and gave him another donation.

I remember telling him a well-known story about Reb Meshulam Igra who, as a young man, was about to be engaged to a certain girl, but she refused, over her father's protestations. The father of that girl once happened to be in a different city and went to visit the city's Rav. The Rav asked him from which city he came, and after the man replied, the Rav asked him if he knew Reb Meshulam Igra. The man replied that he knew the young man, and asked the Rav why he asked. The Rav answered that once he had a difficult halachic question which he had posed to many gedolim but Reb Meshulam gave him an answer which far surpassed all the others. The man felt so terrible that he fainted on the spot. After he was revived, the Rav asked him what the problem was. The man explained that this Reb Meshulam had almost become his son-in-law. The Rav replied, "If that's the case, you should faint another time." When I told this story to Reb Mendel, he said, "I don't like that story. A person has such tzaar over losing such a worthy son-in-law; how could one possibly make so callous a remark?"

I once told him a story which I thought demonstrated the foresight of a certain well-known rosh yeshivah. He had predicted that two boys in his yeshivah would not turn out well despite the fact that they still learned diligently at that time. And so it was. Reb Mendel was unimpressed. "Do you have a story where he saw a bachur who wasn't doing well and predicted that nevertheless he would turn into a fine ben Torah? That would be an achievement."[1]

Reb Mendel was interested in each and every student. He told me many times, "I aim the shiur at the weaker ones; not at the good heads, not at the medium heads, but at the weak boys."

He saw every boy's unique qualities, including those which still lay hidden. If he knew that a bachur came from a distinguished lineage, he would try to bring out any special qualities he might have inherited from his ancestors. I remember one boy who was not much of a masmid but whose grandfather had been a great scholar. Reb Mendel told me about him, "If you give him a good shake, you can get a clear understanding of the Gemara out of him."

I used to sit next to him during davening, and his prayers were filled with such sweetness. He sang the prayers in his own special melody, and many times I had a great spiritual uplift just from listening to him say Pesukei d'Zimrah. I know of people who stood rooted in awe when they watched Reb Mendel daven. They later told me that from listening to his davening, they could feel how the earlier generations must have davened.

His Torah was always clear. Many times I asked him a question and he would simply read the difficult passage to me in a way that made me see that I had read it incorrectly the first time. His Torah was so sweet, so powerful and so clearly explained.

I showed Reb Mendel a quote from the Brisker Rav about the proper approach towards learning: "Do we learn a Tosafos? All we can do is take something out of the Tosafos." Reb Mendel liked that thought very much, as it expressed his own philosophy of learning.

---

1. Reb Mendel was quick to recognize the latent qualities in every person. One day an irreligious teenager walked into the Philadelphia Yeshivah and said he was interested in learning about Judaism. A student at the yeshivah volunteered to learn with the boy and asked Reb Mendel how much time he should spend with him. Rebbe asked to meet with the boy and, after taking one look at him, told the student, "It is worth expending every effort on him." Not much later, the boy became religious and enrolled in a yeshivah, where he soon became one of the top students. Today he is an accomplished Torah scholar and the author of numerous scholarly works.

He loved and admired every Jew, whatever his background. He did not like the term baal teshuvah as it is commonly used today. To be a baal teshuvah, he felt, you first have to have committed sins, but the people of this generation have not done any sins, they just don't know anything. Reb Mendel loved the Midrash that describes how the Patriarch Avraham sits at the entrance to Gehinnom and does not let any circumcised Jew enter, and he personified that attitude. Now that he is no longer with us, I can think of no better advocate for our people in the Heavenly court.

Rabbi Yitzchak Tepper,
Kollel Gur Aryeh, Yeshivas Rabbeinu Chaim Berlin

Reb Mendel built people up without making them feel like they were receiving and he was giving. Anyone who had a relationship with him felt like a very special person because of it.

Reb Mendel would sometimes make comments that seemed odd at the time. But looking back, we could see his ability to discern what was going on under the surface and how to bring out positive results from every situation.

He moaned to a student in private about one of the student's friends, "I don't know what to do. I'm after him all the time and I cause him a lot of pain. If he doesn't take to it, what's going to come out of it all?" At the time, the student considered it peculiar that he would reveal how he felt about another student. Later, however, he realized that Reb Mendel wanted him to repeat what he had said to the friend in the hope that it would help him.

He had a deep concern for everyone, especially for those most in need. One boy who lived near the yeshivah was on a downhill course. Reb Mendel took him under his wing, buying him clothing and giving him money for learning so that he would not find it necessary to steal. He also got other boys in the yeshivah to take an interest in this boy's welfare. Until Reb Mendel came along, this boy was a street child. Reb Mendel gave him back a feeling of self-worth and eventually helped him to lead a normal life.

He always looked at the positive qualities in every person. Though he possessed a penetrating insight into people and could uncover a person's weaknesses at a glance, he never allowed that to lower the person in his eyes and always saw the good qualities as superseding the negative. He viewed any weakness as something that needed to be corrected, and he devoted all his efforts to bringing about the appropriate correction. All this was possible only because of the deep and genuine love he had for every person.

Rabbi Mordechai Kahn,
Maggid Shiur, Yeshivah Chasan Sofer

Almost everyone I have ever spoken to agrees that the masechtos they learned best are those they learned from Reb Mendel. He taught us how to learn honestly. A bachur once asked him to explain a difficult passage in the Ramban. After looking it over, Reb Mendel said, "I could give you ten different ways of explaining it, but I don't know a single true one."

He was in awe of anything said by Chazal or the Rishonim, or even the great Sages of the present day. Discussing a ruling of Rabbi Moshe Feinstein, he said, "I just can't understand how Reb Moshe Feinstein could rule this way. His logic is like that of a Tanna or Amora. It's a wonder that anyone can still think like that today!" Then he added, "Reb Moshe is a sefer Torah."

Rebbe used to give us Reb Elchonon Wasserman's definition of has-madah: "It doesn't mean that you don't interrupt your learning to speak to a friend. Hasmadah means that you don't even lift your eyes from the sefer to see who just walked into the room."

He exemplified this type of hasmadah. He used to learn in the same room with the class when we were preparing for shiur. Even while keeping one eye on the class, his head was still in the Gemara. He never even lifted his head out of the Gemara when, for example, the door slammed.

Reb Mendel had a tremendous love for the words of Torah. After he learned a Tosafos he would say from the depths of his heart, "Ah, the words of Tosafos are so sweet, let's learn them another time!" Then we would go through the entire Tosafos a second time.

We could feel his pleasure in learning. Sometimes when he was learning by himself and we were learning with chavrusos, he would get very involved in the Gemara and begin singing it in his own special, sweet melody. At such times the whole class would become quiet and just watch him in wonder.

§► §► §►

I once read about a rosh yeshivah who received an aliyah while visiting another yeshivah. After davening, someone complimented him on the way he made the blessing, and the rosh yeshivah replied, "I only wish I could make such blessings in the privacy of my home."

Reb Mendel was exactly the opposite: he always concealed his true devotion when he was davening at the yeshivah, but he could not completely conceal the joy and inner fire he put into his prayers.

He used to give a shiur in Chochmah U'Mussar in yeshivah before the morning davening. Sometimes he arrived earlier and would recite the morning blessings with an indescribable sweetness and attachment to Hashem. But such blessings were reserved for those occasions when he didn't notice us. Never would he have dreamed of saying such blessings in public.

Reb Mendel did not limit his prayers to those recited three times a day. Whenever he heard of a sick Jew — even if it was someone he did not know — he would pray on his behalf and urge others to do the same. There was once a boy in yeshivah who went off the path of Torah. Even after he left the yeshivah, Reb Mendel would seek him out and speak to him in the hope of winning him back. Several years later, Reb Mendel met someone who knew the boy and asked how he was faring. He confided, "You should know how many days I fasted on his behalf."

I had the privilege of learning with Reb Mendel privately for half a year. Once he excused himself in the middle of our session. I was curious to see where he was going, so I followed him as he walked past the train station near the yeshivah and into a ravine which contained a thick forest and a stream. When he reached a secluded place, he put on his tallis and tefillin and began to pour out his heart to Hashem with great feeling.

ה ה ה

He once told a student, "A rebbe is not just to teach Torah; his job is also to teach fear of Hashem." Reb Mendel fulfilled both of these requirements to the utmost degree.

He had a different approach for each and every boy. There was one troublesome boy who the roshei yeshivah felt should not return to the yeshivah the following term, but Reb Mendel advised him to come back anyway. The boy was still discouraged until Rebbe said, "You'll show them!" That relit his fighting spirit, and the boy improved greatly.

My background is chassidic, and Reb Mendel urged me to be a chassidishe bachur. He even offered to learn chassidishe works with me. Another boy had a grandfather who was a great talmid chacham. Reb Mendel always talked to this boy about his grandfather and asked him to bring in his grandfather's works. Rebbe made a regular study session of these works with the boy in order to kindle in him a joy in learning.

Every student thought he was the closest to Reb Mendel. The truth is they all were.

Eulogy given at the Shloshim of Reb Mendel Kaplan by Dr. Julian Ungar-Sargon M.D., Professor of Neurology at Harvard Medical School

When Eliyahu ascended to heaven in a chariot of fire, his disciple Elisha looked up and cried out in anguish, "Avi, Avi, Rechev Yisrael — My Father! My Father! Chariot of Israel." The closeness between the mentor and his disciple was not that of a lecturer imparting information to a student; it was the closeness of a parent to a child. Thus when Eliyahu left this world, Elisha's immediate and instinctive response was that of a child who cries out to his parents, "Avi, Avi — my father, my father, you are as close to me as my own flesh and blood parents."

I come here tonight as a talmid of Reb Mendel, zt"l, even though I cannot say I deserved to be his talmid. Yet he was my rebbe. Because I am a bit older than his talmidim in the yeshivah of Philadelphia, I may have a slightly different perspective from my five years of learning with Reb Mendel.

For me, he truly became my father, as well as my mother. He was my father in that he always made demands on me. He was never satisfied with things as they are, never smug in religiosity. He often asked me why I spent so much time "in this world."

"Ultimately it's all for nothing, so don't get so caught up in this rat race," he would quip.

Yet if ever I returned to him with a sense of failure, he was a mother to me — comforting, reassuring, showing unconditional love. He always seemed to understand, and encouraged me with warmth. "Try again — next time you'll succeed," he would say.

He was a rebbe who was interested not only in how much I learned, but whether what I learned would carry me through the day. He was more interested in what was between the lines of the Gemara, what was not said, what was implied, what was incapable of being expressed. Often he would stop in the middle of a line, unable to continue, and muse, "We really know nothing. We know as much about this Gemara as we know about that leaf there outside the window." For him, the ultimate understanding of the simplest fact lay shrouded in mystery.

The days when he was ill or when I was on hospital duty were different from the days that began with a dose of Reb Mendel. As time went on, I could not tear myself away from him. He took the boys' problems so seriously that one could not help but love him. Often he would show up at my home with a student who had a problem to which he wanted me to give my attention. Sometimes he took the boys out of yeshivah just to give them a break and some fresh air.

༄ ༄ ༄

He took great interest in my career. I was involved in the fledging hospice movement, and there were many disappointments dealing with a hostile medical establishment and a regulatory administration that was unwilling to spend more on health care.

Finally the Medicare-Hospice Bill came before the House Ways and Means Committee. Before I was to testify in front of the committee, I told Reb Mendel how afraid I was, how I felt like a Yiddele from Europe with a yarmulke.

He told me, "I, too, was gripped with the same fear, when I was fourteen and I had to appear before a judge in Baranovich with my father." That personal revelation immediately dispelled all my fear. In that moment, the burden of being a Jew was transmitted with love and empathy from a master to his disciple.

He gave me the courage to continue the work that eventually placed this revolutionary form of health care within the reach of all senior citizens in this country. He gave me the strength not to surrender my pride in my Yiddishkeit, and to succeed in a secular world with my dignity as a Jew intact. Who but he could feel so at home in our secular world, and yet so totally strong in divorcing himself from it philosophically. Without ever compromising an inch, either in halachah or hashkafah, he was still sufficiently fluent in the idiom of the day to critique it tellingly.

He was an old man with the wisdom of years, and yet was still moved by little children. How thrilled he was by a yeshivah student in whose soul he saw greatness; how he worried about a boy who was not turning out right. Despite the physical pain and the ailments that plagued him, his impish humor never lost its childlike quality, its purity of spirit.

I learned from him that there are no limits when it comes to chesed. He would come to my house at eleven at night with a non-religious boy whom he had met on an Amtrak train and ask me to give him a meal and to arrange a place for him for Shabbos. I was constantly amazed by his energy, by his ability to get things done on his very own and in his own way. I can only wonder how many people there are in the world whom Reb Mendel met "on the road," whom he "picked up" both physically and spiritually, and whose lives have been touched ever since by this unique man.

Through him I became aware of the ebb and flow of ruchniyus — of the spiritual life. There were times when he was so certain about something that nothing could shake him. And other times when he showed me that one must continue to believe in spite of the tragedies that befell our communities only a generation ago, continue to believe in spite of human suffering, continue to believe in spite of a world for which he no longer had any respect, continue to believe in spite of the failing of individuals.

For me the most lasting lesson was his absolute honesty — never fooling oneself about who one was or where one was going. Humility without naiveté, humility based on an honest self-assessment, however painful, of the image that you might face in the mirror.

Most of all, I miss his inner gentility, his nobility. I am also an orphan. I have lost a father who knew me, knew what I needed, who scolded yet never offended, instructed yet never degraded, loved yet never smothered, enlightened yet never blinded, gave mussar yet never ridiculed. Now that you are gone, how can I carry on?

Reb Mendel! My Reb Mendel!

Glossary

◆§ Glossary

Acharonim — Talmudic commentators and codifiers from 1st century to the present

Aggadah [pl. Aggados] — sections of the Talmud and other rabbinic writings that contain the philosophical, ethical, poetic and historical exposition of Scripture

Akeidas Yitzchak, Akeidah — the Binding of Isaac

alav hashalom — may he rest in peace

al cheit — list of sins recited in Yom Kippur confessions

Aleph Beis — Hebrew alphabet

aliyah — call to the Torah for the public reading

Alter of Kelm — the title of esteem accorded to the revered mussar master R' Simcha Zissel Ziv

am haaretz — ignoramus

Amora [pl. Amoraim] — Sages of the Gemara

anav — humble person

Aron — Ark in which Torah scroll's are kept; Ark in Holy Temple in which Tablets were kept

aveirah — transgression

Avos, Pirkei Avos — Ethics of the Fathers, part of *Mishnah*

baal chessed — one who involves himself in good deeds and acts of kindness

baal gaavah — conceited person

baal machshavah — deep thinker

baal mussar — one who studies and practices *mussar* (ethical and moral) teachings.

baal teshuvah [pl. baalei teshuvah] — one who returns to the Torah way of life

bachur [pl. bachurim] — young unmarried man

baruch Hashem — blessed is G-d

basar vadam — flesh and blood

batalah — time wasting

batlan — one who wastes time

Beis Din — rabbinic court

Beis HaMikdash — Holy Temple in Jerusalem

beis midrash [pl. battei midrashos] — study hall

bekeshe — caftan worn by Chassidim.

ben Torah [pl. **bnei Torah**] — one who studies and adheres the teachings of the Torah

berachah [pl. **berachos**] — blessing

b'ezras Hashem — With the help of G-d

Bircas HaMazon — Grace After Meals

bircas haTorah — the blessings recited on learning Torah

bitachon — trust

bitul Torah — waste time from Torah study

blatt [Yid.] — one full leaf of Talmud

chaburah [pl. **chaburos**] — study group

chacham — wise person

chachmah — wisdom

chasan — bridegroom.

chassid, Chassidim — follower of a chassidic sect

Chassidishe — follower of a Chassidic sect

chasunah — wedding

chavrusa [pl. **chavrushos**] — study partner

Chazal — Our Sages of blessed memory

chazarah — review

chazzan — cantor

cheder [pl. **chadarim**] — elementary school.

chessed — kindness.

chiddush [pl. **chiddushim**] — original analysis and interpretation of difficult points of Torah

Chochmah U'Mussar — Wisdom and Ethics; classic mussar book written by R' Simcha Zissel Ziv, the "Alter of Kelm"

Cholov Yisrael — milk whose processing has been halachically supervised

Chovos HaLevavos — Duties of the Heart; classic book of Jewish thought and philosophy

Chumash [pl. **Chumashim**] — the Five Books of Moses, a volume thereof.

chupah — marriage ceremony; canopy under which it is held

daven, davening [Yid.] — to pray, prayers

devarim beteilim — frivolous talk, unimportant distractions

divrei Torah — Torah thoughts

drashah — discourse

dybbuk — evil spirit

eiruv — legal device which allows one to carry on Shabbos in an otherwise restricted area

Elul — the month preceding the High Holy Days

emunah — faith

Ephod — apron; one of the vestments worn by the High Priest in the Temple

Eretz Yisrael — the Land of Israel

erev — evening

frumkeit, frummer — religiosity

frum [Yid.] — religiously observant

gabbai — synagogue official; attendant of Chassidic rebbe

Gan Eden — Garden of Eden.

Gaon — (pl. Geonim) a brilliant Torah scholar; Sages of the 6th-11th centuries C.E.

gartel [Yid.] — belt encircling the waist or hips, usually worn during prayer

gedolim, gedolei Yisrael — Torah leaders of the generation

Gehinnom — Gehenna, Hell

Gemara — the part of Talmud that elaborates on the *Mishnah;* a volume of the Talmud

gematria — numerical value

gemilas chessed — loving-kindness

geshmak [Yid.] enjoyable; enjoyment

get — bill of divorce

gevurah — strength

guf — body

hachnasas orchim — hospitality

HaKadosh Baruch Hu — the Holy One, Blessed is He

halachah [pl: halachos] — body of Torah law; a Torah law

HaMelech — the King

hasmadah — diligence

havdalah — blessings recited over wine, candles and spices to mark the end of the Sabbath Day

HaYom Haras Olam — prayer from the Rosh Hashanah liturgy

iluy — genius

Kabbalah — the body of esoteric mystical Torah literature

kallah — bride

kapota — Rabbinic frock

kavanos — intentions

kavodik — respectable

kedushah — holiness

Kesuvim — Holy Writings — the last eleven books of the Scriptures

kiddush — blessing recited over wine on Shabbos; also used to refer to the light repast served with it

kinderlach [Yid.] — children

kinnos — prayers of lamentation

kiruv rechokim — outreach to non-religious Jews

Kodashim — Order of the Mishnah dealing with sacrificed offerings

Kohen Gadol — High Priest

Kohen — male descendant of priestly family of Aaron.

kollel — post-graduate yeshivah

Kosel HaMaaravi — the Western Wall; the last remaining wall of the Temple Mount complex

Krias Shema — recitation of the Shema Yisrael prayer

kvittle [Yid.] — note bearing a personal request.

lamdan — Torah scholar

lashon hara — evil speech

levayah — funeral

l'havdil — to differentiate

lishmah — for its own sake

Litvishe — of Lithuanian origin; used in contradistinction to Chassidishe

lomdus — learning

Maariv — evening prayer service

maggid shiur — lecturer of Torah discourse

mashgiach — dean of students in a yeshivah whose function is to be mentor and advisor

masmid — diligent Torah student

mechalel Shabbos — one who desecrates the Shabbos

mechanech — pedagogue

mekubel — kabbalist

menahel — principal or director of a yeshivah

menorah — candelabrum

mentsch [pl. mentschen] — responsible, considerate individual

mentshlichkeit — human decency

menuchah — tranquility

menuchas hanefesh — peace of mind

mesechta [pl. mesechtos] — tractate of Talmud

meshulach — collector

mesorah — tradition

middos, middos tovos — good character traits

mikveh — ritualarium

Mishkan — Tabernacle

mishloach manos — gifts of food sent on Purim

Mishnah [pl. Mishnayos] — Tannaitic dicta compiled by R' Yehudah HaNassi; together with Gemara it comprises the Talmud

misnaged, mishnagdishe — opponent of Chassidism; loosely, any non-*chassid*

mitzvos — Torah commandments

Moreh Nevuchim — The Guide for the Perplexed, a philosophical work written by Maimonedes

moser nefesh — person who is self-sacrificing

Moshe Rabbeinu — Moses our Teacher

Moshiach — the Messiah

Motzaei — the night following

mussar — ethical and moral teachings

mussar seder — study session devoted to *mussar* texts

mussar shmeuss — lecture devoted to *mussar* topics

nachas — pleasure

Nach — Prophets and Writings. Together with the Chumash they comprise Scriptures

ner tamid — eternal lamp in synagogue which burns continually

neshamah — soul

Neviim — Prophets

Nisuch HaMayim — water-libation ceremony

nu [Yid.] — "so?"

Olam Haba — the World to Come

Olam Hazeh — this World

Orach Chaim — section of *Shulchan Aruch* dealing with matters pertaining to everyday life

orlah — fruit which grows on a tree during its first three years. It is forbidden to derive any benefit therefrom; the foreskin

parashah [pl. **parashiyos**] — weekly portion of the Torah

pasul — rendered halachically unfit for use

patch [Yid.] — slap

payos — sidelocks

Pesach — Passover

Pesukei d'Zimrah — Psalms recited as part of the *Shacharis* (morning) prayers

Pidyon HaBen — redemption of the firstborn son

p'shat [pl. **p'shatim**] — basic explanation

Purim — Festival of Lots

Rabbeinu Tam — One of the first of the authors of the Tosafos

Rambam — Maimonedes; Codifier of Jewish law, Jewish philosopher, Royal advisor and physician

Rashi — acronym for R' Shlomo Yitzchaki; "The Father" of Torah commentators

rav [pl. **rabbanim**] — rabbi

Rebbe — teacher; leader of a Chassidic sect

Rebbetzin [Yid.] — rabbi's wife

Rishon [pl. **Rishonim**] — Sage of the period following the Geonim — c.1200-1500 C.E.

rosh yeshivah [pl. **roshei yeshivah**] — dean of a Yeshivah

Ruach HaKodesh — Divine inspiration

seder — learning

sefer [pl. **sefarim**] — book

sefer Torah [pl. **sifrei Torah**] — Torah scroll

segulah — deed or happening that augurs a favorable outcome

semichah — rabbinic ordination

sevara [pl. **sevaros**] — explanation

Shacharis — morning prayer service

Shas — the Talmud

Shechinah — Divine Presence

sheimos — Holy literature which though no longer usable may not be destroyed nor randomly discarded

Shema, Shema Yisrael — Jew's declaration of faith, recited in morning and evening services

Shemoneh Esrei — the *Amidah* section of the daily prayers

sheva berachos — seven blessings recited during wedding ceremony and at meals of celebration during the week following; also refers to the meal of celebration itself

shidduch [pl. **shidduchim**] — marriage match

Shir HaShirim — Song of Songs

shiur [pl. **shiurim**] — lecture

shloshim — thirty-day mourning period

shtender — lectern

Shulchan Aruch — Code of Jewish Law

shul — synagogue

siddur — prayer book

simchah — joyous occasion

Simchas Torah — festival following Succos, celebration of the completion of the cycle of weekly Torah readings

sofer — scribe

succah — temporary dwelling in which the Jew is commanded to dwell on Succos.

Succos — Feast of Tabernacles.

tahor — ritually pure

tallis — large-fringed prayer shawl

talmid chacham — Torah scholar

talmid [pl. **talmidim**] — student

tamei — ritually impure

Tanach — Scripture

Tanna [pl. **Tannaim**] — Sages of the *Mishnah*

Tatte [Yid.] — father

techiyas hameisim — resurrection of the dead

tefach — halachic unit of mesaure, approximately 3-6 inches

tefillin — phylacteries

Tehillim — Psalms

teshuvah — repentence

Tikkun Chatzos — a post-midnight prayer service mourning the destruction of the Holy Temple

Tishah B'Av — fast day commemorating the destruction of the First and Second Temples.

tizku l'mitzvos — may you merit to do mitzvos

Tosafos — twelfth century Talmudic commentary printed in all editions of the Talmud

tza'ar — anguish, pain

tzaddik [fem: **tzadeikes**] — righteous person

tzedakah — charity

tzelem Elokim — the image of G-d in which every person was created.

tzenua — modest person

tzidkus — piety

tznius — personal modesty

vasikin — the morning prayer service held at sunrise

viduy — confession

vort [pl. **vertlach**] [Yid.] — Torah thought

yarmulka — skullcap

Yerushalmi — Jerusalem Talmud

yeshivah [pl. **yeshivos**] — Torah school

yetzer hara — Evil Inclination

yichus — lineage

Yiddele [Yid.] — diminutive affectionate term for Jew

Yiddishkeit — Judaism

Yid [pl. **Yidden**] — Jew

Yomim Noraim — High Holy Days

Yom Tov [pl. **Yomim Tovim**] — Festival

z'chus — merit

Zohar — classic kabbalistic text on the Torah, compiled by R' Shimon bar Yochai

This volume is part of
THE ARTSCROLL SERIES®
an ongoing project of
translations, commentaries and expositions
on Scripture, Mishnah, Talmud, Halachah,
liturgy, history, the classic Rabbinic writings,
biographies and thought.

For a brochure of current publications
visit your local Hebrew bookseller
or contact the publisher:

Mesorah Publications, ltd

4401 Second Avenue
Brooklyn, New York 11232
(718) 921-9000
www.artscroll.com